Contents

Chapter 2

Making a Plan 19

Chapter 3

Decisions, Decisions 35

Chapter 4

Location 45

Entrepreneur
MAGAZINE'S

start*up*

Start Your Own

SUCCESSFUL RETAIL BUSINESS

Your Step-by-Step Guide to Success

Jan Kingaard

Editorial Director: Jere L. Calmes
Cover Design: Beth Hansen-Winter
Production and Composition: Eliot House Productions

This publication is designed to provide accurate and authoritative information in
regard to the subject matter covered. It is sold with the understanding that the publisher is not engaged in rendering legal, accounting or other professional services. If
legal advice or other expert assistance is required, the services of a competent professional person should be sought.

Library of Congress Cataloging-in-Publication Data
Kingaard, Jan.
    Start your own successful retail business/by Jan Kingaard.
       p.   cm.   —(Entrepreneur magazine's start ups)
    Includes index.
    ISBN 1-891984-72-1
      1. Retail trade—Management. 2. New business enterprises. I. Entrepreneur (Santa
Monica, Calif.) II. Title. III. Series.

HF5429 .K525 2002
381'.1'0681—dc21   2002031788

Printed in Canada

09 08 07 06 05 04   10 9 8 7 6 5 4 3

Preface

We're assuming you've picked up this retail business start-up guide because:

- you've worked in someone else's business and are ready to take charge of your own;

- you are an extrovert and enjoy constant contact with people;

- you are comfortable with the unexpected and are a problem-solver;

- you enjoy sales and don't mind working long hours indoors; and

- you know where you want your retail business to be in five years.

Our goal is to tell you everything you need to know to:

- decide if a retail business is right for you;
- get your doors open for business;
- limit the number of mistakes you make; and
- keep your retail enterprise running successfully.

We've tried to make this guide as user-friendly as possible. Experts across the country share their experiences and insights with you to show you what really works and to help you avoid the pitfalls they have encountered. We'll tell you retailers' stories and give you some hard-won advice and cautionary notes so you can operate from best practices. We hope you'll consult the useful contacts in the Appendix as often as you need to for answers and direction.

We've broken this guide's chapters into manageable sections on every aspect of starting up and operating a retail product or service business. We've even included some brainstorming questions to ask yourself to stimulate creative solutions to the particular problems you may face.

The tip boxes sprinkled throughout this guide will give you useful information you can use right away to make decisions. We begin with an overview of the dynamic world of retailing, and each chapter thereafter addresses an important area of responsibility you need to master.

Many people dream of running their own video rental store, gift boutique, or dog grooming business, but they don't know where to start, or they get lost along the way. Maybe you see a dinner theater, secondhand store, or craft cart in your future. Running a retail store or service business is a very different venture from other kinds of businesses. This easy-to-read guide takes you through the steps any small retail business owner must take to be successful.

Retailers have prospered in America since the early trappers of the 1800s. Today, retailing still requires quick-witted and sure-footed responses to dangers in the environment, so we've organized this guide to give you the navigational tools you'll need.

Now let's get started on your adventure. Happy trails!

1

Introduction to
Retailing

The retail industry provides an exciting way of life for the more than 24 million people who earn their livelihood in this sector of the U.S. economy. Retailers provide the goods and services you and I need—from food, auto parts, apparel, home furnishings, appliances, and electronics to

▲

advice, home improvement, and skilled labor. Let's take a look behind the scenes at the many facets of this exciting business.

Welcome to the Big Leagues

Retailing is one of the fastest-growing segments of the economy. As one of the nation's largest employers, the retail industry provides excellent business opportunities for you. At least one-third of the 500,000 or so new enterprises launched each year are retail operations. The entrepreneurs behind these ventures risk their capital, invest their time, and make a living by offering consumers something they need or want. You'll meet several of them in this guide and learn how they created a niche for themselves.

Most retailing involves buying merchandise or a service from a manufacturer, wholesaler, agent, importer, or other retailer and selling it to consumers for their per-

Who Are Your Competitors?

Want to know where shoppers go? According to Chain Store Age magazine, here's how the top 100 retailers break down in sales by retail category:

Supermarkets	24%
Discount stores	14%
Hard-lines stores	11%
Drugstores	7%
Super centers	7%
Department stores	7%
Home centers	6%
Warehouse wholesale clubs	6%
Sears, J.C. Penney	6%
Apparel stores	4%
Electronic retailers	4%
Mail order catalogs	1%
Military exchanges	1%
Convenience stores	1%
Shoe stores	1%
Catalog showrooms	0.2%

sonal use. The price charged for the goods or services covers the retailer's expenses and includes a profit. Each year, this vital sector of our economy accounts for about 38 percent of our gross national product. In 1999, the National Retail Federation (NRF)—the world's largest retail trade association, located in Washington, DC—reported that annual retail sales in America reached $3 trillion.

Storefront ventures run the gamut from clothing boutiques and health-food stores to hardware stores, coffee shops, bars, laundromats, convenience stores, and so on. Among the more recent arrivals on the scene are cellular phone outlets, video and DVD rental stores, cybercafes, and just about anything else you can imagine. The diversity is amazing!

The NRF says more than 1 million retailing companies operate more than 1.4 million retail establishments in the United States. Most are store retailers, though there are other types of enterprises—such as electronic commerce (e-tailing), mail order, automatic-merchandising (vending) machines, direct retailing (door-to-door selling), and service providers.

What About Jobs?

The NRF reports more than 20 million American workers—one in five—are in the retail industry. At present, more jobs are provided in retailing than in the entire U.S. manufacturing sector. Thirteen percent of all new jobs are in the retail sector, says the NRF.

"With the U.S. economy continuing its record-setting expansion, and with good jobs readily available, fewer individuals are going out to start up new ventures," says David T. Kresge, chief economist for Dun & Bradstreet, a leading provider of marketing and financial information in Murray Hill, New Jersey. "The decline is particularly pronounced in retail trade, where starts are down by 12 percent, and new jobs are down by 6 percent." Nonetheless, the service and retail sectors of the U.S. economy continue to report the largest numbers of start-up companies. According to the U.S. Department of Labor, retail employment is expected to increase to 24 million workers by the year 2005.

Basic Kinds of Retailers

Retailing is one of the most mature industries in our economy, and it's constantly being reinvented with the advent of new technologies. Changes in buying behavior, attitudes and buying patterns, and the restructuring of the retail industry, have had a significant impact on small businesses. While some predict the local retailer may become a thing of the past, there is a bright future for those who can identify and respond to

Stat Fact

The National Retail Federation reports that California, Texas, New York, and Florida account for 29 percent of all retail workers and make up approximately 30 percent of all U.S. retail sales.

changing consumer needs faster and better than their larger competitors. With the Internet, television, telephone, overnight delivery, and credit and debit cards, any enterprising individual can find a niche and begin making commercial transactions right away.

To give you an overview of the competitive marketplace, we'll take a brief look at the various faces and configurations of selling to the consumer. Keep in mind that all of these enterprises began as a simple concept and grew to various proportions through popularity and perseverance. At this point in your exploration, anything is possible for you, too.

Store Retailing

The retail scene in America is a dazzling array of independent shops, department stores, discount and off-price enterprises, convenience stores, membership warehouse clubs, national and regional chains, category-killer stores, conventional supermarkets, and other large-scale enterprises that seem to dominate the retail sector.

Store retailers operate fixed point-of-sale locations designed to attract a high volume of walk-in customers. In general, stores have extensive merchandise displays and use mass-media advertising to attract customers. They typically sell merchandise to the general public for personal or household consumption, but some also serve business and institutional clients. These include establishments such as office supply stores, computer and software stores, building materials dealers, and plumbing and electrical supply stores. Catalog showrooms, gasoline service stations, automotive dealers, and mobile home dealers are treated as store retailers by the U.S. Census Bureau.

To understand this diverse business sector, government reporting and other information is broken down into several sectors for easier digestion and fact-finding. The sector groupings are based on one or more of the following criteria:

- *The merchandise line or lines carried by the store.*For example, specialty stores are distinguished from general-line stores.

- *The usual trade designation of the establishment.* This applies in cases where a store type is well-recognized by the industry and the public but is difficult to define strictly in terms of commodities offered. Examples are pharmacies, hardware stores, and department stores.

- *Capital requirements in terms of display equipment.* For example, food stores have unique equipment requirements.

- *Human resources requirements in terms of expertise.* For example, the staff of a computer store requires knowledge that's not necessary in other retail operations.

Internet Retailing

While shopping on the Internet is all the buzz, independent brick-and-mortars (retailers with physical stores) dominate consumer sales and are expected to remain viable for several reasons. Foremost is their real-world presence, having a location that people can drive by, call, and walk through time and time again. A physical building lends credibility as a solid and reliable enterprise. It also provides an outlet, a destination, a gathering place for customers.

Shared experiences and one-on-one exchanges are valued by people of all ages. The ability to look someone in the eye and ask them questions or watch a demonstration appeals to human nature. Another advantage is the ability to feel and smell the merchandise, and to try it and compare it side by side with other items. Shoppers appreciate having a selection of items at their fingertips. There's instant gratification for buyers in carrying their purchase home with them. And there are no packing and shipping charges. People feel more comfortable paying in person than giving out credit information to disembodied entities. Returning items to a store is more convenient than mailing something back. Personal service, community involvement, and local employment are three additional aspects of storefront retailers that will continue to appeal to the public for decades to come.

David *vs.* Goliath

You read a lot about the power retailers—the Wal-Marts, Home Depots, and Targets—with huge physical facilities housing a broad range of merchandise. Faced

---

Every Stripe and Shape

Retailers continue to redefine and plan new shopping environments to provide customers with a variety of places, prices, and merchandise. The most common physical store categories and recognizable examples are:

- ○ Off-price enterprises: Kmart, Target
- ○ Convenience stores: 7-Eleven, Circle K
- ○ Membership warehouse clubs: Costco, BJ's
- ○ National and regional chains: Starbucks, Nordstrom
- ○ Category-killer stores: Home Depot, Best Buy
- ○ Conventional supermarkets: Safeway, Kroger Co.
- ○ Specialty stores: Crabtree & Evelyn, Victoria's Secret

Smart Tip

Successful retailers do not run their business to suit themselves. Retailers must cater to the tastes and requirements of customers. This can mean keeping the doors open on holidays and weekends, and opening early or staying late on some weekdays. You marry the store when you go into business for yourself, so expect many compromises along the way to profits.

with these price-oriented giants, won't the little guy get crushed? Not necessarily. Many "Davids" are learning a thing or two about efficiencies and customer focus from "Goliaths" like Wal-Mart, and they're flexing their own muscles. In fact, the United States is primarily a nation of small, independent merchants: More stores are small, both in size and sales volume.

The typical store is run by the owner alone or by a husband-and-wife team. Such small enterprises naturally lack the substantial resources, purchasing muscle, and sophisticated operations of the large-scale retailers. For the small retailer, there may be a few employees, and one or two may be part-time workers. The store's size is, of course, related to the type of establishment: Furniture outlets, for example, require much more space than shoe stores and neighborhood groceries.

Fred W. and his childhood friend, George M., often discussed what they wanted to do when they grew up. While still in college, they decided that music was what they loved most and could do best, so when they found an empty storefront off the beaten path in Montpelier, Vermont, they opened a music store in 1973.

"I've always been a musician," Fred recounts. "It's an intuitive talent." Fred's brother and a friend ran the business for a year or so while Fred pursued a professional career as a composer in New York. "I probably could have done all right, but when my manager/financial backer was murdered, I returned to Vermont and my cabin in the woods and was glad I had my store to go back to."

Stephanie B. decided to share her love of dogs with fellow enthusiasts by opening an all-natural pet bakery in Newport Beach, California, in 2000. She sees the market as strong and growing because people are having children later and want more affection and companionship in their daily lives. "Pet bakeries are popping up everywhere in Southern California. There are about 10 that I know of," she says. "There are a ton of wholesalers for this all-natural industry. I've been cooking for my own dogs for a long time. I love coming up with new recipes—like the marinara morsels I made the other day."

Specialty Retailing

While power retailers tend to sell "needs," specialty retailers tend to sell "wants." They focus more on neighborhood convenience, the richness of the shopping experience, and inventory that meets the needs of their target customer on a personalized basis. Small stores show surprising strength and resilience in the face of competition from large-scale retailers and Internet retailers. They offer the consumer a warmer atmosphere, and perhaps a broader and deeper selection of merchandise.

Many stores can be owned and operated by one person with minimal assistance. Compared to manufacturing operations, specialty retail outfits are relatively easy to start both financially and operationally. However, a number of failures are due to undercapitalization, poor location, and insufficient market analysis. This guide is intended to help you avoid start-up pitfalls by providing you with tricks of the trade to help you succeed.

There is always room for the right kind of store. Geographic shifts of large numbers of consumers are characteristic of our mobile population; stores need to be wherever people live. Fashions, changing lifestyles, increasing concern about health care, and technological advances all contribute to the need for new variations on old retailing themes. Finally, retail openings continue to occur as established merchants retire, sell their businesses, or close down because of poor management practices or changes in the local environment. Your small store launched today may become the next Lowe's or Starbucks within the next decade.

Stat Fact

"All-natural pet bakeries are an up-and-coming trend in the $26 billion pet industry," says Stephanie B., who researched the industry before leaving her law practice and going into business in Newport Beach, California, in 2000. "It's developing into an industry of its own with about 40 percent of the larger pet retailing market. The oldest [all-natural pet bakery] I've heard of started in 1980."

Nonstore Retailing

When you look at the array of business opportunities in retailing, be sure and include the $123 billion nonstore retailing sector. These businesses are primarily engaged in the retail sale of products through television, electronic shopping, paper and electronic catalogs, door-to-door solicitation, in-home demonstration, portable stalls, vending machines, and mail order. With the exception of vending, these businesses do not ordinarily maintain stock for sale on the premises. They deal in books, coins, computers and peripherals, food, fruit, jewelry, magazines, novelty merchandise, CDs, audiotapes, stamps, and home-shopping ventures, among others.

Fun Fact

According to the Chicago-based National Automatic Merchandising Association, vending dates to 215 B.C. in ancient Egypt. In his writings, the mathematician Hero, of Alexandria, described a device found in places of worship that would dispense holy water when a coin was deposited.

When exploring your options, consider combining one or more retail opportunities. For example, if having a store is the object of your desire, think about adding a toy or gumball machine as an extra revenue stream. If you are thinking about setting up a tax-preparation or insurance-billing service in your home, perhaps you'll want to publish a mail order catalog of topical audiotapes, rubber stamps, forms, and books you can sell to augment your customer base.

There are many advantages to this type of retailing—one being that the buying, maintenance, and protection of a large inventory is not necessary as you contract with others to handle these matters. The U.S. Census Bureau says there are more than 44,000 nonstore retailers in the United States.

Temporary Locations

In your travels down remote roads and through the countryside, you'll find roadside stands offering ripe tomatoes, fresh corn by the bushel, avocados, freshly laid eggs, and other agricultural and dairy products. You might also see handcrafted items, artwork, souvenirs, holiday gifts, regional tokens, and novelties. Many of these businesses sell year-round, though some are seasonal by nature. Carts in malls and by roadways, swap meets, spontaneous garage sales, holiday or summer retail operations, and weekly farmers' markets are additional outlets for the ambitious retailer.

Direct Selling

Direct retailing means selling to the consumer in his or her home using the telephone, the Internet, or direct mail. Home-shopping television channels and infomercials have boosted the popularity of shopping from the privacy and comfort of home. TV-based home shopping was originally touted as a new era in retail, but today its sales amount to only $3 billion, and the sector is dominated by two main players. People have to watch a show in real time to order items before they disappear from the air. Nonetheless, the convenience of ordering from home amidst rising gasoline prices, crowded highways and stores, time crunches, and physical and geographic barriers works to the advantage of direct retailers.

About 10 percent of all consumer goods are sold by direct-selling organizations.

With phone marketing, in less than two minutes, you can complete a transaction—speak with your customer, exchange information, and take an order. For more than a decade, there has been an increase every year of the use of pay-per-call, toll-free numbers, and fax-on-demand for almost every application imaginable. Consumers can purchase advice, news and information, magazine subscriptions, telecommunication programs, investments, videotapes, health supplements, and exercise equipment over the phone. The market is endless. Using telephone technology, you can inform, educate, solicit, and satisfy the consumer and your business needs. Because sales are made by phone to one person at a time, bulk orders, higher-priced items, and contract purchases are the most cost-effective.

In this techno age, many consumers like to be able to ask a real person questions before they buy and feel like the person cares about them. About 10 percent of all consumer goods are sold by direct-selling organizations such as Amway, Avon, Fuller Brush, and Tupperware. House-to-house canvassing, party plans, network marketing, street vending, and route sales are among the techniques used to sell almost everything—clothing, perfume, toys, china and crystal, home furnishings, health and beauty aids, and general merchandise. In 1997, the U.S. Census Bureau reports there were about 28,000 of these firms nationwide, with a total sales volume of $37 billion.

> ### Bright Idea
>
> Even if you're working full time, pick up some part-time or seasonal work in a retail store to get the feel of a small business. Observe how decisions are made, how employees are trained, and what kinds of customer attitudes you encounter. How are resources allocated? See how vendors and inventory are handled. See what works and what doesn't.

Mail Order

From glossy wish books to basic brochures, catalogs are popular with those who live far from shopping areas, the elderly, those seeking the unusual or the obscure, and those who simply hate to shop. What could be easier than calling a 24-hour, toll-free phone number to order clothing, gifts, and gadgets? With direct mail, sales materials can be sent to thousands of potential customers at one time to either make a sale or generate a sales lead. Between catalogs, various direct-mail fliers and brochures, billing inserts, magazine ads, and e-commerce over the Internet, the U.S. government reports that the mail order business has soared to more than $200 billion in sales. Selling products and services directly to consumers by mail is a growing sector because it offers entrepreneurs a high return on a low initial investment.

Mail order enterprises include general merchandise businesses, companies that sell specialty goods of all kinds, novelty firms, various types of clubs (CDs, DVDs, books, audiotapes, gifts), and so on. In most cases, catalogs are sent to consumers in defined niches on a regular basis. Most of the catalog companies offer some form of expedited delivery so customers can receive merchandise quickly.

The extraordinarily versatile medium of direct mail enables you to target people, groups, or organizations within your trading area, all of which may be likely prospects for your retail business. And you can work out of your home, a warehouse, or a brick-and-mortar store.

▲

An up-to-date mailing list is the key to direct-mail profits with back-end fulfillment and relational database support. Most people selling things by mail need at least a 200-percent markup to make money. You shouldn't pay more than $10 for something you sell for $30. If you think this is the retail area for you, Entrepreneur's business start-up guide No. 1015, *Mail Order Business*, will show you where to find the best products, how to save on advertising costs and select mailing lists, and help you maximize your print or online mail order operation.

The Internet

The Internet has changed the retail landscape, connecting companies, markets, and individual consumers. Industry research firm Jupiter Communications predicts that by 2005, 25 to 35 percent of the global consumer marketplace will be connected with Web sites or communities that enable like-minded consumers to do business with a network of companies that offer complementary goods and services. The online business model is accelerating the globalization of retailing. The Internet is the fastest and potentially the most powerful retailing tool the world has ever known.

"The retailer who does not understand the impact of the Internet on its store and catalog channels is likely to underinvest in the Internet, missing opportunities to capture incremental sales in all channels," according to Ken Cassar, a senior analyst with Jupiter Communications.

Consumers who are online represent a large and growing portion of U.S. consumer spending. Jupiter Communications research forecasts that U.S. online users will account for 75 percent of all online and offline U.S. retail spending in 2005.

Regardless of the type of retail business you want to start, you cannot ignore the Internet. Don't let it discourage you, either. Each type of retailing has strengths and weaknesses, so you decide which approaches you want to use in your business.

Specialty Catalogs Deliver

Mail order has evolved from general catalogs to specialty ones. Small entrepreneurs can compete with the large houses and sell at bargain-basement prices because of low operating costs. Improvements in technology and delivery speed merchandise to customers. Specialty mail order appeals to busy people, hobbyists, people located in remote areas, and collectors. Local merchants and homebased entrepreneurs can fill niches and meet special needs for one-of-a-kind and limited-production items, gifts, novelties, leather goods, and personalized products. A recent accounting by the U.S. Census Bureau of 5,000 specialized mail order houses reported nearly $25 million in sales.

Storefront retailers are incorporating the power of the Internet as a strategic business imperative, and you'll hear from some entrepreneurs in this book about how they're doing that. For more information on setting up an e-commerce business, read *Entrepreneur's* business start-up guide No. 1819, *e-Business*.

Vending Machines

Automatic merchandising—or vending machine retailing—has been a proven business concept for more than a century. *Vending Times*, the industry's trade magazine, reports that snacks and soda sales alone totaled more than $20 billion in 1999. As with any other sales venture, having the right product in the right place at the right time is key. This business is highly appealing because of the low startup cost, low working capital, and low overhead. This is a cash business, with you collecting the money when you replenish supplies. In Europe, shoppers can use their cell phones to pay for items in vending machines by debiting their checking accounts online. This is the future for American vendors as well.

Once mostly restricted to gum, candy bars, and canned sodas, today's vending machines sell snack foods, fruit, hot drinks, soups, milk, ice cream, fresh flowers, and an array of impulse goods and necessities. The machines are usually placed in high-traffic locations, such as subway stations, railroad and bus terminals, restaurants, office buildings, and bars. Entrepreneur's business start-up guide No. 1375, *Vending Business*, shows you how to capitalize on the billions of dollars Americans feed vending machines every year.

Service Retailers Are Different

Some retailers offer after-sales services, such as repair and installation. For example, musical instrument stores, electronic and appliance stores, pool and spa stores, and computer stores often provide repair services. Then there are stores that are dedicated to service, such as shoe repair, pool and spa water treatment, and vacuum and sewing machine service. Service organizations include those specializing in education, travel, entertainment, health care, home care, child care, physical training, space planning/organization, coaching, insurance, and countless others.

A service firm is one that derives more than 50 percent of its sales from providing services that may involve a combination of tangible and intangible offerings. Service businesses are currently the most frequently established operations. Since they usually sell a specialty or skill, credibility is very important. Start-up costs are often low, and many service businesses can be operated from home.

Services provided by baby-sitters, real estate brokers, and tax advisors require some knowledge or skill. Selling a service to consumers is usually more of a challenge than

▲

Reinventing Retailing

Until the late 1990s, buyers and sellers conducted trade through three channels: in person, by phone, and by mail. The Internet has become the fourth way for consumers to get what they want. Here's what experts say merchants should prepare for:

○ doing business 24 hours a day, 7 days a week

○ making price comparisons with sources around the world

○ consumers' Web research influencing billions of dollars in offline sales

○ consumers turning to the Internet in record numbers to fulfill their gift-giving and other purchasing wants and needs

○ retail competitors conducting business online and building relationships with customers through e-mail, forums, and chat rooms

selling merchandise. Consumers can touch, handle, and examine goods; this is something they cannot do with most services. Services must be experienced. For example, hair styling and dating services have to be experienced to be evaluated.

You may need to tell the prospective customer what you are going to do, do it, and explain why you did it that way. For example, a carpet-cleaning service that uses a deodorizing process after cleaning the carpet should tell its customers about the special care included in the price and why this extra step is beneficial. Service providers often spend more time with their customers than do merchandise providers.

Many services are essentially perishable. For example, event tickets are only good for the day and time of the baseball game or performance. And dentists, physicians, attorneys, consultants, and accountants cannot recover earnings lost because of an unfilled or lost appointment. In contrast, tangible goods can be held in inventory and sold over several days or months. If a hotel room is empty for an evening, the revenue is lost forever, whereas a book or roll of wallpaper can be profitable for many seasons.

Most service firms are small, single-unit operations, and small size limits service companies' ability to achieve economies of scale. Changes are occurring, however, as tangible-goods firms have established major stakes in service and have introduced tangible-goods merchandising techniques in the services area. One of the biggest growth areas is in franchising service organizations in the convenience industry. There are now child-care, car-care, and home-care franchises. There is also growth in chain dental, medical and legal clinics, and real estate firms. Service industries are typically characterized by low barriers to entry. Consequently, competitors can quickly enter a market and challenge existing businesses.

Many service organizations are labor-intensive. The output of an attorney, florist, or tax preparer cannot easily be increased. These and other services must be personally produced and tailored to the needs of individual clients. This precludes the use of automation and other laborsaving strategies.

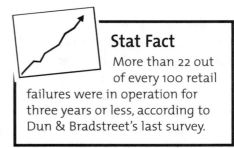

Because of this, and the fact that many services are offered only at the point of sale, standardization in the level of service and quality is difficult to achieve.

The demand for services is often more difficult to predict than the demand for tangible goods. And demand for services can fluctuate widely by the month, day of the week, or even the hour of the day.

Consumers also seem to feel that purchasing services is a less pleasant experience than buying goods, and consumers perceive higher levels of risk in buying services than in purchasing tangible goods. To bridge the "information gap," consumers are increasingly doing their research on lawyers, mechanics, banks, and a host of service providers on the Internet the same way they compare features and prices for tangible goods.

Consuming Appetite for Services

Time is becoming increasingly scarce for millions of people. The 24/7 pace technology has brought us spells opportunity as well as challenge for retailers. New businesses have sprung up to take care of many of life's chores. Personal shoppers, mother's helpers, after-school programs, tutors, handyworkers, maids, valets, insurance and tax preparers, home grocers, pet-walkers, and reminder services are just a few ideas entrepreneurs are cashing in on. The majority of couples are two-income families, leaving little time for preparing meals, picking up the dry cleaning, reading a software manual, remembering birthdays, standing in bank lines, and waiting for the cable installer to show up. People will pay dearly for more time, so figure out what you can sell or do to put people back in charge of their days, and you'll be a winner. Check out Entrepreneur's business service start-up guides No. 1306, *Gift Basket Service*; No. 1334, *Home Inspection Service*; No. 1058, *Child-Care Service*; No. 1313, *Event Planning Service*; No. 1330, *Wedding Consultant*; and other start-up guides for details on how to fill consumers' needs.

Step Up

Whether you are interested in a store, service, or hybrid operation, the deciding factor in your success or failure will be your relationship with the consumer. Get to know your prospects. Consider testing your business concept from home to control overhead costs. After gaining encouraging sales from friends, relatives, and neighbors,

▲

you can extend your reach through catalog, fax, and phone sales. From there, you might want to sell from a cart in a local mall or through a short rental in temporary space to test walk-in traffic and promotional efforts. Then you can determine if your sales and management skills justify start-up costs and long-term commitments. With a realistic view of what you're getting into, you can examine your options for location, size, and format—that is, can you sell more, and more profitably, through one distribution channel over another? Which form would that be—catalog, physical or virtual store, or television and radio sales?

Retailing's Image

Retail businesses exist to make people happy. To the extent that you satisfy customers, you fulfill your company goal. After that's said and done, retailers are in the business of customer satisfaction. This is the key to growth and profits.

The industry continually strives to shift its image from one that profits from others to one that serves people's interests. Image has many sides to it: friendliness of personnel, quality of merchandise, level of service, and ease of access. You must be ever-conscious of the perceived risk the consumer has of doing business with you. One is social risk: What someone buys affects how others view that person—fashionable and smart, or behind the times and ignorant. The second risk is economic. This is the possibility that a purchase decision will greatly reduce the consumer's budget and not yield substantial satisfaction or value.

Social Responsibility

Retailers are improving their image by assuming greater social responsibility. In doing so, they're meeting the needs of society as a whole, rather than just focusing on maximizing profits. They provide their facilities for art exhibits, forums, and community activities. Executives lead fund-raising drives that benefit the community, underwrite programs, sponsor events, and mentor students. Being a business owner provides opportunities for you to be involved in issues that matter to you and your customers.

Some retailers choose to locate in a downtown area that has become blighted over the years. They use some of their profits to help supplement federal funds for revitalizing the area. Locating in an inner city has special challenges because of the problems of vandalism, shoplifting, and other crimes. Nonetheless, some retailers want to make a contribution to society by upgrading the inner city while looking for profits over time.

Long a leader in providing career opportunities for women, retailers have generally made an effort to match the cultural mix of their employees to the community that surrounds them. This is a combination of social responsibility and good business sense. Many retailers have also initiated internal affirmative action programs to provide minorities with equal opportunities for upward mobility. Some retailers make a special contribution by employing high school dropouts and prison parolees in an attempt to train and retain them for the good of society and the firm.

Retailers are also assuming greater responsibility for the products they sell. As a retailer, you will have to be careful in buying products from resources. This involves not only ownership and licensing issues but also labor practices, environmental concerns, and research procedures. Growing numbers of consumers prefer products made with sustainable materials and will not use certain kinds of animal or plant products. They want to discourage the use of chemicals and

Smart Tip

Tip...

Retailers should be people people. But having the gift of gab and being comfortable in diverse and changing conditions are not the only traits that contribute to success. Whether you have a store, vending machine, catalog, or service, organizational skills can make or break you. Your ability to schedule payments, people, promotions, and products requires a remarkable amount of planning, focus, and perseverance.

Retailers' Call to Action

To help fight the problem of so-called "sweatshops," all members of the National Retail Federation endorse the organization's Statement of Principles on Supplier Legal Compliance and pledge that they:

○ are committed to legal compliance and ethical business practices;

○ choose suppliers who share that commitment;

○ include contractual language requiring their suppliers to comply with the law;

○ take appropriate action if a supplier has violated the law; and

○ support and cooperate with law enforcement authorities in the proper execution of their responsibilities.

"Retailers take their responsibilities to their customers very seriously, and we have taken aggressive and proactive steps to help our suppliers obey the law," says Tracy Mullin, president of the Washington, DC-based trade association. "Retailers have answered the call and are doing their part to ensure that the products they sell are made legally, ethically, and morally."

materials that are harmful to people and the environment, are wary of genetically engineered foods, and expect disposable items to be recyclable.

Retailers should be aware of groups like the Sierra Club, People for the Ethical Treatment of Animals, and Greenpeace, which often influence consumers' perception of proper business conduct. The Fair Trade Federation is an association of fair trade retailers, wholesalers, and producers whose members adhere to social criteria and environmental principles to foster a more equitable and sustainable system of production and trade.

Know that you may also be required to have some products tested or review test documentation before selling a product. The reasons are obvious: Government regulations are making it mandatory, the increasing cost of liability insurance is forcing retailers to eliminate some items, and consumers are becoming better informed and more demanding. You'll need to do some homework to stand behind your products.

Air and water pollution, accumulation of toxic chemicals and wastes, and overflowing landfills are just some of the environmental problems of the 21st century. Several existing businesses and franchises are providing opportunities for entrepreneurs to operate and invest in. Selling organic produce and herbs, natural garden services, natural products, products made from recycled materials, and ecotourism are a few of the ways retailers are making a living and a life from their beliefs.

Windows of Opportunity

Today, finding the right goods or services and creatively marketing them no longer assures that a retail firm will grow and prosper. You must run your business with a constant eye on the consumer. You must have a strategic view of your business and focus on your positioning, changing consumer lifestyles, technological advances, and competitive business concepts.

Of all the habits of highly successful businesses that sell directly to the consumer, the ability to assess relationships with the marketplace is perhaps the most crucial. Being able to anticipate and adapt to constant changes in the retail environment more quickly and effectively than the competition is every retailer's goal. The ability to harness the energy of change is what separates innovative, energetic, growing, profitable companies from obsolete, static failures.

Store retailing offers you the kind of business in which you get to meet lots of people. The retail store is a cash-and-carry operation. The day you open your store to the public, you begin taking in money at your cash register. Capital requirements are characteristically lower than for either manufacturing or wholesaling. This ease of entry is very attractive and explains the large number of new stores launched every year.

Consumers 40 and older are more familiar with retail stores than with all other business types because they have shopped in stores all their lives. Younger consumers have a broader perspective on shopping, which incorporates various electronic outlets (telecommunications devices, the Internet, and TV) for purchasing goods and services.

What Now?

Take a look at the demographic trends. Ask your chamber of commerce, local college or university business school, reference librarian, and newspaper marketing department for reports on demographic trends in your city. How are national trends reflected in your market area? Are you ahead of or behind what's going on? Watch what the leaders are doing. What are the master plans for major educational institutions, governmental agencies, and businesses in your community? Leverage their investments to get a higher return on yours in the marketplace.

With a growing population over 50, businesses that sell walkers, jar openers, easy-dressing clothing, large-print books, and other useful items for the elderly are promising.

Another growing business caters to teenagers. Tutor concepts like Sylvan Learning Systems Inc. in Baltimore and Huntington Learning Centers Inc. in Oradell, New Jersey, are two examples of early entrants in this growing field. Plato's Closet, a unit of Grow Biz International Inc. in Minneapolis, sells secondhand designer clothing—just the kind teens are looking for.

Do You Accept the Challenge?

The best retailers are outgoing, verbal people who like to live in the fast lane. Most retail jobs present continual variety, meeting and mixing with people, creating your own opportunities, and generally engaging in self-promoting activities. This is a dynamic field that places a high demand on responding quickly to change, bringing diverse elements and people together, working unscheduled hours, taking rejection, negotiating deals, resolving confrontations, and adjusting to periods of high and low activity.

Is this the kind of atmosphere you want to work in? Do you have the personality for retailing? If you answer yes, read on. The more you learn about retailing, the better prepared you are to make the right choices when starting your business.

In the next chapter, we'll cover more about the personality of a successful retailer and help you decide, based on your strengths and interests, what type of retail business is right for you.

2

Making a
Plan

There are two typical start-up scenarios for entrepreneurial ventures. One: An entrepreneur has an idea and turns it into a business. Two: A business idea turns someone into an entrepreneur.

Dan Dye and Mark Beckloff loved dogs. One Christmas, Mark's mom gave him a recipe for homemade dog biscuits and a dog bone cookie cutter. A few months later, Mark's neighbors and friends were clamoring for freshly baked biscuits from the budding entrepreneur's home kitchen. This unique business eventually grew into the Three Dog Bakery retail and wholesale operations and earned the entrepreneurs appearances on the "Oprah Winfrey" and "Good Morning America" shows.

"Business, by its very nature, is nothing more than a couple of people coming together and creating something where there was once nothing," says Dye. "We've seen people's lives ruined by greed and bad choices. But we have also seen lives enriched and empowered by hard work and creative visualization." Seeing is believing, as you're about to find out, even if the "seeing" is only in your mind's eye. This book will show you how to make your dream real.

Darrell T.'s future came into view quite by accident. Darrell was working with his parents in their construction firm when his parents decided to sell the company and retire. "I walked into my first Thomas Kinkade gallery and was hooked. I actually started inquiring within two months about the availability of [opening] an art gallery. Before then, [my parents and I] had done no retail and never dreamed of selling art for a living," Darrell says. "It's just the effect the art had on us; it caused us to go into this line of work." Darrell and his parents are licensed dealers of the internationally published artist in Seattle.

Retail and You: A Match Made in Heaven?

Is retail the right opportunity for you? Weighing several factors will help you answer that question. Personality, motivations, your strengths and weaknesses, money, and experience should be at the top of your checklist.

Making a good career decision involves both self-assessment and market research. Begin the self-assessment process by examining your skills and identifying what kinds of products or services you can offer. What skills do you most enjoy using? If you are artistic, merchandising a store and designing advertising may appeal to you. Or you may be mechanically inclined, enjoy solving puzzles, or helping people. Therefore an auto parts store, business consulting practice, or birthing coach business may be for you. By tying your skills to your market's wants and needs, you greatly increase the likelihood that your new business will be successful.

When their son graduated from college in 1998, Jim and Mary D. decided to follow Mary's interest in fashion and open a women's and children's clothing boutique in Thomasville, Georgia. "Mary has been in fashion modeling and retailing since she was a teenager, and I have been an administrative financial analyst and pharmacist. We have transferred much of my experience in retail pharmacy into this clothing business. Also, we both love dealing with the public," says Jim.

So what are retailers selling and where? The big picture is that travel services, books, gifts, and music are the best online product categories, according to research done by San Francisco-based consulting firm Cognitiative Inc. For catalogs, the consulting company found that apparel, gifts, music, and computer hardware do best. Storefront retailers fare well with furniture, food/groceries, apparel, and appliances. However, the lines are blurring as brick-and-mortar stores put up Web sites and manufacturers exercise all their options for making a sale. Retailers are no longer limited to one way of doing business. Whether consumers buy online or not, the richness of the online experience has raised the standards for retailers in all channels. Retailers must listen carefully to customers, know what competitive channels are doing, continuously hone their unique selling propositions, and respond quickly to changes.

Old Shoppers *vs.* New Shoppers

Over the last decade, technology—specifically the Internet— has transformed the "old" shopper into a "new" shopper with unprecedented control over the retail industry. These new shoppers use the Internet to identify needs, search for solutions, compare prices, buy what they want, and resolve problems. Many "old" shoppers have become part of this new breed, and as their number increases, the entire retailing experience—online and offline— is changed.

Previous generations have only been able to buy clothing, cars, and household items by going to a store, ordering through a catalog, or responding to a direct sales solicitation. Today's consumers have a full menu of choices, including cell phones, personal digital assistants, television, fax-on-demand, manufacturer-direct purchasing, and Web sites. Can you deal with these new realities?

▲

Personality

Many people successfully make the transition from being an employee to an employer, but many do not. Do you have what it takes to be in business for yourself? Even if you are suited to be a business owner, is a consumer-focused business for you? Are you better suited to be a wholesaler, distributor, or manufacturer? Answer the following five questions honestly. Talk to your spouse, best friend, or prospective partner about your answers as a reality check.

1. *Are you good at multitasking?* In your own business, you have to be willing and able to do everything yourself. When you work for someone else, you are usually responsible for just one thing and have limited control. You are supported by others with expertise or experience in different roles and functions. In retail, every day can be a stretch, as you encounter customers, employees, vendors, and landlords. You can't say "That's not my job." It's all yours.

Do You Have the Stuff?

What's your RQ? People with high "retail quotients"—the ability to weather the ups and downs of this industry—are self-aware, decisive, patient, strategic thinkers, courageous, and good students. Answer the following questions to estimate your RQ.

- ○ Why am I entering retailing?
- ○ Which business am I starting?
- ○ What goods or services will I sell?
- ○ Where will I get my goods or talent?
- ○ What is my market and who is my consumer?
- ○ Who is my competition?
- ○ Can I compete successfully with the competition?
- ○ What is my sales strategy?
- ○ What marketing methods will I use?
- ○ How much money is required?
- ○ Where will the money come from?
- ○ What technical and management skills do I need?
- ○ Where do I want to be in five years?
- ○ Do I want equity, income, or both?

---

2. *What is your risk tolerance?* In a start-up retail business, you worry about being in the right place at the right time with the right goods and services for the right people at the right price. Do you adjust quickly to unplanned events or prefer more predictable, organized projects? Do you see risk as a threat or an opportunity?

3. *Do you count on a paycheck?* New business owners can rarely count on a regular paycheck. Start-ups frequently require more capital than planned. Something's bound to go wrong or change even though everything is penciled out in your plan. If you break out in a cold sweat if you aren't paid on the same day every month, you may want to rethink going out on your own. Most of the money you make will go right back into inventory and other costs of doing business.

4. *Are you a self-starter and comfortable being alone?* Or do you draw your energy from being around others and count on colleagues for support and advice? In your own business, you must lead, knowing what to do and when to do it, and be fully accountable for everything that happens. The buck stops with you. Sometimes that's a lonely place.

5. *Do you value predictability or prize diversity?* Not only are there laws against discrimination in hiring and business practices, but America is a multicultural society. When you open your store or service company, you will be interacting with a wide spectrum of customers, vendors, advisors, and employees. Retailers need to be people-oriented, flexible, and good-natured. Can you manage conflict, see things from others' point of view, and cater to their taste, not yours?

Growth or Income?

What is your business goal—income or equity? The difference between a lifestyle and growth business will factor into your decision to launch or buy a company. The choice boils down to: Are you buying a job, investing in an asset, or both? Many entrepreneurs choose a business that offers both income and equity growth because they want to sell the business down the road and use the equity return as a retirement nest egg. Considering the wild swings in the consumer market, relying solely on the proceeds from selling your retail operation for your retirement is risky.

An income company is one that creates more income than value or equity, such as a

> **Beware!**
> Think about what you want in the long run.
> A number of small video store owners who thought they could sell their stores with enough money to retire on have been disappointed by the low return on used videos. Some companies require continual capital investment without providing profits for years. Can you hang in there financially and endure delayed gratification while you build equity in your enterprise?

single-person professional practice. When the lawyer, handyman, or other principal practitioner retires, the business shuts down with few assets to sell.

Strengths and Weaknesses

There has to be a compelling reason why you want to become a retailer. There needs to be an even stronger reason for the type of retail business you choose. Think about what you're good at, what you really know, and most of all what you truly love doing.

Part of what makes a good entrepreneur is originality, not the ability to catch a ride on somebody else's coattails. Look at "unglamorous" areas for new business ideas. (Insurance billing and pest control businesses can provide a good living.) Be open to all of the possibilities. As an entrepreneur, you will need to oversee the present while planning two stages ahead. First you must raise your awareness of what's out there. Then you must get into the habit of writing down the ideas that you hear.

Money

You may like the security of having a steady paycheck but want to be your own boss. How can you decide what's more important: job security or self-employment? In a workplace defined by constant change, there are very few people who truly have the security they're seeking. There are no guarantees you will have customers tomorrow. To help you test your resolve to be a retailer, you can develop your new business on a

---

Will It Work?

Test your concept before investing heavily in starting up a business. You can gauge consumer response to your business idea by renting a booth at a flea market. Commit to several weeks at the same location and do some market research. Find out what shoppers think of your selection and what they would like that they don't already see. Do you like dealing with the public? Try a few different venues to sample a cross section of your market. Fine-tune your concept, presentation, and prices. Do people want what you're selling? The only way you can tell is if you are converting interest to sales. If you can make a profit at this point, you may want to move up to rent a cart or kiosk in a shopping district. Many shopping malls provide temporary space in empty storefronts between leases to full-time tenants. While these options are more expensive than working from home or going door to door, they expose your idea to a greater number of prospects, which will give you the facts and figures you need to make a wise decision about the future of your business.

---

part-time basis. Perhaps you could see individual clients or sell your products in the evenings or on weekends. This would allow you to test the marketplace and increase your confidence in your ability to market yourself or merchandise.

How solid are your finances today, and what do you project for the future? This is not the place for rationalizing or unrealistic optimism. Most businesses fail because they are undercapitalized or because they are unable to manage the money they have. Does your proposed team have the leadership, skills, and experience to compete? An honest answer here can save you a lot of pain down the road.

How long do you plan to be in business before you retire or sell? Will this be a family-owned and operated business, or are you planning to go public? Whose money will be invested in the business—yours or other people's?

Experience

Another consideration is the extent of your preparation for the business. Your chances for success are significantly improved if you've had prior experience in the particular line or trade.

Three brothers in Thomasville, Georgia, have all the bases covered for running a successful hi-fi sales and service business specializing in equipment for home theaters and live field recordings. Jim O. is a sales and public relations whiz; Doug has business experience and Web savvy; and Carlos can put together or fix anything. Their fascination with sound and the equipment that enhances music, nature, voices, and imagery has sustained a passion for their work for more than 20 years.

Beware!
As you formulate your business plan, you may be looking for any support you can get. Be selective in whom you give your business plan to, and check out people who claim they can connect you with financing for a slight fee or "miscellaneous" expenses.

If you love to cook and entertain, you may be considering a catering business or want to explore the growing personal-chef industry. We suggest you first work with a successful caterer or chef to get an insider's view of the business. You can do some online research at www.4Caterers.com and by visiting the Web site of the American Personal Chef Association (www.personalchef.com).

Technical and Management Skills

Have your co-workers, friends, or relatives always paid you compliments about your ability to organize things, persuade people, or create beauty wherever you are? Ask people who know you what they think you're good at doing.

Take a look at your resume or news articles and memos written about you. Refer to your teachers' assessment of you on old report cards and your boss's comments on employee evaluations. What have you been given awards for? We've talked about what you enjoy; now take a hard look at what others identify as your talents. After all, you will have to rely on strangers—hundreds or thousands of them—for your livelihood. To make a profit from your retail venture, you will need to get people to pay you for what you have to offer.

Accurate and timely record-keeping, fiscal responsibility, and interpersonal skills are the basic requirements for a start-up. Some store types call for technical skills or professional preparation (optical shops, photo studios, beauty salons, pharmacies, electrical supply stores, and plumbing-fixture outlets, for example). Others require special licenses (liquor stores, car dealerships, restaurants, bars, caregiving, and so forth). You will either have to have the proper license or hire some one that does.

> ### Smart Tip
> **Tip...**
>
> Tie into trends. Help the elderly, market extreme sports, or target teenagers or Latino families. Keep your finger on the pulse of American consumers: Look through news outlets like daily newspapers, *People*, and *USA Today*; review industry reports from retail trade organizations; read business magazines like *Wired, Sales & Marketing,* and *Entrepreneur*; and get out there and observe what people are doing. What do people say they're missing?

Who do you know who could help, either in the business itself or as an advisor? Who can you rely on to give you solid information? Who can you bounce ideas off?

Business Goals

What do you want to create? Starting a business is an act of creation, an opportunity for personal expression of goals and values as well as a means to an end. It seems that there are more questions at this point than answers, but keep at it. Remember, persistence is a litmus test for those suited for retailing and self-employment. If you're getting tired of having to think about so many things already, this may not be the right time for you to go into business for yourself.

For those of you who say "What next?" make up a personal goals worksheet to flesh out how you feel about these issues. At this point, you need to clarify what kind of retail business you want to invest your life in. Will it be a socially and environmentally responsible business? A big business that you can sell? A business that doesn't require employees, or

> ### Smart Tip
> **Tip...**
>
> "Surround yourself with people who are inspirational, insightful, and supportive of you and your business venture," counsels Jennifer Kushell, president and founder of the Young Entrepreneurs Network. Don't listen to people who say you're too young to be serious about business. For tips of the trade, visit www.yenetwork.com.

one that provides good jobs for others? A business you can pass on to your family? Or one that provides you with a glamorous lifestyle?

Corporate lawyer Stephanie B. just knew she wanted a change—something very different from setting up wills, trusts, and foundations. She thought about what she could do for about six months. Then she heard about Backer's Annual Pet Industry Trade Show & Educational Conference, where she learned about pet bakeries. Six weeks later, she translated her love of animals into a new venture—an all-natural pet bakery and store in Newport Beach, California.

Is There Enough Time or Demand?

Many entrepreneurs leave companies to do the same thing better on their own. Even though you've worked for someone else's successful retail operation, duplicating that store or service somewhere else is no guarantee that it will do as well as the original. (You could also run into legal problems if you signed a noncompete agreement with your former employer, so tread cautiously.) Timing, trading area, population, and other factors such as your mix of skills and experience impact the outcome of your efforts. It may have taken your former employer 10 or more years to build that business up to the level you found while working there. There may no longer be a need for another of the same enterprise or sufficient reason for the customer to switch to your business. The cost of entering the market now may be too high to survive the start-up and development phase of the business.

> **Tip...**
>
> ### Smart Tip
> The arrival of a super-store or national chain in a retailer's market area need not spell doom for a small retailer. Jack A. Taylor, professor of retailing at Birmingham-Southern College in Alabama, suggests you follow the advice of Jerry Garcia of the Grateful Dead. "You don't want to be considered the best at what you do. You want to be the only one who does what you do."

If you want to get into retail because you want to cash in on the yogurt, doughnut, nail parlor, or discount shoe craze, beware of oversaturation. Just because it's a popular type of business does not mean the market will support one on every block. According to the U.S. Census Bureau, there are more clothing and accessories stores in the United States than any other type of retail operation. Food and beverage stores are next in number of establishments, with motor vehicle and parts dealers coming in third. Visit the U.S. Census Bureau's Web site (www.census.gov) to check out other data for retail trade. In Chapter 4, we'll give you some additional information for a reality check.

At the opposite end of the spectrum from the "safety in numbers" approach is the "break out from the pack" route. Because certain retail types are few in number,

▲

advocates leap to the conclusion that there is ample room for more. Ask yourself if more are needed for a growing population, or if they are few in number because only a small segment of the total population is interested in old maps or bagpipes. Refer to the *Statistical Abstract of the United States* in your public library for the number of stores of a particular type in existence, and see which ones are in short supply and may spell opportunity for your area and interest.

Look at Industry Numbers

Operating results for retail businesses can vary considerably from one year to the next. The retail sector is in a continuous state of flux. So if you're basing your business choice on the rate of growth, businesses that yielded the highest operating profit percentages, or top sales, you still need to keep up with the financial news.

A strong business plan begins with a statement of the mission or purpose of your business.

The 1999 "Top 100 Specialty Stores" listing, compiled by American Express and the National Retail Federation, revealed the strength of specialty retailing in housewares, furniture, and fine jewelry. Retailers in the toys, books, consumer electronics, recorded music, and sporting goods businesses have had to contend with fundamental changes in their markets, including shifts in consumer tastes and the

Profit Prophet

Operating profit percentages say a lot about the health of business opportunities. Operating profit is the amount of money remaining after subtracting operating expenses from gross profit. According to RMA, a Philadelphia-based association of lending, credit, and risk management professionals that serves the financial services industry, the five retail businesses that yielded the highest operating profit percentages for 1998–1999 were:

Used merchandise stores	6%
Jewelry stores	5.9%
Candy stores	5.7%
Bakeries	5.3%
Optical goods stores	5%

pressure of online competition. It is in the nature of specialty stores, with their narrow merchandise mixes, to be more susceptible—both positively and negatively—to the trends, fads, fashion, and other things that influence consumer behavior.

Start Thinking About Your Mission

Can you explain why your business will be sustainable over time? A strong business plan begins with a statement of the mission or purpose of your business. From it, you establish the objectives that you want to achieve, and then you work on your positioning strategy and all the other details that add up to a profitable venture.

So take a moment to write down your mission statement. It will be invaluable in helping you make decisions before and after you open your business. The basic ingredients of your mission statement are definitions of products and services to be offered; customers to be served; geographic area(s) to be covered; how physical assets, financial assets, and human resources will be used to create customer satisfaction; and how the firm intends to compete in its chosen markets.

Smart Tip   Tip...

For retail news you can use, check out these Web sites: Dun & Bradstreet, www.dnb.com; the National Retail Federation, www.stores.org; and Chain Store Age, www.chainstoreage.com.

Your mission statement provides a clear sense of direction for the enterprise and distinguishes your business from all others. It also often reflects the values and philosophy by which you want to run your firm.

Dr. Leonard L. Berry, marketing professor and director of the Center for Retail Studies at Texas A&M University in College Station, Texas, warns that uninteresting stores, unfocused stores, and stores with order-takers, not salespeople, won't make it. Consumers are value-minded and have high expectations for their shopping experience, including choices, fun, convenience, and service. Consider these elements when writing your mission statement.

Stat Fact

Service and retail sectors of the U.S. economy posted the largest numbers of start-ups in 1999, accounting for 47,643 new service businesses and 29,263 retail operations, says a recent report by Dun & Bradstreet.

Jim and Mary D. developed this mission statement for their women's and children's boutique in Thomasville, Georgia: "To meet the needs of [female] shoppers for unique and fancy women's and children's clothing and accessories by providing matchless value and service within our marketing sphere of influence." Fred W.'s Montpelier, Vermont, music store's mission statement simply says, "Music to color silence."

▲

You must clearly and simply define who you are and what you're doing. If you can't clearly state who you are, what you're doing and for whom, you are going to have trouble communicating your value to financiers, vendors, employees and customers. Use the "Mission Statement Worksheet" below to formulate your own.

Be a Trend-Watcher

Newspaper and magazine articles identify trends you can take advantage of or test your idea against. Business news and programs dedicated to entrepreneurs reveal opportunities, and futurists, cultural anthropologists, and industry analysts can help you navigate what is to come. Deloitte & Touche, Jupiter Communications, Ernst & Young, Dun & Bradstreet, Faith Popcorn's BrainReserve (a marketing consulting firm that specializes in identifying and applying consumer trends), and the Trends Research Institute (a trend forecasting company) publish useful information. Refer to the Appendix for more great sources.

Mission Statement Worksheet

Fill in your mission statement on this worksheet. Remember that the mission statement should clearly define the following:

○ *A view to the future.* How do you envision your business down the road—in one year, two years, and in ten years?

○ *A view to your customers' perception of your company.* How do you want them to think of you?

○ *A view to the retail community at large.* How do you want the retail community to perceive your business?

Mission Statement for *(your business name)*

_____

_____

_____

_____

_____

_____

Though the dreams of entrepreneurs have given birth to a multitude of different businesses, identifiable trends exist. Currently, young entrepreneurs are flocking to five distinct industries: high technology, entertainment, apparel, multilevel marketing, and international trade. The retail expression of this phenomenon includes online shops, event ticket resellers, special-event planning businesses, themed restaurants, T-shirt businesses, store-branded merchandise, clothing boutiques, and network marketing of vitamins, makeup, skin care products, and telephone cards.

Paco Underhill, founder and managing partner of Evirosell (a behavioral market research and consulting company), Gerald Celente of the Trends Research Institute, and Faith Popcorn of BrainReserve (all founded in New York) have published books and reports outlining major social trends that suggest areas retailers can capitalize on. Among them are:

- *Cocooning.* Because of a renewed focus on home life, Americans are reading more, chatting online, spending more time with their children, watching more TV, and engaging in other household activities. Home improvement is a $143 billion business. Home-shopping channels send out 62,000 packages per day. Private security is now a $104 billion market. There are more than 10 million at-home workers in America. Today's lawn-care business boasts more than 10 million customers. Home meal replacement is now a $100 billion business.

- *Self-gratification.* People hunger for small indulgences like imported chocolate, special-blend coffees, champagne, caviar, and vehicles for recreation instead of merely transportation. On a typical day, the restaurant industry averages more than $922 million in sales. Personal chefs, beauty spas, specialty foods, and premium-priced sunglasses offer small indulgences for stressed-out consumers who reward themselves with affordable luxuries. Theme parks are booming, with annual revenues of $6 billion.

- *Agelessness.* Baby boomers are enjoying more vitality relative to their age than previous generations have. They don't intend to stop or concede to aging. They find comfort in familiar pursuits and are nostalgic for their carefree childhoods. This creates a booming retail landscape for products from their youth—collectibles, re-creations (the new Volkswagen Beetle and the new Ford Thunderbird), trinkets in Disney stores, and grown-up toys like four-wheel-drive cars, motorcycles, and cruiser bicycles.

- *Personalization.* Consumers crave recognition of their individuality. This includes custom-made clothes and monogramming, personal distinctions (body piercing, tattoos, and hair color), imprinted stationery, and made-to-order bicycles and cars.

- *Female clout.* The way women think and behave is impacting business, making relationships more important than ever. Pay attention. A woman opens a new business every 60 seconds. Women control 80 percent of household spending,

▲

purchase 75 percent of all over-the-counter drugs, buy 50 percent of all PCs, own 52 percent of all stocks, and influence 90 percent of all car purchases.

- *Traditionalism.* Religion is back. Proms, bar mitzvahs, quinceañeras, and weddings are once again spectacular social events. People want the values their parents possessed, such as having a happy family life. Christian bookstores reap $3 billion in annual sales, and the wedding industry is booming, generating more than $32 billion in retail sales a year.

- *Quality reigns.* Consumers want the best value for their dollar. They know what quality is and want guarantees and products that last. This also means quality of life, as in saving time. BrainReserve trend-watcher Faith Popcorn predicts that by 2010, 90 percent of all consumer goods will be home-delivered.

- *Social conscience.* Concerned about the fate of the planet, consumers respond to retailers who exhibit a social conscience attuned to personal and corporate ethics, the environment, and education. Some retailers give employees paid time off for community service. Alice W., owner of a popular restaurant in Berkeley, California, created a foundation to attract support for educational and cultural programs that promote sustainable agriculture.

- *Concern for wellness.* Because people want to lead longer lives, there's a great deal of fear about aging and concern about health. Polluted air, contaminated water, and tainted food stir up a storm of consumer uncertainty. Hand sanitizers are now a $100 million category. Fitness club membership is up 64 percent over the last seven years for those aged 30 to 54. Alternative medical treatments for humans and pets, and the popularity of organic products (a $600 million business), have grown dramatically.

How Will You Compete?

Now that you have assessed yourself, popular culture, and your competition—and gotten a good view of the retailing climate—how do you intend to compete? There are five areas of specialization that can make a retailer a contender. You must focus on being better than any other retailer in one key area. Which one do you want to be known for?

1. *Service.* Nordstrom is the retailer most customers think defines the standard for great customer service.

2. *Experience.* The Disney Store is a destination stop for shoppers who enjoy more than just a transaction.

3. *Price/value.* Wal-Mart is synonymous with offering superior value for the money every day on every item.

4. *Product.* Sharper Image offers the best, most innovative products in its segment.

5. *Access.* CVS is relied on for convenient store hours seven days a week.

What's Your Plan?

Writing a business plan requires a lot of effort, but it all pays off in reducing anxiety, focusing your efforts, and recruiting the right talent at the right time.

In *The Complete Book of Business Plans*, authors Joseph A. Covello and Brian J. Hazelgren say you need to answer these questions when writing a business plan:

- *What is your product or service?* Take off the rose-colored glasses, forget the marketing hype, and take a critical look at what you want to do.
- *Who are your customers?* Who currently buys/uses your planned products/services from your would-be competitors, and who might if the price/place/service were convenient for them?
- *What will be particularly gratifying or rewarding in your business for customers that differentiates you from everyone else?* You've got to know who you are and are not.

Are Antiques Your Bag?

Selling antiques is a growing business. An efficient way to get started is to rent a small space in an antiques mall. Most cities have buildings that rent spaces to a number of independent dealers. Visit several on different days of the week and at different times to make an appraisal of the vitality of the location and caliber of clientele. Talk with the dealers. Are they happy? Do their wares complement what you plan to sell?

For rent, you usually pay a flat fee plus a percentage of sales. You can expect the mall owner to provide cashier services, insurance, utilities, and advertising. About $15,000 to $50,000 in inventory should get you up and running, dealers say. Buying your inventory at trade shows, garage sales, flea markets, estate sales, auctions, and from established dealers, you'll learn a lot about the antique market. You'll need display cases and shelves, business cards, and a place to sit and do your paperwork and clean and price items. You'll probably want to have the most current edition of *Schroeder's Antiques Price Guide* (Collector Books) and *Sotheby's International Price Guide: Antiques And Collectibles* (Rizzoli International Publications Inc.). Some trade magazines that will help you stay informed include *Antique Review, Antique Week, Antiques and Collectibles News Magazine, Antiques Magazine,* and *Collectors News.*

▲

Businesses are built on price, brand, assortment, service, reliability, and convenience.

- *How are you going to differentiate your store from your competitor(s)?* What new products or services can you provide that will keep customers coming in?
- *Can you learn to think three moves ahead?* Don't just focus on what you'll do to set your business apart; also think about how your competitor will counter your move. Do you have a contingency plan to deal with whatever fate deals you?
- What is your strategy for marketing your business? How are you going to reach prospective customers? Through what channels of communication? How can you build a relationship past the "try me" stage into a loyal customer base?

Once you've answered these questions and pursued the leads presented above, you're ready to sit down and put all your ideas down on paper in the form of a business plan.

By now, the plan for your business is really taking shape, and you're ready to move on to the next step of being an official retailer.

Decisions,
Decisions

The long-term goals you set in your business
plan will affect the decisions you make during your first year of
business, and your first year in business will affect your long-
term goals. You may find that there are aspects of your business
you like more than you thought you would and others that are
disappointing. There are some things about running a retail

▲

operation that you cannot anticipate until your business is open. A formal business plan is a tool that forces you to think beyond having "a good idea" to the many factors that go into actually doing what needs to be done to build a business that supports itself. A plan doesn't guarantee that every decision you make will be a good one, but you are better prepared for the future if you carefully think through various "what if" situations now.

All businesses require dedication, determination, enthusiasm, flexibility, and perseverance. Consumers today have a tremendous sense of well-being and wealth, but you should be prepared for a sharp or prolonged decline on Wall Street, a rise in interest rates, or signs of a slowing economy, which could cause Americans to curb their buying. There are all sorts of things that can turn people away from shopping, so plan for good times as well as rocky ones. If you want to get into a retail business because times are good, you may want to think again. If your passion for going out on your own and dealing directly with the public is not extinguished by the prospect of difficult times, read on.

Will you launch your own business or buy an existing one? Perhaps you're thinking about buying a franchise or a business opportunity. Whichever way you decide to go, keep the following in mind.

Buying a Business

The kinds of businesses you can purchase include franchises, business opportunities, network marketing systems, and existing independent businesses. Here are some facts and figures you can factor into your decision-making process.

Franchises

Franchising is becoming the dominant form of retailing in America. One recent year, there were more than 663,000 franchises in the United States, generating combined revenues in excess of $800 billion. Buying a franchise is a very specialized undertaking. There are numerous books and magazines devoted to the subject, and you should read as many of these as you can. There are also lawyers, accountants, and consultants who specialize in franchises and can give you the necessary insight and facts to make a wise decision. For more information, see this book's Appendix under "Franchise and Business Opportunities."

A recent Gallup Organization survey has found that the total average investment entrepreneurs made in a franchise was $143,260. In the United States, there are more than 3,000

In the United States, there are more than 3,000 different franchise opportunities available.

different franchise opportunities available. McDonald's and Burger King are the most popular franchises, but franchises can be found in nearly every industry, in various sizes and requiring a wide range of financial investments. Some smaller franchises, such as childcare and housecleaning services, continue to gain momentum.

Never buy a franchise without retaining an attorney and an accountant who specialize in franchise operations. Make sure they perform audits and assist with your due diligence and negotiations.

> **Smart Tip** *Tip...*
>
> There are two different kinds of franchises. One is a product franchise where you obtain the rights to purchase and sell the product of the franchisor, such as an automobile dealership. The other is called a business-format franchise, such as Chuck E. Cheese's.

Business Opportunities

A business opportunity is similar to a franchise in that you get to market a known product or service, but you don't open your business as an extension of the franchise. This is less expensive than buying a franchise. Some business opportunities have no start-up fees. Hallmark stores, Stride Rite children's shoe stores, and Apple computer stores are examples of licensed dealerships. You get national marketing support and use the product signs and logo of the parent company, but you operate as your own business. Some business opportunities offer a turnkey business package that gives the buyer a business plan and operations support.

Network Marketing Systems

The third form of business you can buy into is a multilevel marketing company (or network marketing system). These are direct-selling companies in which you sell specific products provided by the company based on your personal contacts rather than on the reputation of the brand. With network marketing systems, you get a percentage of the sales of all the new salespeople you bring into the distribution system. The buy-in is usually just a stock of inventory, and there generally is no equipment. But you probably won't receive support in the way of protected territory, product promotion, or operations training. Some network marketing systems offer sales and motivational seminars and will sell you videos, audiotapes, and marketing materials.

> **Bright Idea**
>
> For current information about franchises, check out the International Franchisee Association (www.franchise.org) and the American Association of Franchisees and Dealers (www.aafd.org). In January, *Entrepreneur* magazine publishes the Franchise 500, a listing featuring the hottest franchise trends.

Existing Independent Businesses

Acquiring an established business requires a greater financial outlay than starting one from scratch, but buying a business allows you to realize profits faster and receive a quicker return on your initial investment. A major advantage to this approach is that the business you're considering spending a chunk of money on has a track record to review. Obtaining outside financing may be easy, and projections should be more accurate because of known historical trends. The business already has its financial and marketing plans in action. You are paying for it having an established location, inventory, customer base, and trained staff.

Entrepreneurs wanting to buy an existing business will have to do as much—or more—research and careful analysis as is required when starting from scratch. Carefully evaluate the opportunity cost of entering various industries through acquisition. Do your due diligence and make sure there aren't any hidden reasons for the sale of the business—for example, the opening of a major competitor within your market area, a scheduled road widening that would take part of your parking lot, or increasing crime in the area.

⚠ Beware!

You do not eliminate all the risk of being in business when you buy an existing store. It is just as easy to inherit a bad reputation as a good one from a previous owner. The location may be bad, too expensive, or inadequate for expansion. The facility or equipment may be in disrepair or obsolete. The staff may be incompetent or disgruntled.

Many retailers have bought out failures or near-failures that could not be revived—even under the most skillful management. Complete and careful analysis is essential if a good buy is to be made. Verify the claims made by the seller, and look into the reputation and image of the store.

Experience on your part is essential because you will have to step right in and take over the day-to-day management. There is no time to learn on the job. Without expertise in the field, you are more apt to miss major problems and stall or set back the company's growth. Employees, vendors, and customers all need to feel confident in you from day one, or they'll go elsewhere. Buying an existing retail operation can lead to buyer's remorse without attention to all of these details.

Identifying Opportunities

The best place to begin looking for a business to buy is through your own contacts. Ask friends, relatives, and professional advisors if they are aware of any businesses for sale. Do some research on the Internet. Ask your accountant and attorney if they know of potential opportunities.

Many businesses for sale are represented by brokers. The business may be advertised in the newspaper or a trade magazine, or listed with a brokerage firm. Caution

> ## ⚠ Beware!
>
> There is no substitute for your own due diligence to determine what is a true opportunity and what is not. Remember that the Web is a marketing tool—just like corporate brochures and promotional seminars—and the claims and content have not generally been investigated or guaranteed to be accurate.

should be used in following brokers' leads because high-pressure sales tactics are frequently employed.

Some entrepreneurs simply go into a store they are interested in and talk to the owner to see if he or she would be interested in selling. Others go on the Internet to see what businesses are being advertised for sale. Sell-a-biz.com and BizBuySell.com are two such sites.

Evaluating the Business For Sale

To determine the value of the business, you will need the past five years' audited financial statements and tax returns. In addition, review the most recent financial statement for consistency. Use these financial statements, tax returns, support documents, personnel records, customer lists, vendor contracts, inventory reports, and accounts receivable and accounts payable schedules to help you ascertain the true value of the business.

Some sellers may not want to reveal much information until they are convinced you are a serious buyer. It's your job to convey that you are a trustworthy, serious buyer who must have sufficient information to make a well-informed decision. It is helpful to have your CPA or lawyer accompany you on these fact-finding missions. Generally speaking, buying any company that is less than three years old poses a substantial risk because it lacks a track record.

Objectivity is important when evaluating business purchases. Don't become emotionally attached to the point that your enthusiasm clouds your judgment and you don't ask the tough questions. You must be able to walk away from a questionable transaction. Helpful articles can be found at Business Book Press (www.businessbookpress.com/articles), the Small Business Library (www.bizoffice.com/library/library.html), the Retail Business Resource Center (www.retailadvz.com), and Small Business Advancement National Center (www.sbaer.uca.edu).

Launching Your Own Business

You may believe you have a distinct concept that is different or better than anything else out there, and you want to create your own business from the bottom up.

Most successful small businesses provide something attractive or advantageous by taking what's already there and developing some innovative features. Have you developed an improved technique for delivering goods to the market? Drive-thru coffee

▲

and juice bars situated near freeway onramps offer added value for commuters. Some clothing retailers send store reps to the customer's office with fashions and a laptop computer for taking orders after educating employees on options for Friday casual dress. Using the technology and initiative, these retailers help customers overcome time problems and deliver exceptional service in about half the time the traditional method requires.

May I Cut In?

There are several factors you need to take into consideration to help you determine if it is wiser for you to buy an existing business or start your own. Will buying this business give you a jump-start into retailing or waste precious resources trying to breathe life into someone else's failed dream? Ask yourself these questions:

1. Do I have the interests, skills, temperament, and experience to step in and run this business right away?
2. Do I have enough money to buy and operate the business and still have a reserve fund for unexpected needs?
3. What are the market trends (growth, size, and position) for this business?
4. How many years has this business been in operation, and how many owners has it had?
5. Why is this business for sale?
6. What am I actually buying—physical assets, name, location, customer list, existing business, or projected business?
7. Are the books accurate?
8. Is a profit being earned?
9. Are the operating ratios compatible with industry averages?
10. What is the worth of the business assets?
11. Are the employees highly trained and productive?
12. Are the customers loyal to the present owner or to the store? Will they leave when he or she leaves?
13. How long is the current owner willing to spend assisting in the smooth transfer of the business?
14. Does the business need an immediate cash infusion? Will that solve any problems?
15. Is the owner reluctant or cooperative in providing details and answers?

Perhaps you have an idea that will fill a market niche. A few entrepreneurs have started up successful ventures in ecotourism and other forms of adventure travel for those with money, social consciousness, and a desire for educational value to be added to their leisure time. What is your unique proposition?

Another reason for wanting to go your own way without the safety net of an existing business model is that you have developed new markets or promotional techniques for existing goods and services. For example, several years ago, Lenox Inc. aggressively promoted its bridal registry. Today, this promotional tool is now widely imitated in stores everywhere and online for weddings, graduation, Christmas, and baby gifts.

At this point, you have struggled with the question of whether retailing is for you. You have looked at the personal qualities you'll need and considered how you'd start up. You've narrowed down the type of business you want to go into, revised your business plan draft to reflect your refined thinking, and are about to make some other key decisions you hope will help you be a success in the retail industry. Now you're going to need to enlist the help of some experts.

Professional Advisors

No one said this was going to be easy. Throughout this book, we suggest many resources that have potential value for helping you make good decisions. We also recommend that you build a team of advisors that can guide you along the way. Given the level of your potential investment, industry experts suggest that you budget about 2 to 5 percent of your start-up costs for expert advice.

Lawyers and Accountants

Lawyers and accountants' general business experience enables them to review contracts, legalize your business name, outline the business structure, and counsel you on operational procedures you need to follow to avoid lawsuits. Their experience with retail clients will be invaluable in: helping you negotiate the best lease or buy terms for a business or property, establishing best practices for your store, keeping you abreast of current laws and regulations, and helping you manage risk. The more complex your start-up, the more important it is for you to hire professionals who have worked with entrepreneurs in the retail industry.

Bankers

As a retailer, you will deal with banks in a number of ways. If you accept credit cards, you'll need a bank that can handle merchants' accounts. Since you might want a loan at some time, it is helpful to deal with a local bank or branch with which you can develop a personal relationship. Start by getting answers to these four questions:

▲

Where do other retailers in your area bank? Is the bank you are considering FDIC-insured? What are its hours and merchant services? Does it have online banking that would be advantageous to your type of operation? Where you locate your business may limit your choices, so think about where you would be doing your banking when you are narrowing down the choices.

Average Gross Profit

Recent figures from RMA, a Philadelphia-based association of lending, credit, and risk management professionals that serves the financial services industry, indicate that the average gross profit before taxes for various types of retailers is:

Apparel and accessories	2.0%
Auto parts	2.5%
Bakery items	3.8%
Boats	1.8%
Cameras	3.5%
Candy	5.0%
Catalog and mail order items	0.5%
Flowers	2.7%
Furniture	2.5%
Gifts and souvenirs	3.6%
Household appliances	3.5%
Jewelry	4.8%
Liquor	1.3%
Miscellaneous home furnishings	3.7%
Miscellaneous retail items	0.5%
Motorcycles	3.6%
Musical instruments	2.7%
Nursery items	3.4%
Sporting goods	2.0%
Stationery	1.7%
Used merchandise	4.8%
Variety items	2.7%
Vending machine products	2.4%
Women's clothing	2.3%

One piece of advice you've probably heard before is to have a relationship with a bank before you need it so that when you do, it'll be there. Jim and Mary D., the Thomasville, Georgia, clothing entrepreneurs, used their savings and money from selling his pharmacy to start their shop. But they are planning on expanding both their online prom and bridal business and their store, so they are raising their profile with the bank now so they will be a known entity when they need those extra funds.

Jeff P., a grocer in Dadeville, Alabama, had a personal relationship with a bank for his cars and houses before he needed to approach his banker for start-up capital. "I had used the same bank before, so when I came to this area to start my business, I went to the local branch and was fortunate enough to meet a man who took me through the SBA process and got me an SBA loan," says Jeff. "He told me every step of what to do, and I did, and that was how I got started."

For more on banking, turn to "Bank Locally" on page 70 in Chapter 5.

Consultants

Consultants can provide useful services for your business. They can assist in the start-up or expansion phases of your business and suggest ways to manage and promote your enterprise. You may be approached by public relations firms, store designers or advertising agencies once your dba is published in the local newspaper or you file your business license with the city. Do not take anything for granted. Evaluate each person and company's track record, background, educational degrees, client list, and fees before you enlist their advice or services. Your vendors will provide a lot of free advice, which can be quite useful. Ask your suppliers, trade associations, the Better Business Bureau, and your local chamber of commerce for referrals to retail experts in areas you need help in.

Once you have made some of the important decisions discussed in this chapter, you're ready to move on to Chapter 4, which is all about establishing a location for your business.

Location

Although a great location may not guarantee success, a bad location will almost always guarantee failure. A new retail business needs to be where the customers are. You want a location with a reasonable degree of security, access to public transportation for your customers and employees, adequate parking for commercial as well as personal vehicles, room for an office, and that all-important sales space. Where you locate will determine the hours you keep, who your clientele is, and what types of promotions you do. Also, where you set up shop will impact how long it will take you to grow. Luckily, you have lots of options. Read on.

The Homebased Retailer

The economics of homebased businesses make them attractive. SBA statistics show that 40 percent of new companies launched outside the home will still be in business after five years. For home enterprises, 57 percent will still be in operation after five years. Many such businesses can be started with limited financial investments. The low overhead of operating a business from your study or guest room greatly increases your likelihood for survival.

Financial risk may be reduced by having little overhead, but other risks now replace it. Running a business from home requires the same drive and skills demanded of any business, plus a talent for time management, concentration, organization, and self-motivation.

Thanks to advances in technology, it is getting easier and less expensive to equip your business. Powerful computers eliminate multiple positions that were required only a few years ago. Now you can communicate worldwide, 24 hours a day, seven days a week, via the phone, fax, and Internet, eliminating time and distance barriers. Advanced technologies and outsourcing services at your disposal can help you project the same professional image as a storefront company.

Despite all this, a retail business is one of the few businesses that is difficult to run from home. This is largely due to a conflict between needing customers to come to your place of business and the penalties of having a stream of clients visiting your home.

Beware!

If you're operating your business out of a rental property or a co-op or condominium you own, be sure and check your CC&Rs. Even if the area is zoned for your business, house rules may pose a problem. Check with your landlord or co-op or condo owners' association. Consult a lawyer if you have any questions about the codes or want a special-use permit or a variance.

Everyone accepts the occasional garage sale, but some communities regulate how often you can have one. Most residential zoning excludes retail, so your neighbors can report you to city or county officials if your business creates noticeable traffic, noise, or parking problems. Some communities prohibit commercial vehicles or cars and trucks with signs on them from parking on the street.

One option for retailers who want to work out of their living room is to sell their goods and services from booths or tables at craft fairs, in cooperative booth space at emporiums or expositions, by mail order, or at flea markets. You can also sell retail on the

Internet. Seminar leaders, real estate agents, custom book producers, calligraphers, carpet cleaners, interior designers, direct mailers, catalog companies, tailors, pattern makers, feng shui consultants, personal commemorative makers, and genealogists report thriving while working at home.

There are many things you can do by yourself or by hiring people part time or full time. Do you love music, parties, and people? Try starting your own disc jockey service. If you have a knack for working with computers, your business could be based on computer tutoring, installation services, troubleshooting, or buying assistance. Combine people's concern for security and time, and start a home inventory business, auditing the possessions of homeowners for insurance documentation in case of fire, storm, or robbery.

Stat Fact

Homebased businesses are now widely accepted. The U.S. government estimates that there are now more than 16 million home enterprises estimated to collectively generate nearly $600 billion annually. The SBA says 1.5 million home businesses are launched each year. And Link Resources Corp., a marketing data organization, forecasts an annual growth rate for the home-office trend of 7 to 8 percent.

New York City-based Matt M. designs his high-end "architectural bags," catalog, and Web site from his apartment. He has a small showroom and office in the space, which gives him the freedom to design all night, fulfill orders, and do business overseas without having to hail a cab. "In a perfect, well-financed world, I would love a store," says Matt. "We have considered it several times over the last five years, but it

Home, Sweet Business?

In addition to the legal, logistical, financial, and operational questions of a homebased business, you need to consider your lifestyle and living arrangements. Operating a business from your residence will require some family concessions. Is your home loud and chaotic, or quiet and uncluttered? Does your condominium or apartment have thin walls or heavy-footed tenants upstairs? Can you devote the time and space that are needed to serve your customers? Different businesses require different amounts of privacy, focus, and schedules. You must honestly assess the physical and emotional challenges of having your business in your home before deciding it's the right base for your operation. You also must get the agreement of your family or living partners that they will honor your choice and adhere to rules required for blending work and home life.

has been impossible for us because of cost. My business is as much about image as it is about product, and to produce a shop correctly would be very costly."

Commercial Locations

If working at home is not for you—or it simply won't work for your particular business—be advised that the best location combines visibility, affordability, and lease terms you can live with. Brick-and-mortar retailers need to be where the action is, so deciding where to put your business is every bit as important as the business you decide to go into. It is risky to move into an area where there has always been trade assuming that there always will be. A lot of factors enter into the picture today, so study the business and consumer pages to see where you can find business support services and a growing community of people with regular incomes and interest in the goods or services you plan to offer.

The idea of opening a music store hit Fred W. in 1973. It was an idea born out of the desire to live in Central Vermont and to be his own boss and have time to play music. The search for a store location led to a 450-square-foot storefront in the Vermont capital of Montpelier—population 8,000. The fact that the street was a dark, narrow, practically forgotten alleyway of dowdy offices, a print shop, and a paint store did not dissuade Fred and his partner, George M. "We could not get a loan from our new landlord, which happened to be a bank, because they were not confident we would be able to a make a successful go of it in this location," Fred says. They nearly didn't. Even though there wasn't another music store in town, it was a struggle. After a year, it became clear that the business could not support two people, so Fred bought George out. In 1975, Fred's brother, Dennis, saved the store by becoming Fred's new partner and to this day is "the behind-the-scenes mastermind of all things technical that keeps the store alive," according to Fred.

Fred says his low overhead and the unique services his retail business offers have enabled him to ride the ups and downs of the economy. Business has grown up around him, and being located in the state capital benefits his business because of the tourism. Downtown Montpelier is now a vibrant place to be, and his store has become a destination for musicologists. Over the years, he absorbed two spaces in his building when stores went out of business, giving him more window and floor space.

Smart Tip

Tip...

After more than 20 years in the audio engineering and service business, Thomasville, Georgia-based Jim O. advises new retailers to always rent to begin with because you don't know how long you'll survive. He also suggests finding out where the high-traffic areas are in your market and locating where you can keep your overhead down.

Jim and Mary D. found Thomasville, Georgia, very charming. The population is about 20,000, and there is some industry there—Textron and Caterpillar, for instance. "This is a small town that's done really well," Jim says proudly, as he recalls what attracted them one New Year's Day to the community. "We're in a little town of American Main Street, which is a national project."

For Darrell T., the most difficult part of putting his Washington state-based art gallery business together was locating prospective sites. "In the Seattle area, it's difficult to find available retail space," says Darrell. "It's at a premium up here, so we not only had to target which locations we'd prefer to go to first, but also factor in which ones are likely to be available when the time comes for our expansion."

> **Tip...**
>
> ## Smart Tip
> Across America, revitalization in central business districts is taking place, and retailers are central to that effort. The main thoroughfare of any downtown is frequently named Main Street or Broadway. New shopping areas, mixed-use buildings, and pedestrian malls are cropping up, creating robust economic activity.

Researching Locations

Take the time to analyze the areas that appeal to you. There are three phases of choosing a location for your retail business: selection of a city, choice of an area or type of location within a city, and identification of a specific site.

In choosing a city, investigate these main factors:

- Size of the city's trading area
- Population and population trends
- Total purchasing power and who has it
- Total retail trade potential for different lines of trade
- Number and size of competition
- Quality and aggressiveness of competition

Once you have a general idea of what city you like, choose an area or type of location within a city by evaluating these:

- Customer attraction power
- The nature of competition
- Availability of access routes to the stores
- Zoning regulations
- Geographic direction of the city's expansion

▲

- General appearance of the area
- Sales and traffic growth prospects of the trade area
- Demographics of neighborhoods

These are factors in narrowing down your site choices:

- Traffic flow
- Complementary nature of neighboring stores
- Adequacy of parking
- Vulnerability to competition
- Cost of the site

Match the Area to Your Customers

Whether you're looking at a free-standing building or one in a strip mall, you have to do your homework. If you want to open a clothing store for young women 12 to 24 years old, for example, you would not want to locate in an area where the majority of residents are retired. Rather, you'd want to have schools, music stores, and snack shops that target this age group within walking distance of your business.

Get a county map with ZIP codes on it. Place an "X" where your business will be. Then draw three circles that represent 5, 10, and 15 miles from you. This is where your bread-and-butter customers live and/or work. Will their demographics support 75 percent, 20 percent or 5 percent of the sales you need?

You also want to see if the population is growing or declining. Are there seasonal variations in population that favor your type of business, or will you suffer when students, families, or snowbirds leave town? And you will want to check out the activity during the week, weekends, daytime, and nighttime to see if it's in alignment with your business plans.

Make your own analysis of the market and fact-check the figures a rental agent or developer gives you. In this respect, money for professional help is well-spent. Companies such as Claritas have demographic site reports available for sale online (www.natdecsys.com). You can get lifestyle consumer segmentation reports by ZIP code, retail trade potential in various areas, a list of

Smart Tip

Tip...

For the last seven years, Dun & Bradstreet and *Entrepreneur* magazine have ranked the top cities for small business. When you are looking for the most advantageous environment for your start-up, begin with a peek at the October issue of *Entrepreneur* magazine, and do your own analysis with the same criteria for the areas you are considering.

shopping centers, demographic trends, age by income, and other useful information.

Pinpointing the specific site is particularly important. In central and secondary business districts, small stores depend on the traffic created by large stores or a group of stores. These stores depend on attracting customers from the existing flow of traffic. However, where sales depend on nearby residents, selecting the trading area is more important than picking the specific site.

> **Smart Tip**
>
> A destination store is one to which customers will make a special trip to shop. Customers value the goods and services offered and tend to be more loyal and willing to travel longer distances to reach it.

Type of Products and Location Choice

Another factor that affects site selection is the customer's view of the goods you sell or the services you offer. Customers tend to group products into three major categories: convenience, shopping, and specialty goods.

Convenience Goods

Convenience goods are usually low-priced, frequently purchased items that require little selling effort, are bought by habit, and are sold in numerous outlets. Candy bars, newspapers, cigarettes, and milk are examples. Quantity of traffic is most important to stores handling convenience goods. The corner of an intersection that offers two traffic streams and a large window display area is usually a better location than the middle of a block. Such downtown convenience retailers as low-priced, ready-to-wear stores and drugstores have a limited ability to generate their own traffic. Convenience goods are often purchased on impulse in easily accessible stores.

In addition, the greater the automobile traffic, the greater the sales of convenience goods catering to drive-thru traffic. For the drive-thru store selling low-priced items, the volume of traffic passing the site is key. The consumer makes frequent purchases and wants things like gum, bottled water, soda, and chips readily available. Consumers are reminded when passing a convenience goods store that they need a particular item.

> **Smart Tip**
>
> At C-store (convenience store) locations, customers are willing to pay a little extra for the one or two items they are in a hurry to pick up in exchange for not having to wait in long lines. Express counters are also strong sellers of impulse items.

▲

If consumers must make a special trip to purchase food and drug items, they will want the store to be close to home. Studies show that the majority of people in the central city patronizing these stores shop within one to five blocks of their homes, and in suburban locations, the majority of customers live within three to five miles of the stores. For rural locations, the average driving time is 10 minutes, with 20 minutes being the maximum time customers will travel to a convenience store.

Shopping Goods

Shopping goods usually have a high unit price, are purchased infrequently,require an intensive selling effort , have price and feature comparisons done by customers, and are sold in selectively franchised outlets. Examples include men's suits, automobiles, and furniture.

For stores handling shopping goods, the quality of the traffic is important. While convenience goods are purchased by nearly everyone, certain kinds of shopping goods are purchased only by segments of shoppers. Moreover, it is sometimes the character of the retail establishment rather than its type of goods that governs the site selection. For example, a conventional men's clothing store generally does best in a downtown location close to a traffic generator like a department store. On the other hand, a discount menswear store tends to require an accessible highway location.

In many cases, buyers of shopping goods like to compare the items in several stores by traveling only a minimum distance. As a result, stores offering complementary items tend to locate close to one another. Another excellent site for a shopping goods store is next to a department store, or between two large department stores, where traffic flows between them. Another option is to locate between a major parking area and a department store.

A retailer dealing in shopping goods can have a much wider trading area than convenience

Smart Tip Tip...

The ideal location for a coffee and tea store is an area that has a steady flow of foot traffic, according to research done by the National Business Library. Busy retail shopping areas are generally more expensive to rent but give you the audience you're after. For more information on this $4.5 billion industry, read *Start Your Own Coffee & Tea Store* (Prentice Hall). Visit www.prenhall.com.

Smart Tip Tip...

If you plan to offer shopping goods, you should not locate too far away from your potential customers. Most of your customers will live within 5 to 10 miles of your store. The size of the trading area for a shopping goods store can be determined by a customer survey, automobile license checks, sales slips, charge account records, store deliveries, and local newspaper circulation.

goods stores. Without a heavily trafficked location, this more expensive type of store can generate its own traffic. In this case, a location with a low traffic count but easy accessibility from a residential area is a satisfactory site. Consumers buy these goods infrequently and make deliberate plans for these purchases.

Specialty Goods

Specialty goods usually have a high price tag, are bought infrequently, and require a special effort to make the purchase. Precious jewelry, expensive perfume, and fine furs are in this merchandise category.

Specialty goods are often sought by customers who are already "sold" on the product, brand, or both. Stores catering to this type of consumer may use isolated locations because they generate their own consumer traffic. In general, specialty goods retailers should locate in neighborhoods where the adjacent stores and other establishments are compatible with their operations.

Retail Compatibility

Most merchants prefer to be with other retailers. Only the exceptional operation, such as a restaurant or a freestanding discount house, can survive in isolation. A cluster of stores creates more traffic, exposes more people to your business, and creates a buying atmosphere that a single store cannot. Customers are attracted by crowds and like their shopping trips to be social outings.

Having said this, you want to make sure that you select the right community and site for your particular type of store. Will the other businesses generate traffic for your store? Or will you be located near operations that may clash with yours? For example,

Restaurant Parking

New restaurateurs often underestimate their parking needs when selecting a location. It is important to remember that customers want the most convenient access, especially during bad weather and at night. When scouting your location, see if there is off-street parking, parking meters, or time limits on street parking. Will you provide a paid lot, share a lot with other businesses, or rely on a commercial lot nearby? Check out any fees and business hours, and the possibility of valet parking or validating tickets for private lots.

a children's store in a service center of hardware stores and automotive repair businesses does not get enough exposure to its target audience to be successful.

Merchants' Associations

Most first-time business owners have no idea how effective a strong merchants' association can be in promoting and maintaining the business is a given area. Always find out about the local group of retailers. The presence of an effective organization can strengthen your business and save you money through group advertising and promotion programs, group insurance plans, and collective security measures.

Merchants' associations can be particularly effective in promoting stores using common themes or events and during holiday seasons. The collective action of a merchants' association can accomplish what an individual store owner can't. Some associations have induced city planners to add highway exits near their shopping centers. Others have lobbied for and received funds from cities to remodel their shopping centers, including extension of parking lots, refacing of buildings, and installation of better lighting.

How can you determine if the retail location you're considering has the benefit of an effective merchants' association? Ask other store owners in the area. Ask how many members the association has, who the officers are, how often the group meets, what the dues are, and what, specifically, it has accomplished during the last year.

Be aware that a shopping area with no merchants' association may be an ineffective one, be on the decline, or have contentious tenants or other problems. If you see a lot of litter or debris in the area, vacant stores, a parking lot in need of repair, and similar symptoms, you'll know this is not the area for you. With a little on-site investigation at different hours of the day, you can avoid problems by getting a true picture of retail life there.

Landlords

Directly related to the appearance of a retail location is the reputation of the landlord. Unfortunately, some retail landlords actually hinder the operation of their tenants' businesses. In fact, the landlord may be largely responsible for the demise of the premises and retailers' failure. For instance, some landlords restrict the placement and size of signs, forego or ignore needed maintenance and repairs, or rent adjacent retail spaces to incompatible or directly competing businesses.

Sometimes landlords lack the funds to maintain their properties. Rather than continuing to invest in their holdings and support their tenants, they try to squeeze out whatever they can get.

In addition to speaking with current tenants, talk to previous tenants of the location you have in mind. They can give you helpful information. Find out what businesses they were in and why they left. Did they fail or just move? What support or hindrances did the landlord provide? Would they rent from this landlord again?

Where's It Gonna Be?

While answering these 16 questions certainly won't exhaust all possibilities, it may help you decide on the best retail location for your business:

1. How much retail, office, storage, or workroom space do you need?
2. Is parking space available and adequate?
3. Do you require special lighting, heating or cooling, or other installations?
4. Will your advertising expenses be much higher if you choose a relatively remote location?
5. Is the area served by public transportation?
6. Can the area serve as a source of employees?
7. Is there adequate fire and police protection?
8. Will sanitation or utility supply be a problem?
9. Is exterior lighting in the area adequate to attract evening shoppers and make them feel safe?
10. Are customer restroom facilities available?
11. Does the store have awnings to provide shelter during bad weather?
12. Will crime insurance be prohibitively expensive?
13. Is the trade area heavily dependent on seasonal business?
14. Is the location convenient to where you live?
15. Do the people you want for customers live nearby?
16. Is the population density of the area sufficient?

▲

Zoning and Planning

Your town's zoning commission can give you the latest mapping of the retail location and surrounding areas that you are considering. Here are some questions to think about:

- Are there restrictions that will limit your operations?
- Will construction or changes in city traffic or new highways present barriers to your store?
- Will any competitive advantages you currently find at the location you're considering be diminished by zoning changes that will be advantageous for competitors or even allow new competitors to enter your trade area?
- Most zoning boards and economic/regional development committees plan several years in advance. They can probably provide you with valuable insights to help you decide among retail locations.

Incentive Areas and Agencies

Hundreds of local, state, federal, and private agencies offer programs designed to entice business owners to move into economically disadvantaged areas. Contact your local SBA chapter for information on federal empowerment and revitalization zones in your area. Most operate an information center to help business owners learn more about the various programs that are available and how to apply for services and programs. Businesses located in these areas receive a wide range of technical assistance, tax credits for hiring local residents

Take a look at the prospective customer base as well as direct and indirect competitors.

and training workers, deductions of business equipment and supplies, and opportunities to apply for tax-exempt bonds to help build new facilities.

Main Street Outreach

The Internet allows small-town businesses to reach beyond superstores' geographic influence. Main Street businesses use the Internet to provide better service to local customers and augment sales in brick-and-mortar stores. Moving merchants from malls to Main Street is a trend across America, according to Kennedy Smith, director of the Washington, DC-based National Trust for Historic Preservation's Main Street Center program. "Five or six years ago, Main Street businesses had virtually no Web presence. Now they are discovering the means to expand retail sales on the Web. This presence is an important step for Main Street, where even a 5 percent increase in annual sales can be key to success or failure."

There are 1,500 active communities in the program. A recent survey of emerging trends in historic Main Street commercial districts showed that retail sales are up in 65 percent of these communities, and more than 58 percent reported an increase in the number of retail businesses. Small towns had greater increases than urban districts in upper-floor occupancies and numbers of restaurants and professional offices. Urban districts saw increases in ground-floor occupancies, event attendance, and numbers of retail and independently owned businesses. Larger communities have had dramatic increases in property values and numbers of retail businesses, housing units, and franchises. Smaller communities had increases in personal services businesses and Internet usage, underscoring the change in small towns where superstores affect retail saturation.

Check Out the Competition

To find out how you can get involved in the Main Street movement with the location of your business, contact the National Trust for Historic Preservation at www.nthp.org.

If you're going to run a plumbing store, you have to be the dominant plumbing store against all competition (the local wholesale plumbing store, a home center, a specialty retailer, or all three). So take a look at the prospective customer base as well as direct and indirect competitors. This means if you want to open a flower shop, you need to assess a location's profit potential in terms of what other gift shops, supermarkets with flowers, floral vending machines (yes, these do exist), fresh and silk flower wholesalers, and mass merchandisers there are.

Selecting a Shopping Center Location

Shopping centers are distinctly different from downtown and local business strips. The shopping center building is pre-planned as a merchandising unit for interplay among tenants. Its site is deliberately selected by the developer for easy access to pull customers from a trade area. It has on-site parking as a common feature of the layout. The amount of parking space is directly related to the retail area. Customers like the shopping center's convenience. They drive in, park, and walk to their destination in relative safety and speed. Some shopping centers provide weather protection, and most provide an atmosphere created for shopping comfort. For the customer, the shopping center has great appeal.

Can You Qualify?

Developers and owners of shopping centers look for successful retailers. If you are considering a shopping center for a first-store venture, you may have trouble. Your financial backing and merchandising experience may be unproven to the developer. Your challenge is convincing the developer that the new store has a reasonable chance of success and will help the tenant mix.

Whether or not a small retailer can get into a particular shopping center depends on the market and management. A small shopping center may need only one children's shoe store, for example, while a regional center may expect enough business for two or more.

Darrell T. thinks the main reason the Seattle mall leasing agents allowed him in without prior retail experience is because the artist his gallery exclusively represents has a great reputation—and because of the product line the gallery carries. "In nationwide mall tenant polls, I believe [the artist] is No. 2 in sales per square foot, second only to Sunglass Hut," says Darrell.

To finance a center, the developer needs major leases from companies with strong credit ratings. The developer's own lenders favor tenant rosters that include the triple-A ratings of national chains. However, local merchants with good business records and proven understanding of the market have a good chance of being considered by a shopping center developer. So if you or your store manager has a good reputation and track record in retailing in the area, you may be able to make a strong case for acceptance into the center you want.

Beware!

One or more large department stores or major discounters traditionally draw shoppers to malls. An enclosed mall without an anchor store may not be able to generate enough traffic to be a viable location for your business. If the leasing agent promises that a star store is slated for that role, negotiate for lower rent until the big store opens, and have your attorney put an escape clause in your lease should the anchor back out.

Center Costs

In examining any shopping center location, get answers to questions such as these: Are its shoppers your prospective customers? Would the center offer the best sales volume potential for your kind of merchandise or service? Can you benefit enough from the center's access to a market? If yes, can you produce the appeal that will make the center's customers come to your store? Can you deal with the competition of other stores?

How much space do you need and where do you want it? Naturally, the amount of space you want will determine your rent. Many merchants need to rethink their space requirements when locating in a shopping center. Rents are typically high, so space must be used efficiently. What amount of space will you need to handle the sales volume you expect to have? Be sure that it has adequate interior space for sufficient inventory, an area for an office, and possibly a receiving and shipping area. You should also consider the necessity for adequate space for expansion when business picks up.

Your location in a center is important. Do you need to be in the main flow of customers as they pass between the stores with the greatest customer pull? Who will your neighbors be? What will their effect on your sales be?

"We're in [a mall that] has about 60 specialty shops," says Darrell T., the Seattle art dealer. "We compared it to some of the other sites in the territory that were available to us,

> **Smart Tip**
> Trade journal *Specialty Retail Report* says that carts and kiosks are good start-ups for young entrepreneurs due to the low investment required and the methods' ability to thrive even during economic downturns. Use a cart to find out about price points, who your customers are, what the demand for your products is, and to start a customer database. To succeed, offer something anchor stores don't carry.

and based on the information we received—sales per square foot, other stores—we went ahead and chose [this mall]. We have to be a little picky about our location. Galleries located in a prime spot within a mall do much better than those that are in an out-of-the-way location. Even though the malls are comparable, basically a 'C' location in an 'A' mall is not the same as an 'A' location in a 'B' mall," he says. "And location in the mall is quite possibly the most important factor—even more than the mall you are in—in my mind. As long as you are visible and can catch the shopper's eye, I think you'll do well wherever you go."

What will rent really cost? In most nonshopping center locations, rent is a fixed amount that has no relationship to sales volume. In a shopping center, the rent is usually stated as a minimum guaranteed rent per square foot of leased area against a percentage. Typically, this percentage is between 5 and 7 percent of gross sales, but it varies by type of business and other factors. This means that if the rent calculated by the percentage of sales is higher than the guaranteed rent, you pay the higher amount. If it is lower than the guaranteed rent, then you pay the guaranteed rent amount.

But this guarantee is not the end. In addition, you may have to pay dues to the center's merchants' association. You may also have to pay for maintenance of common areas. Therefore, you must think of "total rent" when considering what you can afford to pay. Can you draw enough sales to cover the true rent of being in a center?

Don't forget that you still have to design and finish out your space. You pay for light fixtures, counters, shelves, painting, floor coverings, and installing your own heating and cooling units. Some landlords provide a cost allowance toward completion of your retail space. This "tenant allowance" is for storefronts, ceiling treatment, and wall coverings. The allowance is a percentage of their cost and is spelled out in a dollar amount in the lease. Some developers will help you plan storefronts, exterior signs, and interior color schemes. They provide this service to ensure storefronts that add to the center's image rather than detract from it.

Specialty Leasing

About 80 percent of America's 1,800 enclosed and regional shopping malls have temporary tenants, which include kiosks and carts. There are between 10 and 40 carts per mall at the Simon De Bartolo Property Group malls of Indianapolis, which rely on carts to add color and variety, as well as to generate income. Entrepreneurs can display their wares in a prime, high-foot-traffic location with little investment. Some cart operators move in just to capitalize on busy holiday seasons, and others remain year-round.

Rent for in-line stores is about four times the rent for carts and kiosks. You can buy a cart for $3,000-plus or rent one from a mall. Many entrepreneurs find carts and kiosks a low-cost way to launch a retail business or to supplement an existing business. You'll see a variety of specialty products introduced this way—silver jewelry, engraved products, imported fragrances, hair accessories, watches, etc. Some retailers use carts as test businesses in potential markets, while others make more than $1 million by operating several carts in several malls and cities.

At Bloomington, Minnesota's Mall of America, about 100 temporary tenants dazzle 40 million visitors a year. Cart rental rates are about $2,300 a month or 15 percent of monthly sales, whichever is greater. All temporary tenants must pay $1,500 in "key money," which pays for a store designer to design and build a cart with the right look.

Street vendors and swap meet and fair concessionaires need to check with the city or county in which they want to do business for the regulations and specifications for the types of products, hours, and displays that are allowed.

Everything Is Negotiable

Once you've decided what kind of space you want, where, and how long you need it, it's time to consult a lawyer to discuss what specific issues you need to address in order to negotiate the best lease for your business. Core points to review carefully are occupancy date, chargeable floor space, which renovations or tenant improvements the landlord will do or pay for, services to be provided, liability, and renewal or termination terms. Once you're close to reaching an agreement with the real estate broker, leasing agent, or landlord, your attorney can make sure that everything is in writing to clearly define each party's obligations.

Retail space is usually rented on what's called a "net lease" basis, meaning that you arrange for most of its services. Unless your premises are tied to the building's mechanical systems, the costs for most services—such as heating and air-conditioning—are your responsibility.

The breadth of your use clause (the specific use intended for the space) will affect your ability to assign your lease or sublet the premises. The broader the definition, the better. If you've leased the space to sell ski equipment, for example, and business lags because of a lack of snowfall, you want to have the option of opening a juice bar instead.

In addition, it's a good idea to get a restrictive covenant to prevent the landlord from leasing space in the same building or nearby to a business that competes with you. How far this provision extends will depend on the type of area you're located in. In a city, it might be a few blocks, whereas in the suburbs, it could be a few miles.

Once you've decided what kind of space you want, where, and how long you need it, it's time to consult a lawyer.

With shopping center leases, you are customarily charged for maintenance of common areas and for the mall's marketing efforts. Find out what the mall's plans are for any structural alterations or remodeling, resurfacing the parking lots, or replacing the roof. These can be devastating assessments for a young business. Requirements for hours and days of operation, employee parking restrictions, participation in community service events, gift certificate and loyalty programs, and storefront appearance may not fit into your business plan or capabilities. Make sure you will be capable of conforming to these requirements.

Starting from Scratch

A few of you will decide to throw caution to the wind and start your new business from scratch, including constructing a new building. You want to take advantage of current market conditions and design a building that's exclusively yours. A disadvantage to this approach is the cost of complex financing and legal clearances required in buying and building out property.

Starting a new business in the mature, densely populated retail industry does not, by itself, immediately present customers. The need to cultivate the market over time delays a return on your investment, which adds to the length of time you'll be paying interest on nonproductive money. This may require the infusion of cash over a longer period of time just to keep the doors open. Plus, your new business will have to compete with existing businesses that may already be successfully established in prime locations. A specialty restaurant may be the exception, as there is roughly a 90-day window of opportunity to get a buzz going among locals, visitors, and food critics to catapult your chef to stardom and you to profitability.

Location in a Nutshell

Selection of a retail location requires time and careful consideration. A retail firm cannot survive in a poor location because customers will avoid patronizing a place that is not easily and safely accessible. Choosing a location should never be rushed through. If you haven't found a suitable location, don't plan to open until you're sure you've got what you want. Remember: Opening a retail business in a poor location is fatal.

Legal and Finance Issues

You're about to fully commit to starting your own business. You're confident you're a retailer at heart with a good idea in mind, a location that will serve your customers, and a written plan to implement your dream. The next step is to cross your t's and dot your i's.

Today's business world is fast and often furious, and laws and regulations are changing all the time. Because of this, it's impossible for you to run a successful business and be an expert in everything.

So you'll want to line up a number of professionals you can rely on to help put your deal together and keep it moving toward your goals. The professionals you'll want to hire may include an architect, a lawyer, an interior designer, an accountant, a graphic designer, a merchandiser, and a buyer.

One of the advantages to having a franchise or licensed dealership is the expertise you can draw on from the parent company. For Seattle art gallery owner Darrell T., his parent company was a one-stop shop for the new retailer. Part of the parent company's training program is to bring in a variety of consultants—business planners, lighting and layout specialists, lease negotiators, and inventory and marketing people—to talk about what they have done with other galleries. Since Darrell and his parents (with whom he went into business) had never done anything like this before, they don't know what they would have done without these resources.

> **Don't wait until the last minute to line up competent legal counsel you trust.**

To ensure that you get off on the right foot, hire an attorney with start-up expertise who can give you advice to grow on. You can use his or her knowledge of the pros and cons of each business structure to determine which one is best for your venture. You can get insight into your lease, buy-sell agreements, licenses, ordinances, bonding, zoning, financing, and other matters. An experienced business lawyer can minimize your exposure to IRS, occupational, employment, and safety problems. Don't wait until the last minute to line up competent legal counsel you trust. You don't want to put your fate into the hands of a total stranger.

Newport Beach, California, pet bakery owner Stephanie B. is a lawyer, so setting up her business was no problem. But she doesn't recommend that the inexperienced try to do everything themselves. Entering into written agreements without the advice of counsel is not wise.

You can reduce the amount of professional fees you have to pay by doing some homework—researching the answers to questions, making some decisions, and knowing how to do part of the paperwork yourself. There's a growing number of books on the subject of forming your own business available from Nolo Press in Berkeley, California; Simon & Schuster in New York City; and the latest editions of Michael D. Jenkins' state-by-state series, *Starting and Operating a Business in...* (Oasis Press), for your state. Write or call the Small Business Development Center nearest you, and visit your local library or bookstore for some of the publications listed in the Appendix.

Even former corporate lawyer Stephanie B. read two or three "how-to" business start-up books to make sure she was not overlooking something. She went online to www.amazon.com and searched the site for retail start-up and new business books, read the editorial description and reader's reviews, and then ordered them.

Forming a Business Entity

Forming a business entity is a big step with long-term consequences. While it is possible to change the legal structure anytime in your company's life, it is time-consuming and costly. Converting from a partnership to a C corporation or limited liability company will pose few problems, as will switching from a sole proprietorship or partnership to an LLC. Converting from a C corporation to a partnership, sole proprietorship, or LLC, however—or getting in and out of an S corporation—is more complicated. Think carefully before you finalize your business structure. To ward off impatience and other pressures, look at the three- and five-year projections you put in your business plan to help you stay on course.

Jim O. and his brothers, owners of the hi-fi sales and service business in Thomasville, Georgia, chose to operate the company as a partnership for years but are now incorporating for tax reasons.

If you're like most retailers, you will open as a sole proprietorship. There are no special steps required other than obtaining a business license. You may need to file a notice of a fictitious firm name and present it to your bank to open a business account, but there's not a lot more required for you to start selling your products or services.

A partnership is formed through an oral or a written agreement, but a written agreement is advisable. To form a limited liability company, you need to file articles of organization with the state. A separate document, the operating agreement, outlines the rules for managing the firm. A lawyer will charge you about $1,500 to $5,000 for filling out the paperwork. Forming a corporation usually costs between $500 and $2,000 upfront, according to Deborah L. Jacobs, author of *Small Business Legal Smarts* (Bloomberg Press). There is a substantial amount of paperwork involved, including filing articles of incorporation and paying a state filing fee, which varies from $100 to $150.

Fred W.'s Montpelier, Vermont, music store is a partnership (with his brother, Dennis), in keeping with his personal philosophy that simpler is better. He started the business in 1973, with his best friend from high school, George M.

Smart Tip

Tip...

There is little paperwork involved in setting up a sole proprietorship. Get the necessary selling permits and other licenses, and notify the city, county, or state of your intention to do business under an assumed name (dba). You pay taxes on the business income as if it were personal salary and assume full liability for anything that goes wrong. You also pay self-employment tax for Social Security and Medicare coverage.

Protect Your Name

Corporations must register their corporate names with the secretary of state, state Department of Corporations, or commissioner of corporations. Each state's laws on this are a little different. But in every state, you must get permission to use your trade name before incorporation. You have to select a permissible name, make sure it's distinguishable from any corporate name already registered in the state, and then send in an application (with a fee) to reserve the legal right to use that name to identify your business.

Audio retailers Jim, Doug, and Carlos O. and Dadeville, Alabama, grocer Jeff P. used their surnames for their businesses. Stephanie B. used a play on words for her business. New York City-based designer/retailer Matt M. is using his full name as his brand.

Any person who uses a trade name other than his or her surname, or any organization that goes by a name other than the last names of the owners, must register the name with the state or county as a fictitious business name. This usually means filing a certificate with the county clerk stating who is doing business under that trade name. This is called a dba (doing business as).

If your state has no central fictitious name registration, you may want to check more than one county's records to see if anyone else in your state is using the name you propose for your business. Otherwise, several businesses might use the same name in your state, and if you want to expand your operation, you may run into difficulties.

Your name is the cornerstone of your brand, and the identity of your company is a major component of your success. Because image is such an important part of marketing, a lot is riding on your name. Your signage, business cards, name tags, uniforms, vehicles, word-of-mouth advertising, private-label lines, and Web site will depend on the integrity of your name, so you'll want to guard it carefully.

A Name to Remember

Fred W. and his then-partner, George M., named their business while "sitting around the kitchen table spewing out words and combinations of words that would create a name that had something—however immediate or remote—to do with music (and maybe books, too)," Fred remembers. "Perhaps it was because there were two of us that we liked names with two words. We have an unusual name with an awkward spelling, but it sure comes out sounding sweet, and it's memorable."

Separate from the state law issue is the question of whether or not your name has any trademark value because it distinguishes your goods or services from those of other companies. If so, you can register the name for federal trademark protection, which entitles you to stop others from adopting or using it. You must complete a registration form from the U.S. Patent and Trademark Office in Washington, DC.

There are two very different contexts in which your business's name may be used. One is the formal name of your business for purposes of bank accounts, creditors, and potential lawsuits. The second is the name you use to market your goods or services (trademark or service mark). Whether someone is using the same trade name as yours is of less practical importance than if they were using the same trademark, or using the same trade name as a trademark as well. If your corporate name figures into your future marketing plans, you must search for use of the name as a trademark in addition to complying with the corporate name registration requirements. If someone else is the first to use your name as a mark, it doesn't make any difference whether you or they have previously registered it as a fictitious or assumed name. They will still have the right to exclusive use of the name in the marketplace. Unfortunately, it's fairly common for a small business to choose a name that's similar to that of another enterprise.

There are several ways you can use to conduct a trademark search to avoid such problems. You can pay a search firm; use a computer database; manually consult trademark registers, directories, industry journals, and other library resources; or use the phone or mail to consult state agencies. This can cost you a few hundred to a few thousand dollars. Trademark searching is a competitive business, so be prepared to negotiate. Nolo Press has a self-help guide, *Trademark: How to Name a Business & Product*, that shows you how to protect your business and lists several books, software packages, and services that may help you.

Domain Name Registration

Once you have your business name, you will want to register a domain name for your Internet address. This will identify your business on the World Wide Web by a domain name with a .com, .net, .org, or .edu suffix. Commercially, this will mean having your product or service easily accessible to millions of prospective customers worldwide.

Stat Fact
At the time of this writing, there are more than 2,000 service providers on the Web who will conduct a search of name availability, register it for you, and notify a specified number of search engines. You will typically pay a $59 to $70 one-time service setup fee for the first year and $35 per year thereafter, plus a service charge to submit your URL to search engines.

What Kind of Money Will it Take?

The SBA says that about 89 percent of all start-ups are financed with less than $100,000. Regardless of outside cash you may be able to raise, it is a general rule of thumb that you will have to put up at least 10 percent of the required cash yourself—maybe even 25 percent.

Fred W. says that he and then-partner George M. pooled their collective liquid resources and came up with about $3,000—what Fred calls "an impossibly pathetic amount with which to start a business." Fred borrowed heavily against his life insurance policy. He believes one of the main reasons his music store has been successful is its low overhead. He started out paying rent of $75 a month, and now comparable space goes for nearly $3,000 where he is. However, his good track record at the same location has minimized his rent increases.

Stephanie B. invested $80,000 of her own money to start her pet bakery, and Jim, Doug, and Carlos O. came up with $100,000 to put their audio sales and service business together.

Grocer Jeff P. got into the business somewhat accidentally. "I didn't think I was ready to go out on my own at 29," he says, "but the opportunity presented itself, so I took it. I heard by word-of-mouth that a gentleman wanted to sell some of the stores he owned and retire. I wasn't looking to buy a business at the time, but there it was. The store originally opened before I was born. I was fortunate to catch it at a time when it was down. It had been up, and I felt like it could go up again." He bought his 8,200-square-foot store in a leased building with an SBA loan for around $375,000. "Since then," says Jeff, "I've bought another grocery store and built a brand-new store to replace the one at the original site."

If you only have $5,000 cash, you should be looking for a business whose total start-up cost is in the $20,000 to $50,000 range. For a list of start-up costs for different types of retail businesses, check out "Retail Opportunities" on page 75.

So what will it take to get you in business? Set up a budget, and list your operating expenses for the first three months—the time it will take to stock the store, advertise your opening, and hire help. Go down the worksheet and itemize everything you will need to open your doors and acquire that first customer. There are so many variables that you might want to talk with retailers in your market as well as a knowledgeable Service Corps of Retired Executives (SCORE) counselor whose background is in retail. The tips

Dollar Stretcher

Network Solutions Inc. is the central registry for domain names, with more than 5 million registrations. Some new registries with competitive pricing can be found at www.internic.net/alpha.html. You can register a name for up to 10 years.

you gather can guide you in seeing if you have enough cash on hand to do the deal, or what you'll need to get from advances on your credit cards, loans, and vendor assistance. Talk over your projections with your accountant. For a sample list of start-up expenses, turn to page 73. For a "Start-Up Expenses Worksheet" you can fill out for your own business, turn to page 74.

Ready, Aim

Smart Tip *Tip...*

Dadeville, Alabama, grocer Jeff P. has been in the food business for years, and he's concluded that if you want to be in the independent supermarket business, you're going to need $100,000 cash and financing for another $400,000-plus, based on the kind of supermarket you buy and where it's located.

Figuring out how much money you'll need is the most difficult yet vital step in the process of opening your business. It is, after all, an exercise in goal-setting. You are asked to predict what you think will happen in the first few months of something that doesn't exist yet. It's a lot easier if you are buying an existing business or a franchise because some historical or average figures can guide you.

Prepare for the unexpected when charting your start-up budget. If your retail business will be your sole source of income, you will need to bankroll money to support yourself until your new venture turns a profit. Typically, the amount of money you need will equal six months' to a year's living expenses for you and your family.

Homebased Businesses Aren't Free

Although a homebased business won't have all the expenses of a leased-space business, it is rare for any type of retailer not to have start-up expenses. You will need supplies and business equipment. Laws and ordinances governing homebased businesses vary widely from community to community. Know what is required before you start your pet-walking, hair-braiding, bridal consulting, or other kind of homebased business.

A homebased business needs a license to operate, a seller's permit, and a federal ID number, depending on your industry and local

Smart Tip *Tip...*

A resale number or seller's permit is required by all states that collect sales tax. The permit allows you to buy merchandise at wholesale prices without paying sales tax, but you must pay the state sales tax on taxable merchandise when sold at retail. Usually, the consumer pays the sales tax at the time of purchase.

▲

requirements. You should also check fire department permits if you use flammable materials; air and water pollution control permits if you plan to burn any material or discharge any waste into the waterways; liquor, wine, and beer licenses if you sell liquor, even through the mail; and health department permits if your business involves food or food preparation.

You may be sufficiently covered under your existing homeowner's or renter's policy, or you may need additional insurance coverage. Check with your insurance agent. And to find out what tax benefits you may qualify for with your homebased business, seek the guidance of an accountant who is familiar with homebased deductions. He or she can calculate your cash needs with and without the tax deductions, in case tax laws change and you receive no benefits beyond savings on rent and utilities.

Bank Locally

Regardless of your location, as a businessperson, you'll need to set up your accounts. You want a bank that wants your business. Look for a full-service financial institution that caters to small businesses in general and retailers specifically. Your goal is to find one that has the products, services, and fees that fit your needs.

The basic items you will want to compare among financial institutions are:

- Business checking account
- Business interest checking account
- Business savings account
- Cash management services
- Merchants' deposit
- Payroll service
- Online banking services
- Lines of credit (seasonal and revolving)
- Small-business loans (short-term, long-term, collateral, equipment, accounts receivable financing, factoring accounts receivable, cosigner)
- SBA-approved status
- Wire transfers
- Safe deposit box rental
- Foreign currency exchange

Even if you're like pet bakery owner Stephanie B. and Thomasville, Georgia, clothing store owners Jim and Mary D., and you've saved up enough money to start your business

> **Smart Tip** *Tip...*
> Weigh the fees charged and services offered by different banks against their proximity to your business, hours of operation, cooperativeness of personnel, and the bank's reputation for working with retailers.

without having to take out a loan or get outside investors, it's always a good idea to be on a first-name basis with your banker. Put the bank manager and head of the loan committee on your mailing list; say hello or wave when you're in the bank; and make a point to share some exciting news with them about sales, new personnel, or your community involvement. By being someone they know and respect who doesn't want anything from them, when you do approach them to get some new equipment or remodel your store, they will know who you are. If grocer Jeff P. hadn't established a good consumer record with his bank, he might not have been able to buy his grocery store when he did.

> **Tip...**
>
> ## Smart Tip
>
> There are five things an entrepreneur should be prepared to show a loan officer: a business plan that shows how you will use the financing to operate the business; proof that you pay your obligations when due; that you have enough equity money; that your team has enough experience to implement the plan; and that your sales prospects are strong enough to repay the loan.

"Financing a business can be a problem," says Jim D. "My advice for people is to have a consistent banking relationship. Do all your banking with the same bank all the time. Even if the banker is not your lender, he can become someone who is a reference.

"Even if you're small, you can present a record that shows progress from month to month or year to year," Jim continues. "It doesn't have to be big. You then have the objective proof that says 'This is what we want to do, and this is why we know it's

Unsolved Mysteries

Some unforeseen expenses that can throw off your start-up expenses projection are:

- ○ Increase in taxes
- ○ Difficulty attracting customers
- ○ Changes in consumer styles, preferences, and demand
- ○ New competition in your market that takes away some of your revenue
- ○ Price increases from your suppliers
- ○ Accidents involving you, your employees, or best customers
- ○ Increases in insurance, utility costs, or vital supplies like heating oil or gas
- ○ Lawsuits
- ○ Fines

▲

going to be successful. For example, we can produce a volume of orders that shows a progression, even if unfulfilled. These are orders that should have sold.' In other words, you're asking a banker or a sponsor for financing by saying 'Here's where we could have been if we hadn't had problems financing.' That's exciting. I think somebody will say 'All we have to do is give him money, and I can see where he's going to go.' I think this is an important part of having a relationship with the bank."

Start-Up Expenses

Here is a start-up expenses chart for an aftermarket sales and service motorcycle shop in Montclair, California.

Montclair Motorcycle Shop

Accountant setup fees	$500
Advertising	$4,000
Computer system	$9,700
Fixtures	$8,700
Grand opening	$2,500
Insurance	$6,500
Inventory setup and pricing	$3,000
Legal fees	$2,700
Licenses and permits	$350
Miscellaneous expenses	$1,000
Office equipment	$10,000
Opening inventory	$55,000
Payroll account	$5,000
Remodeling	$12,000
Rent/security deposit	$12,000
Retail seller's permit deposit	$1,500
Shop equipment and tools	$15,000
Shop supplies	$1,000
Signs	$9,200
Start-up checking	$10,000
Supplies (office, cleaning)	$1,200
Utility deposits	$1,500
Total Start-up Expenses	$172,350

Start-Up Expenses Worksheet

Advertising and promotion for launch	$
Building construction/remodeling	
Cash (reserves and on hand)	
Computers	
Construction costs	
Displays	
Equipment	
Fixtures	
Installation costs	
Insurance	
Interior design and decorating costs	
Lease payments	
Legal fees	
Licenses and permits	
Miscellaneous	
Opening inventory	
Payroll	
Professional fees	
Rent	
Services	
Signage	
Supplies (office, cleaning, store)	
Unplanned expenses	
Utility and other deposits (telephone, water, gas, cleaning)	
Total Start-up Expenses	$

Retail Opportunities

Here is a sampling of businesses and ballpark revenue and start-up cost figures gathered from researchers and retailers. Your actual investment and rewards will vary according to these key factors: location (home, cart, store), size (square footage, number of clients, breadth of inventory/services, capitalization), market, and structure (franchise, purchase, start-up).

Business Type	Average Annual Revenues	Estimated Start-up Costs
Alterations	$9,000–30,000	$500–3,000
Amusement arcade	$70,000–130,000	$90,000
Antique dealer	$25,000–80,000	$15,000–50,000
Apartment finder	$35,000–90,000	$40,000
Art gallery	$30,000–1 million	$35,000–100,000
Balloon decoration	$12,000+	$500–1,000
Bed-and-breakfast	$15,000–170,000	$50,000–450,000
Carpet cleaning	$50,000	$500–20,000
CD exchange	$50,000–130,000	$60,000–100,000
Child care	$25,000–45,000	$500–15,000
Coffee shop	$6,000–500,000	$15,000–250,000
Costume/novelty shop	$60,000–170,000	$30,000–50,000
Dance instruction	$40,000	$20,000–45,000
Dating service	$50,000–500,000	$15,000–100,000+
Detective agency	$25,000–100,000	$10,000
Doll houses	$20,000–75,000	$6,000–15,000
Editorial service	$40,000–100,000	$3,000–7,000
Elder care	$25,000–60,000	$5,000–11,000
Flower shop	$80,000–100,000	$30,000–90,000
Genealogy service	$30,000–55,000	$3,000–10,000
Gift baskets	$10,000–100,000	$2,000–40,000
Graphic design	$50,000–140,000	$5,000+
Hair stylist	$20,000–100,000	$1,000–90,000
Health food store	$40,000–110,000	$30,000–80,000

Retail Opportunities, continued

Business Type	Average Annual Revenues	Estimated Start-up Costs
Home health care	$100,000+	$7,000–200,000
Image consulting	$10,000–70,000	$6,000–15,000
Interior design	$30,000–150,000	$3,000–19,000
Jewelry design	$25,000–80,000	$5,000
Mail order	$5,000–150,000	$200–70,000
Makeup application	$20,000–50,000	$4,000–10,000
Massage therapy	$20,000–50,000	$4,000
Meeting/event planning	$12,000–100,000+	$1,000–8,000
Mobile disk jockey	$25,000–130,000	$1,000–10,000
Party supply store	$12,000–110,000	$40,000–120,000
Personal fitness training	$20,000–80,000	$2,000–5,000
Personal shopping	$20,000–40,000	$1,000–4,000
Pet grooming	$25,000–45,000	$16,000–20,000
Pet shop	$75,000–180,000	$30,000–400,000
Photography	$40,000–300,000	$3,000–175,000
PR agency	$40,000–80,000	$1,000–12,000
Restaurant	$100,000–1 million	$35,000–500,000
Resume service	$20,000–60,000	$3,000–8,000
Secondhand store	$30,000–120,000	$1,000–15,000
Sign painting	$15,000–50,000	$1,000–2,000
Tanning salon	$40,000–70,000	$45,000
Tattoo studio	$65,000–270,000	$10,000–25,000
Tax preparation	$40,000–60,000	$6,000–8,000
Toy store	$35,000–100,000+	$90,000–125,000
Travel bureau	$40,000–120,000	$10,000–40,000
Tutoring service	$30,000–90,000	$2,000–100,000
Wedding consulting	$25,000–150,000	$2,000–11,000
Women's clothing store	$75,000+	$40,000–80,000

6

Operations

The glamorous side of retailing is where the merchandise is located and customer action is taking place. What goes on behind the scenes, however, is vitally important because the support systems you put in place are what keep your business alive and well.

Store Policies

Store policies are the broad guidelines that outline the general practices to be followed by all employees to achieve your goals. Take time to think these various details through and then schedule times for each task to be done and who is to do it. Policies are more than daily procedures and work rules; they are a road map for success.

Rather than running your business in an informal, by-the-seat-of-your-pants manner, before you open your business, write down rules that outline every one of your expectations. Once you are open for business, things will happen very quickly, so you want to be able to create the work ethic and atmosphere you want in your business before you open. By focusing on the details now—under fairly unpressured circumstances—you will be able to meet decision-making demands when under stress, and your employees will do what you want them to do. In a few pages, you'll learn what several retailers' days are really like.

Hours

The retailers we interviewed for this book told us this line of work has two kinds of hours: business hours and store hours. There are many tasks that need to be done besides selling—receiving, preparing and tagging merchandise, cleaning and facing shelves, freshening displays, counting the cash in the cash drawer, ordering new merchandise, checking on special orders, notifying customers of the status of their purchases, returning damaged goods, recording markdowns, answering the phone, and a multitude of other invisible, but necessary, tasks. These are all included in business hours because you obviously can't accomplish all these tasks during store hours.

Determine your hours of operation. If you locate inside a mall like Seattle-based art retailer Darrell T. did, your hours may be predetermined. If you are like pet bakery owner Stephanie B. in Newport Beach, California, and locate in a free-standing building, you will have complete freedom to determine the hours that work best for your particular store.

> **Tip...**
>
> **Smart Tip**
>
> Homebased workers need a lot of self-discipline to grow a retail business. Keeping standard 8-to-6 weekday hours keeps you in sync with most storefronts (8-to-5 for most service businesses) and gives you a set time frame in which to complete your tasks.

In the beginning, Montpelier, Vermont-based music store owner Fred W. worked two full-time jobs: one on the early shift at a local assembly plant to earn a paycheck, and the other in the afternoons and evenings to build his music business. "It was a plan

From the moment Stephanie opens her doors, the store is like a three-ring circus.

too unrealistically unworkable to be true, but I did it anyway," Fred recalls. "Sleep deprivation was a way of life."

Now, Fred and brother Dennis run the business. Dennis, however, has another full-time job, so daily operations are Fred's responsibility alone. "The typical things I do all day long are related to inventory control, sales, and customer service," says Fred. His store hours are Monday through Thursday, 10 A.M. to 6 P.M.; Friday, 10 A.M. to 8 P.M.; Saturday, 10 A.M. to 5 P.M.; and Sunday, 11 A.M. to 4 P.M. "I get here between 8:30 and 9 A.M., vacuum and sweep, and check everything. UPS deliveries arrive at 10:30, and it takes one to two hours to inventory arrivals. Then I'm fielding questions and ringing up sales until closing. I cash out the drawer and print out everything sold during the day. If I can make my distributor's deadline, I place orders. Finally, I go home at about 7 or 8 P.M."

Fred has learned over time what the typical flow of customers is and takes into account what hours other stores in the area are keeping. "We're closed on Christmas, Thanksgiving, Labor Day, and the Fourth of July," Fred says. "After school, between 2 and 6 P.M., we're really busy." He is very visible all day, managing by walking around and giving customers personal service. Having a Web site extends the store's operating hours and provides a convenient way for customers to browse through his 13,000-title catalog and place orders when the store is closed.

On the West Coast, Stephanie B. is up early. "I usually try to get in at 7 A.M. and start baking," she says. "But it's always different. I don't have to get up at any time or be here at any time as long as the store is open at 10. We're open 10 to 6 seven days a week. I should bake about three times a week but don't always have time because of all the interruptions." She leaves at night between 7 and 8 P.M. after cleaning the store, balancing the cash register, and catching up with the day's paperwork.

From the moment Stephanie opens her doors, the store is like a three-ring circus. Her dogs are playing behind the counter and get very excited when customers visit with their pets. The phone is ringing, one of her friends is looking up something in one of the catalogs for herself or a customer, and there's always lively chatter about the latest product arrival,

Smart Tip

Tip...

Be ready for business by having the right assortment of coins and bills to fill the till each morning. This money is set aside the night before when the register is balanced and the next day's deposit is readied for the bank. Always start with an even amount—$100, for example. Plan ahead for busy weekends and special events. Make sure you plan around bank holidays so you're not caught short.

▲

recipe for dog treats, or dog-training tip. When UPS rings the delivery bell, conversation halts for a split second, and then the excitement starts up again. The smell of freshly baked dog biscuits permeates the store, and Stephanie goes back and forth between the sales floor, the phone, the oven, and the cash register. Between customers, she checks on special orders, responds to e-mail, and processes incoming stock.

> **Bright Idea**
> Keep yourself organized by following the tips in *How to Get Control of Your Time and Your Life* (Mass Market) by Alan Lakein, attend a Franklin Covey seminar, or use a software program like Microsoft's Meeting Maker or a personal digital assistant such as a Palm Pilot or Casio Pocket PC.

The small location is a popular walking area for tourists and residents, so there is a constant flow of new prospects and old friends. In the midst of doing business, she arranges for homes for rescued dogs, and commits to being a sponsor for a charitable event then decides what she will donate for a silent auction.

Darrell T., who runs a gallery inside a mall, has a less-demanding schedule. "When we get here at 9 A.M.," Darrell says, "the gallery is in pretty good shape. We make sure the gallery is presentable and stock up those items that were sold the day before, and just basically do general organization before we open at 10. We keep mall hours, which are 10 A.M. to 9:30 P.M., Monday through Friday; 10 to 8 on Saturday; 11 to 6 on Sunday."

Credit Policies

Many small retailers sign up for MasterCard, American Express, or Visa and willingly pay the small percentage to let a bank operate their credit departments for them. You will need to decide which credit cards, if any, you will accept. Base this decision on what sort of merchandise you sell. Is it a high-ticket item your customers will be unable to pay cash for?

Also determine under what circumstances you'll accept personal checks. Most retail businesses that accept checks ask for a form of picture identification from the customer writing the check. Other businesses ask for more detailed information, such as a home or work telephone number. Your bank may be able to recommend policies that will help you cut down on the cost of accepting bad checks.

You may also want to consider providing a layaway option for your customers. See page 85 for a "Layaway Record."

Customer Service Policies

How do you want returns and exchanges handled? Will you offer gift-wrapping? What about alterations? Deliveries and special orders? Customer service can be as simple as saying hello to customers as soon as they step through your doors.

Your employees are the front line of customer service. Set your policies in writing and make sure everyone understands how you expect your business to be represented.

See the "Merchandise Return Form" on page 86 and the "Discount Worksheet" on page 87.

Housekeeping

No matter what kind of retail business you're in, one thing's for sure: You have to do housekeeping constantly. Retailers believe that a consistent standard for cleanliness and orderliness gives them several advantages over stores that don't have a cleanliness standard. Customers are safer, their confidence in you is higher, and your sales are enhanced by a well-kept enterprise. Business owners all try to set an example for employees by sweeping, restocking, filing, and dusting as needed rather than waiting for a set time.

Depending on your lease, your landlord may take care of exterior landscaping and building maintenance. If you own the building, as Jim O. and his brothers do, it's all up to you. Add one more list of tasks to oversee. Air conditioning, elevators, lighting, and computer terminals all require technical maintenance. Floors, restrooms, and workrooms also require care and daily attention. Retailers who neglect repainting, cleaning windows, replacing worn fixtures, and basic janitorial service often pay for it in reduced customer traffic.

Security Policies

Each year, American retailers suffer billions of dollars in crime losses. To decrease the chances of robbery, retailers say to limit the amount of cash you have on hand. Bank deposits should be made at different times of the day so that potential robbers cannot be sure when cash will be leaving your business. A safe should be located on your premises that is not visible from outside the store. Do not keep large amounts of money in it for any length of time or for predictable time periods if at all possible.

Although the retailers interviewed have not had many problems with crime, they say that it is something you need to be on the lookout for in your daily operations. See page 84 for a "Petty Cash Form," page 88 for a "Cashier's Till Record," and page 89 for a "Daily Cash Record."

You will find more information on security in Chapter 14, "Risk Management"; ask your local sheriff's department or police agency to suggest what instructions you should include in your employee manual and training. When law enforcement agencies distribute fliers notifying you of scam artists working the area or shoplifters hitting other retailers, make sure all employees get the information right away. Keep an employee bulletin board in the back of the store where you can post important notices.

All in a Day's Work

In addition to selling products, Jim, Doug, and Carlos O., the audio brothers in Thomasville, Georgia, have a service center that offers a wide range of repair and installation services. "Our reputation in the field of digital equipment repair began in the early days of our store due to our ability to repair the Sony PCM units then used to encode digital data onto a VCR tape," Jim says. "[Our business] grew rapidly as many factory service centers were unable to repair the complex units used to master CDs and archive live musical performances." The fact that the service side of the store has processed more than 11,000 digital units gives you some idea of the volume of work done by the company's four full-time and one part-time employees, plus the three brothers. They put everything into a computer database, which enables them to diagnose what ails a customer's gear. They do extensive post-repair testing to ensure that their redo rate is kept enviably low and customer satisfaction remains high.

For the audio business, it's a five-day workweek. "We lost some car stereo and local business when we started closing on the weekends," Jim says, "but our Internet business has grown, so we don't regret our decision. Having more time to spend with my kids is most important to me. We're open 10 A.M. to 6 P.M. Monday through Friday. We have some walk-in traffic, but we're more a destination place than a drop-in business. We get in at about 9 A.M. and take it from there. There is no typical day; we're just busy all the time answering e-mail and phone calls, designing systems, overseeing everyone, checking parts, selling, solving problems, and examining new things."

An important part of most retailers' operations is keeping abreast of what is going on in their particular industries. Stephanie B. goes to H.H. Backer pet industry shows and visits dog lover Web sites. Jim O. goes to trade shows like the Consumer Electronics Show (CES) and the National Association of Broadcasters (NAB) show, participates in Internet forums and discussion groups, and reads trade magazines. Staying up on industry and consumer news has to be incorporated into their monthly tasks so they don't get left behind.

Bright Idea

Part of operating a business is establishing ties with your community. Get to know the other retailers in your area and join community groups and business associations. Attend monthly meetings or send a representative to keep you visible, involved, and informed.

For some retailers, sometimes a day's work stretches well into night. Matt M., the New York City designer we interviewed, admits to sometimes working around the clock to meet deadlines. He's on the phone or e-mail all day tracking shipments, negotiating prices for materials, checking on production, and planning his next collection. Essentially, his business is never closed because he has catalogs to plan, pricing to strategize, showrooms to visit, and retail buyers to sell. Once or twice a month, he does an interview with the print or broadcast media, and he also has to go trade shows and be seen at fashion functions. On top of that, there are special orders to fill, signature fabric to design, and prototypes to create. Despite the hectic pace, he finds time to teach a class in environmental design for his alma mater, Art Center College of Design, which keeps Matt active in a global network of visual artists. In the fashion business, you need to stay dialed in.

Business as Usual

Here are just a few of the tasks you will need to perform to operate your business:

- ○ Meet with customers, suppliers, and employees
- ○ Fulfill orders and deliver service
- ○ Keep the books (general ledger, accounts payable, accounts receivable)
- ○ Order supplies
- ○ Prepare balance sheets and profit-and-loss statements monthly, quarterly, and annually
- ○ Maintain employee records
- ○ Do payroll
- ○ Buy, manage, and control inventory
- ○ Display merchandise
- ○ Market the business through advertising, promotions, and public relations
- ○ Correspond by Internet or mail with suppliers and customers
- ○ Prepare and print daily cash reports, purchase orders, and necessary business forms
- ○ Create and maintain relational database for sales, service, and supplier records
- ○ Print mailing labels
- ○ Make signs
- ○ Print and affix price tags
- ○ Draft and print direct-mail offers
- ○ Design and print promotional pieces
- ○ Prepare personnel schedules
- ○ Prepare budgets and compare year-to-date figures against those that were budgeted
- ○ Track shipments in and out of store

▲

With their Thomasville, Georgia, women's and children's clothing boutique, Jim and Mary D.'s schedule echoes a similar refrain to the other retailers. They, too, have a Web site that takes time to keep fresh and responsive to customer inquiries. They, too, are committed to providing timely customer service. If the customer doesn't find something right away, Jim or Mary will find it for them.

Whether you're selling prom dresses, groceries, or stereos, you have to take time to make intelligent use of the data you collect on a daily basis. Everyone interviewed said this is one of the most difficult challenges they constantly have to deal with. Keeping track of the numbers on a daily basis, then interpreting them on a weekly, monthly, and annual basis and deciding what they mean in terms of buying, pricing, discounting, and profit-taking can be stressful.

"You really have to be adaptable in retail," comments one retailer. "Every business is different. There is no standard practice or manual you can follow. A lot of it is learn

---

Petty Cash Form

Keep a petty cash fund of about $25 for small store necessities. When the cash is depleted, write a check to bring the balance back up after posting disbursement to the appropriate accounts listed on the petty cash slips. Do not mix the petty cash with cash register funds or the till will not balance with the sales report at the end of the day. Petty cash receipts can be purchased through stationery or general merchandise stores, or you can print some up on your computer.

Received by: _____

Date: _____

Item: _____

Amount: _____

Account: _____

Item: _____

Amount: _____

Account: _____

Total: _____

Please staple sales receipt(s) to back of petty cash form.

---

as you go. I talk with other retailers to get some ideas on how to manage my people and handle customers better. There are so many variables in location, capabilities, product mix, customers, and computers that you just have to try what you think will work, do it, and see."

In retail, every day is different, which appeals to people in this industry. (See the "Motorcycle Retailer's Daily Diary" on pages 90 and 91 for an example.) While much is unpredictable, all the retailers we interviewed said if you don't attend to business, you won't have one. You'll learn more about retail operations in upcoming chapters as we expand your perspective from the owner's viewpoint to a close-up on employees and customers.

Layaway Record

Salesperson:		Date:	
Customer:		Telephone:	
Address:			

City:	State:	Zip:

Quantity	Item/description	Price/unit	Total

Pickup date:	Total due:	
Delivery schedule:	Deposit:	
	Balance:	

Merchandise Return Form

Date: _____

From: _____

Address: _____

_____

Telephone: (____) _____

Quantity	Invoice/order	Item/description number	Price per item	Total
				$
				$
				$
				$
				$
				$
				$
				$
				$
				$
				$
				$
				$
				$
				$
				$
				$
				$
				$
				$
				$
				$

Reason for return:

Credit as:	Total return:
Exchange:	Quantity:
Store credit:	Amount:
Cash:	Check number:
Charge:	

_____

_____

_____

_____

Discount Worksheet

Clearance: _____ Date: _____

Special Promotion: _____

Advertised in: _____ Prepared by: _____

Run dates: _____

Item description	Wholesale price	Retail price	Dates valid	% discount	Final unit price
	$	$			$
	$	$			$
	$	$			$
	$	$			$
	$	$			$
	$	$			$
	$	$			$
	$	$			$
	$	$			$
	$	$			$
	$	$			$
	$	$			$
	$	$			$
	$	$			$
	$	$			$
	$	$			$
	$	$			$
	$	$			$
	$	$			$
	$	$			$
	$	$			$
	$	$			$
	$	$			$
	$	$			$
	$	$			$
	$	$			$
	$	$			$
	$	$			$
	$	$			$

Cashier's Till Record

Date:
Name:
Amount start of day:
Amount end of day:
Over/under:
Deposit:
Deposit date:

Item	Start of day	End of day
Pennies		
Nickels		
Dimes		
Quarters		
Half-dollars		
Ones		
Fives		
Tens		
Twenties		
Fifties		
Hundreds		
Checks/other		
Total:	$	$

Cashier's signature: _____

Daily Cash Record

| Date: |
| Page No.: |

CASH PAID OUT

Name:		Total paid out: $
Amount:		Total receipts: $
1		Total receipts: $
2		Less paid out: $
3		Balance: $
4
5
6
7
8

CASH RECEIVED FROM

Name:		Total paid out: $
Amount:		Total receipts: $
1		Total receipts: $
2		Less paid out: $
3		Balance: $
4
5
6
7
8

Remarks:

_____

_____

Motorcycle Retailer's Daily Diary

7 A.M. Unlock door and turn off alarm system. Open safe and set up cash drawers. Check phone for messages. Check for special orders. Order inventory items. Set up employee duties for the day.

8 A.M. Check stock on floor. Arrange sales displays. Clean up store interior. Check yesterday's sales for reorder and stock. Check service schedule. Greet employees. Have a short sales meeting and go over day's schedule and "to do" items. Get coffee ready for customers.

9 A.M. Open doors for customers. Make necessary telephone calls. Get bank deposit ready. Make tour of store and double-check for items to do. Greet customers in department. Make sure that all parts needed for service orders are in stock. Check for e-mail and faxes.

10 A.M. Take deposit to bank. Return to store. Greet customers and answer questions. Go through mail and check out new items from vendors. Check e-mail. Review specials for next week. Tour the floor and service area to let customers know the owner is available. Talk with employees about responses to advertisements currently running. Get suggestions from employees about what customers are asking for.

11 A.M. Check for items done that were on employee's list. Greet customers. Check service area for jobs completed. Check e-mail. Check restrooms and coffee area for cleanliness and supplies. Make floor patrol again. Check Web site for orders and enter in system.

12 P.M. Start lunch break schedule. Check e-mail. Fill in on floor for employees on lunch break. Meet with customers and talk about upcoming events in the area. General conversations always lead to customers expressing needs and desires. Floor patrol again. Check on service department.

1 P.M. Check e-mail. Check in deliveries and check shipping tickets against orders. Print price tags for new inventory. Meet with customers. Put new arrivals into computer inventory. Do morning sales count. Check on service schedule for delivery time. Check floor for tasks completed. Have one salesperson getting packaging ready for afternoon shipper pickup. Check shipments against orders. Check with vendors on backordered items. Check with vendors on ordered items.

2 P.M. Floor patrol and check exterior of store. Check e-mail. Enter orders in computer from Web site. Check service department. Check floor for coverage of salespeople. Check shipment for accuracy. Greet customers. Make necessary phone calls.

3 P.M. Floor patrol. Check service department and exterior of store. Check restrooms and coffee area. Check e-mail. Check Web orders. Make up order list for today's sales and orders. Take time to talk to salespeople; make them feel like they are part of the family.

4 P.M. Floor patrol. Get daily shipment out. Make sure that all service orders will be ready at delivery time. Start general store rearrangement of things out of place. Check e-mail. Get ready to finalize daily order. Make any necessary phone calls.

5 P.M. Check service area and be available to go over items on invoices with customers. Check sales floor for cleanliness. Check for all items in place. Final patrol of exterior. Make sure all customers are satisfied with their service work.

6 P.M. Store closing. Make sure all cash drawers are balanced. Do day-end closeout on computer. Check computer for items to add to daily order. Make sure all areas are clean and ready for the next day. Make sure all employees' time cards are completed and entered in computer. Check e-mail and Web site for orders. Make all changes to daily orders and fax to vendors. Check store for lockup. Check cash drawers and organize deposit for tomorrow. Check stock for all service orders for tomorrow and set up in service area. Double-check store for lockup and get ready to leave. Turn coffee machine off. Make sure all equipment is shut down.

7 P.M. Set alarm and lock store. Go home.

7

Store
Design

Imagine you are a customer walking through your store's front door for the first time. What impression do you have of the store? What benefits are being offered to you? Do you have a sense of excitement and confidence? The physical setting and visual cues of your business set the stage for the consumer's experience with you. So what will it be?

Are you an upscale, trendsetting store? A discount or mainstream business? Are you futuristic, contemporary, or traditional? Take your positioning statement from your business plan and present it in the 3-D world of location, architecture, and interior design. Use scale, colors, textures, materials, amenities, and layout to convey your store's philosophy. Should you use a chandelier, neon, or spotlights? Elegant columns, contemporary angles, or casual corners? Hot colors or subdued hues? Marble floors or industrial carpet? Set the stage for your customers.

The Store Planning Process

Your store plan has two key elements: store design and store layout. Store design is concerned with atmosphere, image, interior design, and exterior design factors. Store layout involves the internal arrangements of each department, selling and sales support allocation, and the evaluation of space productivity.

To set up your store, consider consulting with architects, interior designers, and lighting engineers. Working with skillful designers gives you an invaluable resource: Not only will they know the best location for air conditioners and elevators, but they can help build flexibility into lighting, sound, and wiring systems that will keep you from incurring costs when floor layouts are altered. Designers keep abreast of the hottest color schemes, materials, sources, and trends to a degree that would be impossible for someone outside the trades to do. You can save yourself a lot of aggravation and a fair amount of money with thoughtful preparation.

Most good design firms are used to working within a budget, but you must be very organized in order to control costs. One of the best ways to prevent expensive mistakes or unnecessary changes is to think through what you want before you contract outside services. Preparing a "design brief" forces you to formulate what you want in specific terms and raises questions you will rely on design professionals to answer.

If you choose to do the work yourself, get out there and do your research. Visit retail businesses. Make sure you visit stores similar to the one you plan to open as well as ones that are different. You never know where you might find a good idea. Take notes on elements that work and don't work—then figure out why. See the "Store Planning Worksheet" on page 95 for more information.

Exterior Personality

Customers enter your business partly on their impression of its exterior. It communicates many things to them: stability, friendliness, style, service, value, safety, etc. Therefore, it needs to be distinctive and easily recognizable from a distance. The external lighting, signage, size and shape of the windows, and style and positioning of the entryway should project the image you want them to.

When you're contemplating building a new store or remodeling an existing structure, you have many options, but you may have to compromise your ideal with the reality that your landlord and local authorities have final say over what you can do. You may have to work around a facade that is subject to a preservation order, or use specified materials or colors to ensure a blend with surrounding buildings. One of the most common restrictions

Store Planning Worksheet

In evaluating your physical facilities plan, answer the following questions:

1. Is adequate emphasis placed on space productivity?
   ❑ Yes   ❑ No
2. Are flexible fixtures used wherever possible?
   ❑ Yes   ❑ No
3. Does signage provide adequate information to shoppers?
   ❑ Yes   ❑ No
4. Does the atmosphere support the other elements of the marketing plan?
   ❑ Yes   ❑ No
5. Is merchandise arranged for easy cross-selling wherever possible?
   ❑ Yes   ❑ No

The key information you'll want to have ready for your design team includes:

❑ A profile of your target customer (age, ZIP codes, lifestyles, spending patterns)
❑ Requirements for the types of products to be stocked
❑ The store's positioning (fashion attitude, price levels, philosophy, etc.)
❑ Planned product mix for store (required stock density and presentation needs)
❑ Proposed departmental complements (what goes next to what)
❑ Window and internal display considerations
❑ Stockroom requirements
❑ Back-office requirements
❑ Staff room requirements
❑ Checkout requirements (wiring needs for electronic point-of-sale equipment, credit authorization telephones, and security equipment)
❑ Specific needs for fitting rooms, customer service desks, seating areas, showroom, etc.
❑ The length of time the decor is required to last before updating
❑ A target price per square foot you are prepared to pay

Smart Tip

To find a firm that can handle your new construction or remodeling project, contact the Institute of Store Planners (www.ispo.org), the National Retail Federation (www.nrf.com), your particular trade association, or look in your local business-to-business telephone book for designers who specialize in retail businesses.

is in the size and design of external signs. Retailers advise that it's best to start out with a clear picture of what you want so you can negotiate toward that, rather than succumbing totally to what others think you should have and losing your well-crafted identity.

Let's take a look at your store design opportunities from curbside to checkout counter.

Overhead Sign

A sign identifies a store and provides information about the type of goods carried. Like all other components of the storefront, the overhead sign's tone, character, and design should be perfectly in sync with your desired image. As a new business, you need to make people aware of your existence. Your sign is a major magnet to drawing people in, so spend time and money to come up with a strong one. Signs can attract customers from freeways or from blocks away if they are distinct in color and design, well-lit, and unobstructed by trees, utility lines, or other signs. Be sure you check the line of sight from various angles and distances to determine the most appropriate signage for your type of business.

Signs come in many varieties: lettering (in block or script) made of wood, plastic, or metal set against a background of metal, stone, wood, stucco, or other material, light boxes covered with translucent facings that carry imprinted lettering and/or designs, glass tubing with neon for nighttime illumination, and so forth. The question of signage can be a deal-breaker in negotiating a lease, so address this matter upfront with your landlord and the city.

Make sure your sign will look as attractive after the first rain and two years from now. Chipped or damaged letters, sections of neon tubing that fail to light up, electric bulbs that go out or are broken, and other defects will need to be repaired immediately. Ignoring or putting off this simple task will cost you sales. And while we are on the subject, make sure your entire premises are kept clean and orderly. The sidewalk should be kept clear of dust, dirt, trash, snow, and slush. Retailers in snow country suggest keeping a bag of rock salt in the back room or basement during the wintertime to use on ice. Develop good habits from day one, and your customers will reward you.

Show Window

The principal promotional tool for the majority of small retailers is the show window. Often referred to as "the eyes of the store," it usually starts several feet above the sidewalk, has a flat or elevated wooden base, and is protected on several sides by panes of glass. Lighting fixtures are set into the ceiling; sometimes, they are also set along one wall that is solid, not glass.

Discounters and food retailers tend to use a lot of the glass for promotional posters. Fashion clothing and footwear retailers use it to promote the latest look. Luxury goods specialists often go for minimalist window displays that are pure image-builders rather than specific product-promoters.

What kind of windows will appeal most to your audience? Should the glass go all the way to the ground? Should the windows have flat beds or be raised? What sort of equipment and lighting should be used to advertise what you're selling?

"We light up our windows very brightly at night," says Jim D., the women's and children's boutique owner (with his wife, Mary) in Thomasville, Georgia. "Mary's sparkling windows make people stop to admire them. The windows draw people into the store. We have a sign across the window that says 'New Arrivals.'" Other than that, we don't have any signs pasted on the windows. It's critical that people can see through them."

Despite her claim that she's not very artistic, pet bakery owner Stephanie B.'s Newport Beach, California, storefront window is alive with color and variety, enticing shoppers to venture in to explore. "I change my windows at least twice a month," the dog and cat supplier says. "The last one I did was themed around ceramics and featured lots of bowls. I work very hard to have good displays so that the store doesn't look cluttered." Her love of animals and her art history major show in her window displays.

Montpelier, Vermont, music store owner Fred W.'s window backs are left open so consumers looking at the window display will be able to see directly into the store. Looking in, people see very high ceilings and exposed pipes painted different colors; rows and rows of CDs line cases; and pictures, posters, and collages fill the walls. "Sensory overload," Fred laughs. "Some retail consultants have come into the store and said that the collages are too distracting and should be taken down. But I like them. They're part of the character of the store."

Closed-in window backs, used in many lingerie and fine jewelry stores, enable the window decorator to exercise a lot of creativity in the display. The closed back shuts out interference from the store interior and blocks "peering" eyes from watching people in the store. The display should be kept current with fresh price or other eye-catching signs that are professionally prepared, not handwritten on an old square of cardboard. Rotate the items and change the color scheme every two weeks or so. Keep your display free of clutter, dust, moths, and falling visuals.

Dollar Stretcher

Talk with your suppliers and find out what racks, displays, shelving units, or wire spinners they have for their products that they will let you use for free, or at a price offset by free merchandise. They visit hundreds of stores, so they usually have good ideas.

Consider your window a stage when planning displays. The center foreground is the location of your prime display items, with the sides and rear being good choices for secondary displays. Take advantage of themes, seasons, holidays, and other events to make your display interesting and appealing. Refer to *Chase's Annual Calendar* (NTC/Contemporary Publishing Group) for holidays and anniversaries you can tie into, such as Women's History Month, Mark Twain's Birthday, and National Healthy Heart Month. Tell a story with your products so you can connect with passersby in unexpected and interesting ways and convert window-shoppers to buyers.

Fred has four windows, each with its own theme. The three large ones are 8 feet by 6 feet. One displays CDs and other products, images, and posters. The second sells "wild, weird, wacky, wicked, witty, and just plain funny cards (and bumper stickers, too)," as the banner proclaims. The third window showcases local painters, sculptors, and artisans. The fourth, small 3-by-3-foot window is reserved for political commentary. "Most people would think this would be risky, but I've had people tell me that they don't agree with my politics but respect my courage to stand up for what I believe in," says Fred.

Beware!

Budget restrictions are not the only limitations on how your store will look. There are fire regulations, building codes, zoning regulations, possibly Occupational Safety and Health Administration standards, and standards set by the Americans with Disabilities Act. Contact your local planning department to see what requirements apply to your situation.

Whatever type of window display you choose, make sure the design is economical to maintain and update. Make the windows easily accessible for regular cleaning. Don't clutter them up with signs, except for special-occasion window painting. Display dressing is a specialist skill and is usually provided by a display team brought in on a part-time basis. Care should also be taken in the specification and design of window-lighting systems to ensure that light bulbs can be changed easily by the shop staff without disturbing the displays or having to call an electrician. Plan lighting carefully to minimize window glare. Do not have spotlights shining outward to dazzle window-shoppers.

Entrance

Ease of entry into your store is important. In this respect, stores located inside shopping centers have an advantage because often the entire storefront can be the entrance. Where is the entrance in the building you are considering? Does it draw people inside or scare them away? How will most of your customers be arriving—on foot or by car, bus or bicycle? At night or during the day? Alone or in groups?

The doorway should be inviting and make it easy for people to enter your business, permitting people to pass both ways comfortably. The door itself can be constructed of glass, wood, metal, or other sturdy material. Clearly mark "Push" and "Pull" on the door to ease traffic flow. You won't have doors in enclosed shopping malls because the storefronts encourage shoppers to go in and out of stores when open and use security cages when closed.

Studies show that a pedestrian will normally enter a store that has the largest number of customers already inside and offers the brightest, most colorful interior. The average motorist will normally enter the parking facility for a retail operation that is the easiest to drive into, is not expensive, shows the least possibility of congestion and danger, and has clear signage.

Designing Your Store Interior

Layout is one of the most critical factors in retail stores. Retailing is about selling, and the way a store is laid out can maximize or impede sales. Designing the layout also consists of allocating internal space to specific supporting activities, such as storage, workrooms, receiving sections, etc. It also includes the strategic placement of all fixtures and equipment. Moreover, it involves the flow of shoppers, employees, merchandise, and supplies.

Access for the physically challenged requires special attention. For the convenience of your customers, you need aisles wide enough to permit shoppers to pass each other without colliding. Similarly, you want to allow passageways behind counters and showcases of at least 28 to 30 inches for salespeople to travel back and forth. A skilled designer will see things you may not notice but your customer will feel.

"We had a few different firms help us with the layout of our 643-square-foot store," recounts Seattle-based art gallery owner Darrell T. "Build-out designers gave us presentations showing different storefronts they had done and various layouts."

Dadeville, Alabama, grocer Jeff P. handled store layout himself. "My father has been working for a large wholesale operation and oversees about 350 different independent stores. So I spent about a year and half traveling around looking at other stores and taking pictures of what they had done. I kind of pieced it all together and came up

with something simple that works. Then I hired an architect to draw up the blueprints and take them through the approval process with the planning commission. This is a small town, so it wasn't [difficult]. The officials were so tickled that we were making the improvements that they approved them eagerly."

Of the four main approaches to retail store layout—grid, free-form, boutique, and maze—the grid (also known as the "gridiron") is the most popular. (see "Four Approaches to Retail Store Layout" on page 103.) This style is based on rectangles and is generally found in small stores. Shoppers most often turn right when they enter a store. They pass showcases or sales counters, make a sharp left turn and walk by displays, and then come up along the other side of the store toward the register. Variety stores and supermarkets favor this format because it uses space efficiently, promotes a formal and businesslike atmosphere, simplifies shopping, ensures maximum exposure of store merchandise to the shopper, and is ideal for self-service. However, it is rarely used in specialty-goods stores because customers like to browse leisurely before purchasing.

A free-form pattern permits flexibility and frequent changes. Free-form environments are characterized by curves and arcs. This type of design doesn't compel shoppers to follow predetermined paths. Free-form designs are more graceful and pleasing to the eye than grid layouts, and they encourage leisurely shopping. They allow customers to stay longer and can even encourage impulse buys. However, the disadvantages of this layout are that the space is not used in the most efficient way, and there are often more stock-control and shoplifting problems than with other layouts.

In some cases, designers combine the grid and free-form layouts into a boutique. This layout creates small specialty shops on the selling floor. For example, there might be a "candle shop," "stationery stop," "children's corner," and "kitchen center" arranged around the store. This layout makes it easy for a customer with a particular interest to see the complete offering in one small area. Boutiques are intimate and create a climate where customers feel they are getting more personal attention.

The maze strategy deliberately controls traffic flow, setting up blocks to channel customers into special areas. Proponents believe that this forces the customers through the store or requires customers to ask salespersons for assistance. Opponents of this store design say that it creates consumer frustration and therefore discourages buying, in addition to creating blind sections and corners for shoplifters.

Every Foot Counts

Every square foot of your store costs money, so apportion your space carefully. Usually, the largest area in your store is the selling area. A menswear shop, for example, may devote 15 percent of its selling space to sport jackets because sales figures indicate that this is the percentage of total sales accounted for annually by those jackets. Check with your trade association or the National Retail Federation in Washington, DC, for this kind of information for your specific type of retail business.

Use space effectively. Know the value of your space and locate merchandise accordingly. Learn from the experts: Items with the highest profit should be placed near the front of the store since that space is the most valuable. It is here, in the highest-traffic area, that impulse merchandise and convenience goods should be located.

Cash register areas are also good locations for impulse items. Place sale merchandise or other special items in a wide aisle in a special display "obstacle" rack for effective merchandising. Customers will become accustomed to looking for specials in that particular location.

Flow of Store Traffic

You want to draw customers through the space, exposing them to merchandise and services all the way. One trick of the trade is to separate departments by light and dark color and value in flooring and/or wall coverings. Walls that do not touch the ceiling, undefined aisles, and limited use of carpeting create open, flowing spaces and allow customers to move freely. Do you want a clean, uncluttered look for a more passive, low-key shopping experience? Or do you want to create a sense of urgency—a busy and stimulating atmosphere that encourages shoppers to aggressively go after what they want?

Circulation is a key factor in store ambiance. Movement through your store should feel fluid to customers. At the same time, you have to maximize customers' exposure to displays and merchandise. The easier it is for time-pressured customers to move around, the more they will buy. Keeping the store open and airy, with wide aisles and lots of directional signs, helps shoppers find what they want.

Jeff P. started with an 8,200-square-foot leased building and now owns a 22,000-square-foot food store. "We have a deli/bakery, which we didn't have previously. We

▲

have more than tripled our frozen food section because it has been a fast-growing category for years. And with all the demand for ready-made meals, we had to add that. We also added wider aisles. Now you can get two shopping carts to pass each other in the aisles. Our sales per square foot are about the same as before, maybe a little bit lower, but we were doing a remarkable amount of business in a cramped atmosphere before. When we opened [the store] up, it made the atmosphere more spacious and cleaner for customers to shop in."

Inventory Influences Layout

The layout of any store depends on the amount of space available and the type of products or services offered. For example, a grocery store will have a completely different type of display and layout from a clothing store or snowboard shop. In very small stores, layout is inflexible. A counter, at which one or more employees can work, separates customers from the entire merchandise display that is behind the counter. In larger stores, there may be more display areas along the remaining walls. In even larger stores, there may be counters or rack displays around which customers must circulate to select items.

Whether you have dressing rooms, display suites, personal shoppers, locked cases, or open displays—everything has to have a place. Make it easy for the customer to buy what you're selling. This includes seeing what you have, finding the right size and color, knowing the price, trying the item out or on, getting someone to complete the transaction, and taking the purchase home. Whatever the size of your business, you want the overall result to be a customer-friendly store with ambience.

Does your inventory call for an open and airy space to inspire buyers, or does an intimate, cozy atmosphere put your customers in the mood to buy what you're selling? Is the buying decision an impulsive, emotional one that is complemented by a lively, bright, busy spot, or does the decision-making process require a calm, organized, simple setting? Does the product need to demonstrated or tested?

Any positive sensory triggers in the environment you can create will enhance a shopper's stay and make them want to return. If your store is an emotionally fulfilling social destination as well as a retail destination, you are your own advertisement. Make your customers feel as comfortable in your store as they feel at a friend's house, and you will build goodwill and loyalty. What sorts of friends do your target customers have? At what volume do they play their music? What kind of music? If you capture the feel of a friend's living room, eventually you become a friend, too

Aisles

Customers entering the store should find a main aisle. The counters on either side of a main aisle are generally more effective than subsidiary aisles in catching customers' attention. Subsidiary aisles, if there are any, should be off to the sides.

Four Approaches to Retail Store Layout

Grid

Freeform

Boutique

Maze

KEY

1. Entrance

2. Cashier

3. Storeroom

4. Restroom

5. Dressing Room

▲

Seven Principles of Space Allocation

Once you've decided on a layout for your business, turn your attention to space allocation. Seven fundamental principles should guide you:

1. *Show all merchandise to all customers.* The more merchandise customers see, the more they will buy. You want to design your store to entice customers to visit all departments or at least to see what the store has and return another time. You can accomplish this objective through strategic location of signs, special values, escalators, stairs, dressing rooms, and certain merchandise. (Many supermarkets place convenience items such as bread and milk at the rear of the store to drive traffic storewide.)

2. *Give choice locations, where inside customer traffic is heavy, to the most profitable items.* High-markup and impulse items should be very visible.

3. *Discourage shoplifting.* Keep small, expensive items under lock and key, use convex mirrors where blind spots cannot be eliminated, and install video monitors. By keeping everything wide open, salespeople can observe everyone in the store.

4. *Experiment to stay exciting.* To accommodate changes in layout and merchandise displays, you need to have fixtures that are movable and adjustable, so keep this in mind when you're buying cabinets, shelving, lighting, and other furnishings.

5. *Locate related lines next to each other.* Ties should be located close to dress shirts, printers next to computers, vases next to flowers, and so forth.

6. *Locate related departments next to each other.* Fashion departments complement each other. Cosmetics, accessories, and jewelry often go well together. Cookbooks and gourmet utensils stimulate interest in one another. Departments and merchandise categories should be coordinated as much as possible for customer convenience and cross-selling.

7. *Give the most important lines the best locations in your store.* Play the winners. Anything that is moving fast should be exploited in every way.

Counters at either end of aisles are also good spots for catching attention and are good locations for special displays, sale items, new items, loss leaders (items sold below cost to attract customers), and similar goods. All aisles should be as wide as is practical to minimize crowding and better display merchandise. Displays in the aisles should be planned according to the buying habits of your customers.

There are basically two types of retail store customers: those who know what they want when they come into the store and seek it out or ask for help immediately, and those who just browse without specific items in mind but who might buy something if it appeals to them.

Make it easy for the customer to buy what you're selling.

Studies show that browsers tend to move counterclockwise around a store, while those knowing what they want tend to move clockwise after entering the store. If you can categorize the majority of your customers as being of one type or the other, you may be able to plan your interior displays to your advantage.

Self-Service Techniques

Is your store going to be mainly self-service or customer-assisted? This makes a difference in your layout and how you place your check stands, fixtures, displays, and so forth. Stores of the 21st century are information-intensive. The familiar cosmetics department's enclosed rectangular counters staffed by lots of salespeople is becoming a thing of the past. Female shoppers won't wait for a salesperson to give them assistance on lipstick selection, so self-service testing kiosks and open shelving are proliferating.

Many retailers are attracted to self-service operations because of customer preference, the high cost of labor, turnover, and lack of salespeople's professionalism. Notice we said "customer preference" first. Most consumers today like to have the freedom to look over merchandise, read the print on the packaging or garment tags, compare one item with another, and make a selection without assistance. However eye wear, automotive parts, cosmetics, computers, furs, jewelry, designer clothes, floral arrangements, and some other items require more attention, which customers expect.

To make it easy for customers to serve themselves, you may want to include shopping baskets or carts. To operate on a self-service basis, you will need wide aisles, a flowing floor pattern, easily accessible merchandise, informative signage, and a speedy central exchange system. You might consider installing TVs with VCRs in certain departments for demonstration or entertainment purposes.

The Cash Wrap

A shopper's decision whether or not to purchase is deeply influenced by lines at the cash register. Look closely at this area with an eye to efficiency. A well-designed checkout area cuts transaction time and employee fatigue, according to studies done by New York City-based behavioral research firm Envirosell.

Studies show that the number of transactions per hour a cashier can handle drops the more he or she has to bend down to find the right size bag for a customer. The problem can be solved with vertical shelving and by color-coding shopping bags. This solution will not only increase cashier productivity but also reduce the cost of having to throw away wrong-size bags that were trashed.

▲

Scripted Spaces

Self-defining, media-savvy consumers are hungry for substance and true experience, according to Brian Sullivan, senior associate at retail design firm Fitch & Co. in Worthington, Ohio. "Retail will shift to creating personal experiences that are meaningful and sustainable. Consumers will demand full immersion and participation, and expect that each return visit be a progression from the last. Consumers will reward such experiences with interest and loyalty. The death of brand loyalty is a myth—most retail brands just aren't delivering."

Store design will evolve along two complementary yet distinctly different paths to address consumer mind-sets, say industry analysts. Specialty stores will deliver very personal and meaningful solutions. Products will be organized around people's aspirations, solutions, and narratives. For example, Donna Karan retail stores reflect an attitude about how women aspire to live. She wants to bring customers out of their lives and into an experience. She aims to present a nurturing environment where people feel that they will be taken care of as people, not clothes buyers. Specialty stores like these focus on quality purchasing.

On the other hand, mass merchants and category killers will leverage breadth, providing sophisticated tools that help shoppers select the right product from a vast array of choices. Their store designs focus on quantity purchasing. Visit other stores often to see what they are doing and how you can adopt what you have learned to improve your presentation and sales.

Flooring

When determining which materials to use for flooring in your store, look for surfaces that wear well, especially those that can bear lots of foot traffic and stand up to the demand of ladders, casters on display units, and the bumps and grinds of stocking shelves. Durability is a particularly important consideration in entrances and near checkout stands. You have a choice of asphalt, vinyl, and other tiles in an infinite variety of shades and patterns, along with carpeting of many kinds. Your floors can be of wood, stone or terrazzo, or you can cover them with linoleum. Vinyl wood flooring is a practical material in locations where snow falls most of the year. In addition to durability, look for floor coverings that are pleasant to look at, safe to walk on, and easy to keep clean.

Bright Idea

When choosing flooring for your store, it's important that it not only look good when it's new, but that it's durable, safe, and easy to maintain. Flooring has both an aesthetic and a functional purpose and takes a lot of abuse from foot traffic, box-dragging, and fixture-moving.

Ceilings

Ceilings may simply be painted, or they may be covered with such materials as plasterboard, acoustic tiles or cork. They may be high or dropped, depending on the effect you want to project. Low ceilings can have a positive effect and create a feeling of informality and warmth in some types of stores, or they can have a negative effect by creating a sense of closeness and confinement in shoppers. On the other hand, high ceilings convey a spacious atmosphere that is often equated in the consumer's mind with quality merchandise and leisurely shopping. Yet to some, there's an aura of impersonality, even coldness, in the large, high-ceilinged store. Of course, the lighting and acoustics in your store have a great deal to do with how your customers feel about your ceiling.

Walls

The interior walls and perhaps one or more partitions can be treated in an infinite number of ways. These range from paints of every conceivable shade to cloth materials, tiles, paneling, wood and plastic strips, printed and photographic murals, and wallpaper, to mention just a few. The primary considerations here are the costs, the attractiveness of the wall coverings, their resistance to normal wear and tear, and the expense of keeping them looking good. Often, display shelves of glass, wood, chrome, or other materials are affixed to one or more walls. Mirrors can make the store look wider or longer than it is, and shadow boxes, illuminated from within, are often used to feature special merchandise.

Use of Color

The use of color can breathe life into your premises. It can set the tone and mood, as well as create the kind of atmosphere that will enhance your entire presentation. For example, See's candy stores use gleaming white showcases, black-and-white checked flooring, and crisp white uniforms on employees to show off the chocolate and to reinforce the message that the company's candy is high-quality, special, and pure.

As another example, a store that sells high-quality men's footwear might have thick, luxurious, dark maroon carpeting, wood paneling on the walls, gleaming chrome-and-glass stands for displaying the shoes, and impressive chandeliers to illuminate the selling area—all to convey a sedate, clublike atmosphere.

Use colors on walls, ceilings, and floor coverings with discretion. Bold colors can appear aggressive and inappropriate, except in special situations. Colors that blend in well are preferable in most cases, since they should serve primarily as a backdrop to your merchandise displays and should not overwhelm them. However, bright colors like orange, yellow, or white (in moderate amounts) can be helpful in highlighting merchandise.

Fixtures

Having attended to the major structural elements of the store and its décor, you need to think next about the type of fixtures and the kinds of equipment required by your particular operation. Typically, a retail business needs fixtures for several purposes: display, selling (or self-service), stock, and certain work activities.

To outline what you want, visit stores similar to yours, speak with members of your trade association, and visualize what customers and employees will see as they walk through your store.

Use display fixtures and equipment that complement the décor of your interior. However, if you have only a limited budget for fixtures, you may be wise to purchase or rent less expensive fixtures rather than cut back on the amount of inventory on display. Selling inventory provides you with profit and cash flow, after all.

Look for fixtures that will stand up under heavy usage, are easy to move around, and are flexible enough to use in different ways. But don't invest too much of your initial capital in fancy fixtures or equipment. Look into pre-owned items that can be purchased for a fraction of the cost of new ones and can be refurbished to meet your standards.

Lighting

Lighting is essential to your operation because people like to see what they buy. Additionally, lighting can increase the effectiveness of your displays and work area. A frequent complaint retailers receive is that things look different under the lighting in the store than they do in natural light. This is particularly disastrous for cosmetic, apparel, accessory, paint, and fabric businesses. Interior designers, lighting consultants, and some utility companies can advise you on a selection that would be cost-effective as well as aesthetically pleasing.

> **Tip...**
>
> **Smart Tip**
>
> Lighting can enhance the appeal of different types of merchandise. For example, you can bring out the tempting colors of food by using fluorescent lamps rich in red energy around meats, fruits, and vegetables.
> Concentrated beams of bright, incandescent light will add highlights to jewelry or cut glass.

Nonselling Activities

You should separate selling from nonselling activities. Keep accounting areas, credit offices, public telephones, and similar functions separate from the main selling areas. Generally, these nonselling functions should be at the back of the store since the front of any store is prime selling space. Generally, office/storage space should take up only 10 to 25 percent of your total floor area.

Visual Merchandising

Do not overcrowd displays. Crowded displays can confuse customers and may prevent them from spotting something they would buy if it were more visible. Making a choice among three similar products is easier than a choice among six.

Group displays into obvious categories, and if your customers are generally repeat ones, do not constantly move products to different locations since that can irritate some people. This is particularly true for grocery store, office supply store, and drugstore customers.

Try to create an air of spaciousness in displays, and wherever possible avoid displays that block the view of other parts of the store or the locations of cashiers. The objective of good display is to make the items most customers want stand out. Display signs can help, but don't overdo them. Poor signs or too many signs detract from the actual merchandise, so have a professional make them neat and easy to read.

If you advertise on the radio or in the newspaper that you have a sale on certain items, be sure to highlight the location of those items in the store with special sale signs. Sign colors are important for visual impact. Sale signs are often made in hot colors like red or orange, lettered on a yellow background. Black or red letters on white also stand out well.

Convenience Counts

The term convenience store is being redefined by the consumer to mean a store that has everything they want to buy when they want to buy it. So to attract more frequent shoppers, place the highest-demand consumables in the front of the store for ease of shopping. Customers should be able to understand how the store is organized as soon as they enter so they get the feeling that they can find what they're after.

8

Inventory

In a retail business, you make your money when you buy your inventory. If you haven't bought right, even the most astute pricing strategies won't help you grow a healthy business.

▲

Innovative buying opportunities are everywhere. Your task is to find the right goods to impress the buying public and build the image of your business. Your buying approach needs to be creative and resourceful whether you are dealing in the latest goods, seconds, antiques, or commodities. At all times, remember what your market is and who your customers are; people will try to sell you what they have to sell, which is not necessarily what you need to buy. Know what you need, and stick with it. Be strong. Be smart.

You Are What You Sell

Your selection of merchandise is what will set you apart from other stores. Your decision to go into retail was based on the desire to meet an unmet need. Don't lose your focus now and undermine all the effort that went into planning by buying any old thing. Product selection is all about positioning. It's one thing to stock every item in a category; it's quite another to selectively choose those products that enhance your reputation.

"I had no idea how to set up my inventory," says pet bakery owner Stephanie B. in Newport Beach, California. "I just guessed and made tons of mistakes, but you just live with it," she says. "I could have ordered a lot more of a few things rather than a

---

Inventory Checklist

Here is a list of the most widely mentioned inventory items retailers need, in addition to merchandise, of course. Check off the ones you have and make sure you've put the ones you need in your budget.

❑ Bags (merchandise, garment, and shopping)

❑ Boxes (takeout, gift, and shipping)

❑ Feedback/suggestion cards

❑ Gift cards

❑ Gift certificates

❑ Gift-wrap

❑ Guest book for mailings

❑ Layaway/installment contracts

❑ Promotional items (magnets, pens, key chains, pins, mouse pads, visors, baseball caps, T-shirts, etc.)

❑ Promotional literature (catalogs, fliers, brochures, posters, etc.)

❑ Web page ordering and store location information

---

lot of a lot of things, but I wanted to know what went over, what was popular, and what wasn't. As it turns out, the variety of my inventory is part of the charm of the store. If you buy two collars instead of 10, when a customer comes back to get a collar you had a week ago and it's gone, some people don't like that. For others, they know if they like something, they'd better buy it now or lose out."

"Successful inventory forecasting and management comes from being in the business," says 20-year veteran hi-fi sales and service retailer Jim O. in Thomasville, Georgia. "There are no shortcuts or formulas. In the beginning, we went to the manufacturers' reps and asked them what the most popular items were and what was selling. Now we go to home theater forums on the Internet to see what people are talking about. We look at the market and what others are doing. There's so much competition—and the margins on fast-moving popular items are slimming down—so you have to stay alert. This is true of any type of inventory, not just ours."

Quality Merchandise

What will the quality of your merchandise be? Buying products made in the United States and environmentally safe products has become a hot subject in recent years. But is the quality there? You owe it to your customers to make sure it is. Don't just accept label claims at face value. As much as the customer may be looking for those tags, if the merchandise falls apart in two weeks, they really won't care where or how it was made. They bought the merchandise from you, so they will hold you responsible.

What customers see should be what they get, and what you promise must be what you deliver. To some customers, quality will extend from the point of origin of the materials used in the item through the production process to the distribution chain and onto your shelves. Check your sources, and stay abreast of consumer action groups. Low-wage or sweatshop labor sources and animal testing are a few of the hot buttons that could push you into hot water.

Selecting Your Portfolio

Buying inventory is easy; selecting the right things to fill your store's shelves poses more of a challenge. You know what kind of retail operation you have and who your customers will be. Now how do you put together your merchandise portfolio?

Mary D. says she is very careful with the inventory in her 2,000-square-foot Thomasville, Georgia, dress shop. "Overstocking can mean death to any retailing business," she says. "We started with just $8,000 of inventory and have parlayed that investment by reinvesting it every 30 days or so." Her husband and business partner Jim adds: "Mary really knows how to establish good working relations with buyers, what to buy, and what fads to stay away from."

Most of the retailers we spoke with said there were big-box retail stores in their markets. "Wal-Mart sells more music than anyone else," says Montpelier, Vermont, music store owner Fred W. "We cannot compete with them on price in Top 40 sales, which is too bad because they're high-volume. Where we have the edge is in our deep catalog. We order every weekday, which makes people happy," says Fred. "Most customers are willing to wait 24 hours to get what they want."

Choose products that enhance your reputation. Your prices should reflect your image and your target market. This means that you should establish your price lines and price points before you buy. You must get the highest possible markup consistent with competition and customer price satisfaction. The better the buy, the higher the markup you can take.

Jim and Mary D. picked the top of the line. "We order from the same suppliers who do the Miss America and other pageants across the country," Jim says proudly. "We reduce the profit margin aggressively like we did in the pharmacy business, and sell very few duplicate outfits, so people really get good value. We aim for the 'wow effect.' We talk about it all the time. The 'wow effect' is great value and great service." For more on pricing, see Chapter 10.

Establishing Your Inventory

Here is a simple procedure to follow to help you decide which merchandise you should offer and which you should not. If you are dealing with electronics or clothing, you may wish to do your breakdown on the basis of brand names. If you are organizing a food business, simply list the food supplies you would have on hand the day you open.

We asked a motorcycle dealer to explain how he would use this model.

1. Divide your inventory into broad classifications, such as $30,000 for motorcycle hard parts.

2. Divide each broad classification into sub-classifications—for example, engine parts, wheel parts, frame parts, transmission parts, dress-up parts, drive-line parts, and tuneup parts.

3. Allocate a certain percentage of your capital to each sub-classification—for example, 20 percent engine parts, 5 percent wheel parts, 5 percent frame parts, 5 percent transmission parts, 30 percent dress-up parts, 10 percent drive-line parts, and 25 percent tuneup parts.

> **Tip...**
>
> **Smart Tip**
> Customers will pay more if they know they are getting a better quality of merchandise for their dollar. Now more than ever, value (the relationship between quality and price) is the most important area of merchandise management.

4. Locate resources that will sell you the products you want to stock. Read *Hot Bikes* magazine, the *Motorcycle Dealer News Annual Buyers Guide*, *Thunder Press* newspaper, and *Easy Rider* magazine. Get catalogs from *Custom Chrome*, *Parts Unlimited*, *Drag Specialties*, and *Nimco*.

5. Make sure each item purchased gives you the best possible markup and that the retail prices will fit the price lines you have set for your operation. The store's target markup is 50 percent on services, 40 percent on accessories and clothing, and 35 percent on hard parts.

You only have so much money allocated for merchandise. The challenge you face is to achieve maximum sales from what you buy. By first determining how much of what you are going to buy, you discipline yourself to be discriminating and to keep your buys in balance with your overall inventory needs. Faced with an enthusiastic salesperson, an attractive deal, and a hunger to buy, you need all the will you can muster to remember your priorities. Overstocking in one area at the expense of other areas is a dangerous proposition. Take your buying plan with you and stick to it.

Finding Products

Thoroughly investigate the types of products you want to sell. This means being aware of nationally advertised products, what competitors are selling, and the offers of major suppliers. Your trade association and business publications report trends and identify resources you can use. Keep on top of your reading to stay informed about sources of product.

The Real Deal?

Counterfeiting is one of the fastest-growing economic crimes worldwide. Such crimes account for about 5 percent of world trade, representing about $250 billion annually, says the Counterfeiting Intelligence Bureau at the International Chamber of Commerce. Music, software, videos, games, design-led products, and branded goods are the prime targets of counterfeiters. Knockoffs are inferior in content and performance and can be dangerous. Fake pharmaceutical products, for example, not only fail to cure but have also caused deaths. Aircraft and vehicular accidents have been caused by the use of counterfeit parts. Buy only from legitimate manufacturers, dealers, and verifiable sources. Don't put your business and customers at risk. If an item's price seems too good to be true, it's probably a fake!

Using Buying Offices

A resident buying office is composed of buyers in national or international market centers who shop the market daily to offer their member stores information and to choose and purchase items for them. Resident buying offices primarily provide advice and counsel. Their staffs also do actual buying for their members on a contract basis.

A buying office can be your eyes and ears and can help you evaluate resources, identify price fluctuations, and keep up with trends. A buying office has its own staff of domestic and foreign buyers and can invite your buyer to information clinics.

Most professional buyers are located in or around merchandise markets. Visiting one or more of the regional markets listed in "To Market, to Market" below is an efficient way to begin building your network of buying information and sources. For example, you'll find most professional clothing buyers near the New York market.

To Market, To Market

These markets are found in major cities where a large number of suppliers are located. Many may be in a single building, such as a merchandise mart, and can be important sources for you. Regional markets include:

- ○ *Atlanta:* Atlanta Apparel Mart for men's, women's, and children's apparel and accessories
- ○ *Charlotte, North Carolina:* Carolina Trade Mart
- ○ *Chicago:* Chicago Mart and McCormick Plaza (for women's and children's apparel, furniture, and hardware)
- ○ *Dallas:* Dallas Market Center complex includes the Apparel Mart, Home Furnishings Mart, and World Trade Center
- ○ *Denver:* Denver Merchandise Mart
- ○ *High Point, North Carolina:* Furniture Mart
- ○ *Kansas City, Missouri:* Trade Center
- ○ *Los Angeles:* Garment District (for women's, men's, and children's apparel, with emphasis on sportswear and accessories; also, Furniture Mart)
- ○ *Miami:* Miami Merchandise Mart
- ○ *Minneapolis:* Radisson Center
- ○ *San Francisco:* San Francisco Mart
- ○ *Woburn, Massachusetts:* Northeast Trade Center

Look in your business-to-business Yellow Pages to see what merchandising services are available in your area for your type of business.

Mary D. is the buyer for her store and travels to the Garment District in Los Angeles, where she buys her inventory and meets with other buyers she has established relationships with to exchange tips and ideas. It's helpful to have a list of markets as resources for variety and category needs.

Independent resident buyers usually deal with small retailers, providing few services other than the procurement of merchandise. The buyer can represent many manufacturers and gives the retailer the advantage of choosing from a large assortment of items without paying a fee. The commissioned buyers are considered merchandise brokers.

Whether you're selling gloves, candy, carpets, or lawn mowers, knowledge is king. As a start-up business, you will most likely be doing the buying and will rely on your vendor to get you started with the right inventory. If you engage the services of a buyer, select one who knows your customer, market, and geographic area.

Finding the Right Suppliers

Many manufacturers sell their goods directly to retailers. When there is no middleman or supplier involved, you can negotiate terms more easily. Most retailers buy from wholesalers. Some advantages of dealing with a warehouse include access to a wide assortment of items close to your business, reducing the number of sources you have to deal with, and the ability to purchase in smaller quantities than going directly

Suppliers and Demand

Harmon Tobler of the Retail Success Institute has five suggestions for developing and maintaining the best suppliers.

1. Limit the number of vendors in each category and become important to them.
2. Compare the benefits of the manufacturers' programs and how they fit in with your strategy.
3. Evaluate the distribution pattern, sales margin, and gross margin potential of each potential supplier.
4. Make sure each resource's service and warranty policies meet your standards for customer satisfaction.
5. After you've selected your key vendors, continue to evaluate their product, service, and distribution methods.

Supplier Evaluation

Here are some areas in which you can rate your suppliers' services as excellent, good, average, or poor. Likeableness and price alone won't satisfy your needs. Suppliers are your life support; choose them wisely.

	Excellent	Good	Average	Poor
Company Profile				
Size and/or capacity	❏	❏	❏	❏
Financial strength	❏	❏	❏	❏
Operational profit	❏	❏	❏	❏
Manufacturing range	❏	❏	❏	❏
Research facilities	❏	❏	❏	❏
Technical service	❏	❏	❏	❏
Geographical locations	❏	❏	❏	❏
Management				
Labor relations	❏	❏	❏	❏
Trade relations	❏	❏	❏	❏
Products				
Quality	❏	❏	❏	❏
Price	❏	❏	❏	❏
Packaging	❏	❏	❏	❏
Uniformity	❏	❏	❏	❏
Warranty	❏	❏	❏	❏
Services				
Timely deliveries	❏	❏	❏	❏
Condition on arrival	❏	❏	❏	❏
Follow instructions	❏	❏	❏	❏
Number of rejections	❏	❏	❏	❏

Supplier Evaluation, continued

	Excellent	Good	Average	Poor
Handling of complaints	❏	❏	❏	❏
Technical assistance	❏	❏	❏	❏
Emergency aid	❏	❏	❏	❏
Supply up-to-date catalogs, sales sheets	❏	❏	❏	❏
Supply price changes promptly	❏	❏	❏	❏

Sales Personnel

	Excellent	Good	Average	Poor
Knowledge	❏	❏	❏	❏
The company	❏	❏	❏	❏
Products	❏	❏	❏	❏
Your industry	❏	❏	❏	❏
Your business	❏	❏	❏	❏

Sales Calls

	Excellent	Good	Average	Poor
Properly spaced	❏	❏	❏	❏
By appointment	❏	❏	❏	❏
Planned and prepared	❏	❏	❏	❏
Mutually productive	❏	❏	❏	❏

Service

	Excellent	Good	Average	Poor
Obtain information	❏	❏	❏	❏
Furnish quotes promptly	❏	❏	❏	❏
Follow orders	❏	❏	❏	❏
Expedite delivery	❏	❏	❏	❏
Handle complaints	❏	❏	❏	❏

to the manufacturer. Some importers are excellent resources and connect you with manufacturers in foreign countries. However, buying inventory from suppliers is the cornerstone of many a successful retail business, so you need to know how to establish good supplier relationships.

As soon as you file your business name or take out a business license, suppliers will start approaching you for business. Ask for catalogs, brochures, business addresses, and who they bank with to avoid scams. Established suppliers can not only be a great source of necessities but can also offer you insight into the market. Your suppliers should partner with you to succeed. They should help you interpret consumer demand, guide you in the operation of your business, and assist in solving problems.

Beware!

Be sure any bargains you are offered don't end up costing you more in the long run. Clearly state your expectations for quality, delivery, and service, and hold your suppliers to the terms you've negotiated.

"We get fliers, phone calls, and sales visits from record distributors all the time," says music store owner Fred W. in Montpelier, Vermont. "We read the trade magazines and talk to our customers a lot to make our buying decisions."

Dealing with vendors involves active and continuous negotiation. While a good sales rep may tip you off to specials or price reductions, many discounts are available for the asking. Quantity discounts, invoice dating, shipping terms, return privileges, trade discounts, seasonal and cash discounts, as well as free merchandise all translate into dollars on your bottom line. Ask so you can receive.

"I've known a lot of the vendors I use for years," says Dadeville, Alabama, grocer Jeff P. "They are people who are around forever, and then you get into the business, and they come and see you. You build a relationship with them. They know that I'm fair with them. I'm stern with my vendors and make sure they understand where I'm coming from. [Retailers] also [need to] understand that [they] won't survive without them. You have to have a good relationship with all your vendors. They want volume out of a deal, and you want reliability, quality, and service."

Smart Tip

Tip...

If you're opening a secondhand clothing store, the majority of your inventory will be women's clothes. Used clothing stores for men are a rarity because of low demand. Business suits, winter coats, tuxedos, and dinner jackets are a few items that men will buy used.

Once you have chosen your suppliers, you want to maintain good relations so that you both profit. You have to work at understanding each other's position and be willing to deal openly and fairly with problems that arise. Both retailers and suppliers rate each other on a scale of A, B, and C. Class A is highly profitable because the partner is dependable and very cooperative. Class B is usually dependable and cooperative, and the line contributes significantly to profitability. Class C relationships have to be watched carefully and need to be abandoned before they become unprofitable.

The more money a supplier makes from you, the better you will be treated, and the more money you make from a supplier, the better the treatment this supplier deserves from you. A business relationship will survive only if there is give and take, and the bottom line is mutually rewarding. Don't make unreasonable demands on sales reps, or you will lose a valuable ally and damage your reputation in the industry.

Controlling Inventory

A computer is essential for controlling your inventory. You can program it to tell you when stock reaches a maximum level or minimum level. Automation saves you time, personnel costs, and lost opportunities by helping you act quickly to respond to the ups and downs of consumer preferences.

> **Bright Idea**
> Use a different color tag for new inventory monthly or quarterly, and you'll have a visual dating system for your stock. As you walk through the store, you can see the older merchandise and be aware of the general rate of stock turnover.

"We're always struggling with how to break down the inventory into various groups: jazz, world sound, reggae, rock and roll, etc.," says music store owner Fred W. "We've found that sales increase if we give each artist [his or her] own divider, so we're working on that. We use a Brother label-making machine to make the headers so we can do it anytime we want." From low-tech to high-tech, Fred relies on his proprietary computer system to keep everything straight.

Electronic data interchange, bar-coding, and computer operating systems: All these can be invaluable for managing inventory, but they are no substitute for a culture and procedures that make inventory management a top priority. Efficient inventory management can have a much greater impact on your store's bottom line than a sudden spike in sales. In fact, retailers who espouse accurate and timely record-keeping, an organized storeroom, and very little dead or slow-moving stock can handle just about anything that comes their way.

Always use written purchase orders, itemizing what you ordered and how much you are being charged. Without documentation, you may be billed additional charges or sent the wrong merchandise.

From Shipper to Shopper

Almost half your time will be spent getting merchandise from receiving to the selling floor, properly displayed, and merchandised. Inspection is the first thing that must be done to make sure the merchandise is in good condition. Once accepted, process items, give them an inventory control number, and get the items onto the selling floor. You don't make any money when they're sitting where no one can find them.

Cover the basics of unpacking and handling with your employees. Don't assume that they know how to properly take care of all the different types of merchandise that come into the store.

Selling Seasons

Most buying is done on a seasonal basis. There are certain items that sell through-out the year, and there are those that drive consumers into your store during a specific period of time. Winter means long sleeves, boots, coats, snow shovels, cold remedies, hot food, heaters, and cross-country skis. Summer sells bathing suits, air conditioners, sunscreen, cold drinks, barbecues, and pool supplies. April is tax season, which raises the demand for photocopying services, tax preparers, and software programs. During August and September, sales spike in sales of school supplies and clothing for students and educators.

Factor these realities into your analysis of your store's sales activity. How hot is a "hot" item? Is the interest a passing fad or a sustainable trend? Make sure you can obtain new items and promote them in time to profit, or the risk may be too great for being left with excessive stock you'll have to mark down.

"You have to order early for the holidays," says pet bakery owner Stephanie B. This is the first year for her in all categories, so she's not quite sure how much of what to buy. She's just going on instinct and what people at trade shows and customers have told her to expect. Halloween, Christmas, and Valentine's Day are the three major holidays for specialty items in her store. With her Newport Beach, California, location near Newport Harbor and the Pacific Ocean, nautical-theme pet clothing and accessories are standard stock items, which are particularly good sellers in the summertime.

> **Tip...**
>
> ### Smart Tip
> The more descriptive you are in tracking what is selling and what isn't, the better you will be at servicing your customers. Retailing is rich in nuances and sub-tleties. You won't want to miss a beat in knowing what's going on.

What's Enough?

A common ratio during normal demand periods is 3 to 1. That is, to reach a certain sales figure, a retailer must have three times that amount in inventory. For example, if you have an action sports retail business, it might take a $90,000 inventory in snowboards to generate $30,000 in sales in that category during a given month. Other merchandise classifications have different ratios. In a furniture store, it might take $500,000 in inventory to generate $100,000 in sales—a 5:1 ratio. In fine jewelry, it could take $300,000 to generate $50,000—a 6:1 ratio.

A major retailing goal is to develop as much as possible in sales from the smallest possible inventory, but it is dangerous to run out of merchandise customers want. Thus, keeping tabs on sales-to-stock ratios helps you know how much merchandise you should have on hand. Trade associations usually maintain the most up-to-date ratios to assist retailers with buying. It is common to use such ratios on a month-to-month basis. Sometimes, more frequent use may be called for to measure what is needed for unusually strong demand periods, say during special weather conditions, the holidays, or tourist season. In perishable-goods retailing, stock-to-sales ratios on a weekly basis are needed in most merchandise classifications for food and plant matter.

Inventory and Consignment Items

Building your stock by taking goods on consignment is a smart business practice for retailers who market new goods as well as antique, art, and secondhand dealers. Because you don't have to pay for merchandise outright, you'll be able to build a sizable inventory without a cash outlay. Consigned goods can be displayed for a set period of time and should be kept in a separate category from ordered goods.

You need to establish a policy on how you want to handle consignment items. For example, will you give a store credit to the seller (usually about half what you would sell the item for), or will you pay the seller a certain percentage of cash (50 to 75 percent) when the item sells? Will you require that the seller (frequently an artisan) sign a contract that is renewable every two months, or that they automatically pick up

What Is It?

Classification is the assortment of items by classes. Fundamental merchandising units change little from year to year even though the actual merchandise within each classification will change. Sub-classification breaks goods down into smaller identifiable units. Depth is about variety—an array of styles, colors, and prices. Width is about different product categories that can accompany the sale of your primary item.

▲

items that don't sell after 60 days? Who will be responsible for the display of the merchandise? Can you put it on sale or donate it to charity without the seller's permission if the items are left after a prescribed period of time?

Keeping Up with Change

Focus on the specific merchandise categories your business carries and stay abreast of the trends and market fluctuations influencing the merchandise you sell.

Get out there and look at what's going on. You can spot trends by visiting airports and attending cultural and social events. Visit school campuses and spend time at local resorts. Shop your competitors and go to trade shows. And monitor what people are watching on television and at the movies. Dadeville, Alabama, grocer Jeff P. gets printouts from the Grocers' Association, the Alabama Retail Association, and the Food Marketing Institute. He also reads *Progressive Grocer* and *Supermarket News*. "That's how we try to keep up with the trends. Obviously, you have to try to watch out on your own. There is no one way [to do it]. If you try to look at national formulas, they won't work for Alabama. Alabama's much different from the national scene. What sells in Costa Mesa, California, is not necessarily what's going to sell in Dadeville, Alabama. If I had chitlins in my market in California, I would sit on them. [Likewise], if I get tofu in here, I'm not going to be able to move it."

All the information in this chapter will help you develop a combination of courage and insight to make some profitable inventory choices. You'll find some of the forms that will aid you in keeping track of inventory in this chapter. See the "Back-Order Record" on page 125, the "Items Needed" form on page 126, and the "Receiving Slip" on page 127. Sense what is happening so you'll have the right merchandise for your customers before your competitor does. Retail buying is a fast-track operation.

Back-Order Record

Date from: _____ Date to: _____

Item/ description	Number ordered	Number back-ordered	Date ordered from supplier	Date due/ received

Items Needed

		Date submitted:	

Submitted by:		Department:	
		Attention:	

Item/description	Quantity	Date needed	Price	Date ordered
			$	
			$	
			$	
			$	
			$	
			$	
			$	
			$	
			$	
			$	
		Total cost	$	

Specifications/suppliers to contact:

_____

_____

_____

_____

_____

_____

Receiving Slip

Shipped by:	Date:
	Order/invoice no.:
	Shipping/package no.:

Received from:

Quantity	Item/description	Accept	Return
		Received by:	

Equipment

Now that you own a business, occupy your space, and have ordered your inventory, what's next? You need equipment—equipment to support the various functions of a retail business. You must have the right equipment to help you order, store, display, and sell merchandise or services; manage information; and keep track of everything else.

The equipment you choose should be consistent with the volume and type of operation you run. For example, a service firm will generally not have the same storage or display requirements as a business that sells products. If you don't have a lot of customer traffic, your furnishings-and-amenities needs will be minimal. A single store selling nonperishable items has different needs than a three-store supermarket chain. Likewise, a furniture retailer generally requires fewer display fixtures than a women's clothing store.

You will buy, lease, or rent every piece of equipment you use. Many retailers recommend that you purchase equipment if you have the capital, since they believe it is the most economical choice in the long run and you can depreciate the equipment on your income tax. Lease equipment if you do not have enough capital to buy it, or if you want to establish a credit rating. If you lease, you may have the option to trade the equipment in on upgraded models down the line, or perhaps buy it at the end of the lease term for a preset price. Rent equipment if you want to try out a particular kind, test a retail concept, or have a seasonal rather than year-round need for it. Use the "Equipment Checklist" on pages 140 and 141 to make sure you haven't forgotten any vital equipment.

Equipment Sources

There are plenty of places to get good equipment. Check with other retailers to get leads on equipment sources. Then consider the following sources.

Auctions, Garage Sales, Swap Meets, and Thrift Shops

Auctions are an excellent way to get equipment and supplies at good prices. Watch the business and classified sections of the newspaper for ads. At most auctions, there will be a preview where you can view the equipment before the bidding begins. You will pay a fee for a bidder registration number, and you will probably be required to pay by cash or a personal check for the full purchase amount on the day of the auction. You can also find incredible bargains at garage sales, swap meets, and thrift shops. Some retailers decide to put in the time to shop this time-intensive way to save money to put into new computer systems and merchandise. It goes without saying that shopping through catalogs and showrooms is easier, but these alternative sources can often supply unique equipment.

Online Equipment Sources

Searching for equipment online is easy. Retail.com, RetailExchange.com, and Trade weave.com can give you vast choices and cost savings. Or try sites like KillerBiz.com and Onvia.com.

At Market Max (www.marketmax.com), you can search, select, plan, collaborate, and negotiate directly with suppliers in its virtual marketplace. If you have equipment from a previous business—or something desirable you want to trade—you might want to go to the exchange. Tradeweave.com uses an auction business model. UCCnet.com, which is governed by the Princeton, New Jersey-based Uniform Code Council, is geared largely to the grocery arena. The not-for-profit organization aims to create an Internet-based electronic trading community that permits companies of any size to communicate with their trading partners.

Existing Businesses

If you are buying a business, you may be able to negotiate to buy some of the existing equipment. Pay scrupulous attention to what is and is not part of the purchase price. Ask for copies of all purchase documents, warranties, and service records. You want all the equipment you purchase in good working order, so check it out yourself or hire someone to inspect it for you. Do not take the seller's or broker's word for it. When the refrigerator, safe, or cash register doesn't function properly, you'll lose more than sales. You'll lose face and credibility with your customers and employees.

Office Equipment

There are so many different kinds of office equipment that you will need for your operation, we could not possibly cover them all here. But we will cover computer hardware and software, cash registers, credit card verification systems, bar-code readers, and a few other types of technology that will help you stay on the cutting edge of the retail world.

Computer Hardware

In today's world, no retail operation can be effectively managed without some type of computer system. You need information so you can solve problems and make decisions as effectively as possible. A major function of any system is to predict today what is going to happen tomorrow. It also has to reduce the time required to make decisions. One of the major functions of a retail computer system is to process useless data into useful problem-solving and decision-making information.

Computerization of critical management tasks can make small retailers competitive in this fast-paced business. The hours you save will keep your lights on and cash register ringing up sales. The retailers we interviewed gave us this checklist to help you decide what you want your computer system to do:

❑ Automatic billing
❑ Balance the books

❑ Calculate and file taxes electronically
❑ Electronic cash register
❑ Financial analysis and projections
❑ Generate sale and trends reports
❑ Handle payroll
❑ Maintain customer and supplier files
❑ Maintain employee records
❑ Manage shelf space effectively
❑ Manage accounts payable and accounts receivable
❑ Prepare balance sheets and profit-and-loss statements
❑ Prepare budgets and compare actual figures against plan
❑ Prepare cash reports, purchase orders
❑ Print and store correspondence and mailing labels
❑ Produce business forms
❑ Produce promotional materials
❑ Profile customers by ZIP code, interests, buying habits, preferences
❑ Replenish stock quickly
❑ Set up and maintain customer files
❑ Set up and maintain supplier files
❑ Track activity by time periods
❑ Track advertising and promotion response
❑ Track orders, generating sales, and trends reports
❑ Track responses to advertising and promotion
❑ Track sales tends by product/service and category
❑ Update inventory

Retailers tell us that your hardware requirements will be determined by the software you use. For example, office suites from Lotus, Corel, and Microsoft with word-processing, spreadsheet, e-mail, information management, desktop-publishing, business and customer management, and database management programs list their requirements on the packaging. Although every business is different, to operate the applications you'll need in your retail business, you'll probably need a 128MB Pentium-class computer with an 8GB to 10GB hard drive, running Windows 95, 98, 2000, Millennium Edition, or NT. A 200 MHz or better computer is recommended, and you should have at least 1GB of free disk space. If you'll be creating sophisticated graphics, you'll need an additional 16MB or more of memory; for Web site creation and management, you'll probably need an additional 8MB.

Surge suppressors prevent damage to electronic equipment when there is a fluctuation in voltage. Some power strips look like surge suppressors, but they simply increase the number of outlets you have. Make sure you know what you're buying. Also, a $50 surge suppressor will not protect unsaved data in the event of a power failure. For that, you need an uninterruptible power supply, which will cost $125 to $250.

Jim and Mary D. use a 733 MHz Hewlett-Packard Pavilion PC with 64MB RAM, a 30GB hard drive, and a CD-RW to manage their women's and children's clothing store.

Think ahead. Compare the features you need now with those you will need when you expand your inventory and number of employees. Be sure the system can grow with your business, and that there is tech support. It's very expensive in terms of time and money to have to convert to a different system later. Get the best system you can afford.

Computer Software

Sales representatives and other retailers can help you zero in on the right software and hardware products for your type of business. Retailers told us that there is simply no best application for all retailers' needs. Retail is too diverse an industry to have a standardized software package.

Personal computers generally come with free software. Typically, you'll get a word-processing program (such as Microsoft Word), a basic personal finance program, a spreadsheet program, and an Internet browser. The right combination of hardware and software has the capability of delivering reports once considered too labor-intensive for the time-harried store owner to accomplish. For example, customer buying habits can be detailed to profile personal preferences and frequency of visits, and what referrals they have sent to your business.

A few of the software packages you might want to take a look at for your bookkeeping needs are QuickBooks, Peachtree Accounting, and M.Y.O.B. (Mind Your Own Business) Accounting. Programs like this will enable you to enter your store's daily transactions, track invoices, pay bills, report sales, and schedule employees. Explore your options with your accountant and tax advisor. Check with your trade association for the names of programs widely used in your field. Two examples are Wordstock for bookstores (about $400 a month to lease or $10,000 to $30,000 to buy) and Saltware for liquor stores (about $3,500 per station).

Smart Tip

Tip...

It's not the computer's fault if you lose your data. Save. Save. Save. Then back up daily and store a copy off-premises. Many computers now come with readable/writeable compact disc drives capable of storing 150,000 pages of text per CD as well as complex graphics and sounds. Whatever storage medium you use to safeguard your records, it is only as efficient as your habit of backing up your hard drive.

▲

> ## Smart Tip
>
> **Tip...**
>
> Don't expect a computer to make decisions for you. To be successful, you need to develop a magic feel for your customer, merchandise, and store, and you can only do that upfront and in person.

Look in the smaller ads and classifieds in the backs of trade magazines for the names of some software programs written specifically for small retailers in various markets. You can probably find one for every conceivable type of retail business.

Stephanie B. uses an application called QuickSell on a Windows-based computer to run her Newport Beach, California, pet bakery business. She selected her hardware and software by conducting research online. Pull up a listing for retail/inventory systems from www.google.com and begin your search. Ask other retailers' advice by visiting www.retailernews.com or www.retailowner.com.

The brother of Montpelier, Vermont-based music store owner Fred W. is a computer programmer; he developed a proprietary system for the store because they didn't like the program they had. They felt it was obvious that the person who wrote the commercial software had never operated a retail business.

Cash Register

You can buy a fancy computerized cash register that provides built-in inventory control or settle for a simple unit that allows you to keep track of income. Most of your revenue will come through cash register sales, so it is important to select a cash register system that can do much of the work for you. There are two basic electronic register functions: generation of customer receipts and generation of detailed records of the time of purchase, type, department, salesperson, sales details, and SKU. You'll need sales broken down as taxable and nontaxable for sales tax reporting. In addition, you'll need to know which sales were made by cash, check, and credit card so you can balance each account at the end of the day.

The register should feature four or more departments or category breakdowns, enabling you to classify merchandise purchased by type as each sale is rung up. You'll use the special department category to monitor promotions, a new line, or special items. You'll use the data you collect to analyze and evaluate trends and peg exactly how your business is doing. The more expensive point-of-sale (POS) systems will generate detailed reports for you.

Many low-volume retailers use PC-based solutions for back-end operations and an electronic cash register at the sales counter. While not as efficient or rich in information as a point-of-sale system, this will work. However, to be competitive, a business needs to grow, and volume means more sophisticated tools are needed. A POS system is a computerized cash register system, usually used to read the Universal Price Code (UPC) on each product and match it to the price. The system feeds information about each sale directly into your computer's data bank. A POS system can be used with a bar-code scanner or by entering numeric codes from price tags into the system manually.

POS systems help control sales operations at both the shelf and sales-counter level. They also help identify individual customers. POS systems enable targeted marketing and sales promotion through the continuous analysis of transactions. But a small, single-location store may be hard pressed justifying buying such a sophisticated system. When making a decision, compare the price and features of any technology against the cost of doing a lot of things manually in terms of competitive pressures, time, and accuracy.

POS systems vary dramatically in cost depending on the features and functions as well as the number of stations in your store's network. Here are some sample prices for hardware and software to give you a ballpark to play in:

- Magnetic strip reader, $235
- Credit card software for processing credit card transactions, $395
- Thermal receipt printer, $375
- Cash drawer, $185
- Laser bar-code scanner, $595
- Pole price display, $185
- Bar-code scanner, $225
- QuickSell 2000 for Windows software, $685
- Cash register, $150
- Canfield POS complete Windows system, $1,099
- Touch-screen POS system, $1,995

Credit Card Verification System

There are several advantages of using a swipe-the-card electronic credit card verification system over a manual system: It reduces errors, charges are credited immediately to your account, paperwork is reduced, and it's fast. Debit card and check verification are available with some of the newer credit card verification systems.

Bar-Code Reader

The use of bar-code labeling is increasingly widespread, but not all items come with bar-code labels yet. If you want to, you can print your own bar-code labels using your PC and special bar-code software and a label printer. Some POS systems come with this software and equipment as part of the program.

Tip...

Smart Tip

Bar-code labeling feeds information about each sale directly into the computer's data bank by scanning the numeric codes assigned to an item. It can help you track stock, generate restocking orders, monitor purchase orders, and track sales/margins, stocks, and payables.

Bar codes typically enable better register management. With a bar-code reader, the clerk simply scans the machine-readable numerical codes (vertical bars of varying widths) printed on consumer items, and the item is identified with the price, a print-out is generated, and payment is made quickly.

Other Equipment You May Want

Other technologies transforming the retail industry are electronic funds transfer (EFT), electronic data interchange (EDI), and data warehousing. EFT allows buying and selling electronically. EDI enables you to access the databases of your suppliers and position your inventory accordingly. Data warehousing helps you convert data into useful information. IBM and NCR are leading solution suppliers for the retail sector.

Interactive Shopping Equipment

Experts say retailers need to consider investing in in-store technologies to attract wired shoppers and to tie together their physical and online capabilities. A recent study by Siren Technologies, a Chicago-based company that develops new technologies for retailers, found that approximately half the retailers surveyed use interactive technology tools, including kiosks and electronic messaging. Nearly 80 percent of those polled suggested that injecting different types of technology into the shopping experience is extremely important to be competitive.

Stores of all sizes can utilize multimedia capabilities to capture customer awareness. Fred W.'s music store uses the touch-screen Muse system, which enables customers to sample music. According to Fred, besides being convenient, the system has an added benefit: It encourages special orders.

Marco Scibora, founder of Advanced Communication Design Inc. (ACD) in Bloomington, Minnesota, has thousands of his interactive digital audio and video

Kiosks: the Missing Link

Malls are finding ways to link in-store kiosks to Web sites and corporate headquarters to provide e-commerce options for shoppers. Large retailers are exploring the possibilities, but it takes a long time for the behemoths to implement new systems. Small retailers are more flexible, so by knowing what your competition is up to, you can provide the benefits the technology is trying to deliver right away. In this case, kiosks are simplifying the shopping experience, reducing time spent in checkout lines, and increasing consumer convenience.

devices installed in large retail outlets around the world, including Borders Books & Music, Discovery Stores, and Fred Meyer. Scibora firmly believes that traditional brick-and-mortar outlets face great opportunities and will continue to flourish in spite of e-commerce—and here's the caveat—as long as retailers embrace new technology and electronic merchandising. The ACD retail merchandising system takes the concept of a kiosk to the next level, providing consumers with the means to access specific information about items for sale.

> **Smart Tip**
> Digital signs can deliver customized, real-time point-of-purchase messages. Using these signs is a way to make the in-store experience more entertaining and appealing.

Using the device, shoppers can view listings of a music store's most popular artists, sample CDs not in the store, or find more titles by the artist or more albums in a particular genre. The book-size device is integrated right in with the products on the shelves and operates with headphones or speakers, allowing more than one person to listen to the music at the same time. Any kind of retailer can use it and can customize the content on their system to include daily or weekly advertising specials, electronic coupons and discounts, as well as full integration of point-of-sale cash registers. Retailers can cross-promote products in the store or on their Web site, cross-reference titles, and more, simply by scanning or pushing the ATM-like button.

Sales Floor Equipment

There are many kinds of sales floor equipment (see "Equipment Checklist" on pages 140 and 141). Here, we provide an in-depth discussion of display equipment.

Display Equipment

Whether you choose to display products on high-tech shelving or in antique armoires, you must plan to spend money in this vital area. The decorating scheme of your store is an important promotional device. In addition to the aesthetic appeal of your fixtures, consider safety and convenience. Which fixtures will show off the benefits of the products you sell and make it convenient for customers to examine and buy while minimizing damage and theft? Our "Store Design" and "Risk Management" chapters explore logistical elements of this issue.

> **Smart Tip**
> Jim and Mary D. in Thomasville, Georgia, bought some of their equipment at a "going out of business" sale. "Fixtures were purchased at 10 cents on the dollar," Jim says. They converted an old building into a women's and children's clothing store by installing track lights, bright fixtures, and wall decor. Their total fixtures cost was less than $5,000.

Suiting Up for Selling

Some of the kinds of fixtures you may need are:

- back counters
- baskets
- build-ups
- carts
- counters
- display cases
- display shelves
- display tables

- dumbbells
- easels
- floor stands
- island displays
- pegboards
- racks
- register stands
- sales counters

- self-service stands
- shelving
- showcases
- stock bins
- storage cabinets
- tiered tables
- work tables
- wrapping desks

Use display fixtures and equipment that complement the décor of your interior. If you have a limited budget for fixtures, you may be wise to purchase or rent less-expensive fixtures rather than cut back on the amount of inventory on display. Selling inventory provides you with profit and cash flow, after all.

Look for fixtures that will stand up under heavy usage, are easy to move around, and are flexible enough to use in different ways. But don't invest too much capital in fancy fixtures or equipment. Look into pre-owned items that can be purchased for a fraction of the cost of new ones and can be refurbished to meet your standards.

Use display fixtures and equipment that complement the décor of your interior.

Contact your merchants' association, trade association, and business-to-business telephone directory for referrals to manufacturers, information technology specialists, service providers, and other suppliers. Visit their Web sites or call them for catalogs or a meeting with a sales rep. Talk with other retailers to find out which brand of equipment they use and why they prefer it over other choices on the market. Independent dealers who carry a broad line of equipment for retailers can give you insights on maintenance, longevity, service contracts, and prices. They will also be able to tell you when to expect a drop in price for the item you are interested in.

The closer suppliers are to your business, the better for reducing delivery times, shipping costs, and service. You need reliable equipment that is backed up by warranty. Whatever your decision on brand, make sure you are protected by doing business with companies that stand behind what they sell. You've got to be selling every day, so there's no room for equipment downtime.

Whew! Equipping your business is a lot more complicated than going shopping, isn't it? Balancing your bank account with the record-keeping and merchandising needs of a retail business is a challenging task. But one thing's for sure: Consulting with those who've been there and done that will help you run a successful venture.

Equipping Your Eatery

Fast-food outlets, dinner houses, specialty restaurants, and other types of food-service retailers require specialized equipment. Here are some necessities you should budget for:

- Broilers
- Convection ovens
- Dishwasher
- Freezers
- Griddles
- Ovens
- Steam tables

- Cold tables
- Coolers
- Dry storage
- Fryers
- Toasters
- Woks
- Warming stations

- Kitchenware
- Pasta cookers
- Refrigerators
- Steam kettles
- Pizza ovens
- Steamers

Equipment for a 250-seat restaurant is estimated to cost between $272,250 and $287,250, and breaks down as follows:

○ *Small wares:* (cutlery, dishware, glasses, table accompaniments)	*$12,500-17,500*
○ *Kitchen equipment:* (cooking and storage equipment, stainless steel fabrication, sinks, counters, and dishwashers)	*$120,000-130,000*
○ *Cash control system:*	*$17,500*
○ *Sound system:*	*$6,500*
○ *Liquor control system:*	*$72,000*
○ *Furnishings at $175 per seat:* (chairs, stools, tables)	*$43,750*

In comparison, a 150-seat restaurant's equipment costs might run about $138,250 (small wares, $9,000; kitchen equipment, $100,000; sound system, $3,000; furnishings at $175 per seat, $26,250).

Equipment Checklist

Office Furniture:

- ❑ Office chairs
- ❑ Conference table
- ❑ Desk(s)
- ❑ _____

- ❑ File cabinets
- ❑ Credenza
- ❑ Computer table

Office Equipment:

- ❑ Calculator(s)
- ❑ Copy machine
- ❑ Scanner
- ❑ Phone system
- ❑ Sign maker
- ❑ Alarm
- ❑ Cash register
- ❑ Safe
- ❑ Modem
- ❑ _____

- ❑ Fax machine
- ❑ Computer(s)
- ❑ Printer
- ❑ Credit card equipment
- ❑ Specialty equipment
- ❑ Bar code reader
- ❑ Point-of-sale computer equipment
- ❑ Computer system for Web
- ❑ Pricing machine

Office Supplies:

- ❑ Bulletin board
- ❑ Pencils and pens
- ❑ Sales receipts
- ❑ Computer paper
- ❑ General office supplies
- ❑ _____

- ❑ Employee rights board
- ❑ Stationery
- ❑ Copy paper
- ❑ Note pads

Equipment Checklist, continued

Sales Supplies:

- ❏ Paper bags
- ❏ Shipping supplies
- ❏ Hanging bags
- ❏ _____

- ❏ Gift-wrapping supplies
- ❏ Note cards
- ❏ Hangers

Sales Floor Equipment:

- ❏ Gondolas
- ❏ Wall racks
- ❏ Mirrors
- ❏ Display cabinets
- ❏ Specialty lighting
- ❏ Snack machines
- ❏ Fire extinguishers
- ❏ Restroom signs
- ❏ _____

- ❏ Sales showcases
- ❏ Hangers
- ❏ Display tables
- ❏ Customer seating area
- ❏ Dressing rooms
- ❏ Drink machines
- ❏ Exit signs
- ❏ Hours sign

Back-Room Equipment and Supplies

- ❏ Broom
- ❏ Trash cans
- ❏ Vacuum cleaner
- ❏ Toilet paper
- ❏ Soap
- ❏ _____

- ❏ Dust pan
- ❏ Mop
- ❏ Paper towels
- ❏ Cleaning supplies
- ❏ Window cleaning supplies

Pricing

In retailing, the price of an article is the amount of money the retailer asks for the item. So how do you set prices? How do you arrive at the "right" prices for your goods? For some retailers, pricing is easy: Take the manufacturer's suggested retail price and double it. For the most successful merchants, pricing is a strategic act.

▲

Your pricing strategy is important for two main reasons. For one thing, the difference between what you pay for products or services and what you charge customers determines the margin, which has an immediate effect on your business's profitability. Also, price directly affects the demand for what you have to offer.

If they are right, prices have the power to attract customers. The majority of items advertised in newspapers are priced to pull customers into the store. But you must put high enough retail prices on the merchandise you sell, or you will not be able to pay your overhead expenses and make a profit. If your prices are too low, you will lose money and go out of business.

Your Pricing Philosophy

Decide on your basic pricing philosophy: Will your prices be above the market, competitive, or below the market? You may have already answered this question when you decided what kind of business and image you wanted and formulated your business plan. (See Chapters 2 and 3.)

Pricing for profit is vital to your business. But pricing should not be driven by profit motives at the expense of fair, ethical tactics and competition. Profits should be the result of smart business, not a means to an end. With good business relationships and

Name Your Price

Price is the centerpiece of your relations with your customers, the weapon competitors use to steal market share, and the reason for many sleepless nights. Learn from the experience of others by considering the top 10 pricing factors in your decision-making:

1. Availability (number of suppliers, quantity produced, and delivery)
2. Perceived image
3. Growth stage of market
4. Price sensitivity of the market
5. Legislative and financial climate
6. Prestige of the product
7. Differences in available products or services
8. Quality
9. Competition
10. Your financial goals

products priced correctly, you will generate sufficient sales to provide the capital you need to stay in business and enjoy some profits.

In making your pricing decisions, you need to answer these questions:

- What prices are shoppers willing to pay for the merchandise?
- Where do you want to be in comparison with your competitors' pricing: equal, above, or below?
- What is the suggested real price proposed by the supplier?
- What are the qualities or characteristics of the merchandise that influence a shopper's perception of quality and value—style, perishability, scarcity, richness, commodity, or other?

Narrowing the decision-making process even further, give careful consideration to your specific pricing objectives:

- *Return on investment.* Establish retail selling prices that will yield a specific return-of-profit percentage on your investment.
- *Maximum profit.* Set prices designed to produce the highest possible profit percentage you can expect to earn on the goods you sell.
- *Sales increase.* Work up prices that should produce a specified percentage increase in overall store sales. Usually this involves reducing prices to sell more merchandise.
- *Improved cash flow.* Establish short-term prices to bring more sales dollars into your business.

Sometimes feelings of guilt are involved in pricing. Some price specialists claim that most consumers with limited discretionary income often have guilt feelings about buying certain items, especially nonnecessities. However, if the retailer can appease these guilt feelings, the customer is more apt to buy. Therefore, consider giving incentives to buy expensive items or give a shirt or tie away with a three-piece suit.

Price Impression Psychology

Attracting customers is so important to some retailers that they will take a loss on an item to drive traffic to their business. Supermarkets often keep prices low on a few basic items that customers can easily compare prices on to give the impression that all merchandise in the store is priced lower than the competitors. Tour operators retailing holiday packages use lower prices to stimulate demand in off-seasons. Home

Tip...

Smart Tip
Consumers tend to equate higher prices with higher quality. Fine restaurants, designer shops, and consultants practice prestige pricing to convey an image and capture elite customers.

Tip...

Smart Tip

In the secondhand busi-
ness, there is no such thing
as a manufacturer's suggested retail
price. Every item is unique in terms
of age, condition, rarity, and desir-
ability. The longer you're in the business, the more knowledgeable you'll
be about pricing unusual objects.
Read catalogs and books, speak with
contacts at auctions and estate
sales, and use your common sense.

improvement stores might discount home-
insulation materials during the summer
months to get an off-season head start on
competitors.

"You cannot [buy merchandise] if you
don't [have] money coming in. So sometimes you sacrifice," says clothing retailer
Jim D. in Thomasville, Georgia. "You sell
at cost to buy another [item], but then you
sell the other [item] at a profit."

If the image you want for your store is
one of high-quality luxury goods, then the
prices charged would need to be higher than
average, or you will lose credibility with
your target customers. If your stock is lower-priced merchandise, your customers might
doubt the exclusivity of your store. Be consistent and know who you want to serve.

You do not always have to sell for the lowest price. For example, most consumers
will pay a little over normal supermarket prices for goods at the local convenience
store. They are willing to pay for the ability to buy certain products late at night and
on Sundays and holidays. These are perceived as extra customer benefits.
Remember, the majority of people weigh retail prices against their perception of
value for money.

"[Our] audio store is positioned as the low-price leader in DAT, CD recorders,
multitrack recorders, microphones, home theater gear, and DVD players," says
Thomasville, Georgia-based audio retailer Jim O. "We [also] provide world-class
after-sale support on the products we sell. We have earned a reputation for dependable sales, service and applications support." Every element helps, Jim says, as he has
to compete with "kids in apartments going to huge distributors and ordering out of
catalogs and driving prices down with minuscule 5 percent margins.

"We can't survive on less than 20 percent," continues Jim. "These type of retailers
drop-ship the product to the end user so they have practically zero money invested,
and they give the impression that they're a big operation. It's very difficult to be the
price leader. Fortunately, we've built a good business with our specialty products and
service that makes it difficult for others to compete with us. We get 30 to 40 percent
margins with our own products and 10 to 15 percent on car stereos."

Price and the Product Range

The more variety you have in your product range, the easier it is to combat lower
price activity by the competition or to test a new line. If you have other product types
you can rely on to sell at full margin, you can afford to be more flexible in your pricing activities than if you rely on a narrow portfolio.

If you stock mostly branded goods, then your pricing will be largely determined by the competition, either locally or nationally, because there are not usually large variations in the prices charged by the major brands to small retailers. After all, a pair of Levi's 501 jeans is the same product wherever it is purchased, and it is readily identifiable, so the only comparison a customer needs to make is on the price.

20 Questions

New business owners are often tempted to give the business away to get sales, but this is not an advisable practice. Realistic pricing indicates your confidence in what you are selling, and if you value your service, so will customers. Keep these questions handy and use them over and over again to keep you true to your brand identity:

1. What role do you want price to play in your overall retailing strategy?
2. Will you price below, at, or above the market?
3. Will you set specific markups for each product?
4. Will you set markups for product categories?
5. Will you use a one-price policy rather than bargain with customers?
6. Will you offer discounts for quantity purchases or to special groups?
7. Will you set prices to cover full costs on every sale?
8. Will the prices you have established earn the gross margin you planned?
9. Do you understand the market forces affecting your pricing methods?
10. Do your prices reflect which products are slow-movers and which are fast-movers?
11. Will you experiment with odd or even price endings to increase your sales?
12. Do you know which products are price-sensitive to your customers? At what point will a slight increase in price lead to a noticeable drop-off in demand?
13. Which products will draw people when put on sale?
14. Do you know the maximum price customers will pay for certain items?
15. Do you know what the lowest price point is on some products before customers hesitate to buy because of the perception that something must have less value, functionality, or quality?
16. Is there a specific time of year when your competitors have sales?
17. Do your customers expect sales at certain times of the year?
18. How will you react to competitors' price changes?
19. Have you developed a markdown policy?
20. Will you take markdowns on a regular basis or as needed?

Private Label

On the other hand, if you have products made especially for you, or if your products are mostly unbranded, then careful price planning can provide profit opportunities. Private-label products can usually be bought at lower prices than branded goods since they don't carry marketing costs. Since your private-label goods are unique to you, they give your business the chance to price them according to what you think the market will bear.

Social Price

The social price is the nonmonetary cost of buying a certain item. One social price is time. Time spent doing one thing means the buyer has to give up time available for another activity. This is the "time is money" concept. Another social price is effort. When you have to bring your old refrigerator to get a discount, this takes effort and causes fatigue. Lifestyle is another social price. The last social price is psyche, meaning to forfeit some of your self-esteem, privacy, or peace of mind. You can not only use this awareness in your pricing structure, but also in your selling activities, advertising, and promotion.

Think about ways you can make your customer comfortable doing business with you. For Thomasville, Georgia, clothing retailer Mary D., it's a lot of time spent on the phone and writing e-mails to advise parents about appropriate dress styles for their teenage daughters. In customers' minds, $200 for a dress is well-spent, and they usually return to the store time and time again.

Pricing Restrictions

There are several restrictions on the prices you can charge your customers. For example, art dealerships, consignment shops, and auction houses set minimum prices and bids that items can be sold for, or the items are taken off the market. Cards, magazines, and books have prices printed on them, so the maximum markup is predetermined. Be sure to learn all the regulations affecting your business. Check with your lawyer, small-business counselor, CPA, or government consumer protection agency about price-setting practices in your state.

Pricing Strategies

The most commonly used pricing strategy retailers can employ is cost pricing. Simply stated, you calculate all your expenses—direct and indirect—and then add a profit. The second strategy is competitive pricing. This involves meeting the going price for similar products in your local market. The cost you paid is not taken into account here. Finally, market-value pricing looks at what the market will bear.

Dollar Stretcher

You may be surprised to know that many retailers have tried to increase prices to make a profit, but all they actually did was lose money. Always look for hidden costs to calculate the true costs of special offers.

Market-value pricing is generally used for unique products or services that have few or no competing products on the market. You can take higher markups here. For example, by buying their clothing from specialty companies and not carrying a lot of duplicates, retailers Jim and Mary D. can make a healthy profit on their fancy clothes.

Adopt a pricing policy that fits your needs. When you decide on a price, make sure you can still be profitable. Determining your company's total costs to operate can be a tedious and slow process, but it is imperative to assess costs when you are establishing pricing.

Unfortunately, you cannot control all items that go into the calculation of costs. For example, prices of raw materials may fluctuate. Or your utility company may approve a rate increase for your service. How quickly you are able to respond to those items may impact the viability of your business. The soundness of your assumptions should be carefully tested before you risk all you have invested.

Whatever your pricing philosophy and objective, remember that you must always be ready to react quickly to changes in market conditions. A successful pricing policy is sound, logical, and flexible at all times. Pricing merchandise and price adjustments require time and thought. Whether or not you achieve a net profit will probably depend largely on your skill in this area.

If all of this seems too overwhelming, you can hire a retail pricing service or marketing specialist to develop a pricing plan for you.

Price Lines

Few stores can be everything to everybody. Most retailers must be satisfied to target only part of a given market. You identified your target customer in your business plan. Once a market segment has been determined, then you should purchase the merchandise and price it to reach those within the segment. Price lines should reflect a store's overall image. If you want to reach the middle- and lower-income levels, you'll search for lower prices in the marketplace. If, on the other hand, you want to draw from upper-income populations, you will search for higher-quality and higher-priced items.

Smart Tip *Tip...*

Menu pricing in food-service businesses will vary at different times. If you cater to the business lunch crowd, base your prices on fast service, midday portions, and table turns. Dinner selections are usually higher-priced because portions are larger and people linger longer.

Dollar Stretcher

Look for unique items customers don't have a preconceived idea of how much they should sell for so you can price this merchandise at a higher profit than keystone. For example, buy a bundle of items and then price them separately, or create a gift set of baby or kitchen items to add value and consumer appeal.

A price line is the top, middle, and bottom prices at which a retailer offers a certain classification of merchandise to customers. For example, writing instruments can be purchased from a large number of resources and offered at 30 or more retail prices. However, dozens of prices complicate the inventory and confuse customers and salespeople. So to simplify the operation and demonstrate good merchandising, a retailer might restrict the price line to three categories: under $5, $10, $20, and over $35. This price line would indicate that the retailer is after the middle to low end of the market. If you have a selection of 20 different price points instead of four, your salespeople will have five times as many prices to keep track of in terms of price and features, your customer will have a wider selection to choose from, and there will be more difficulties with inventory control. Price simplification is an important merchandising tool.

Pricing Principles

Price points are the specific prices you choose within your price line. They are important because research indicates that more people will buy an item at one price than at another—even if the difference between the two is only a few cents. Suppliers can often help you select the best price points. For example, should you sell an item for $12.95 or $13.50? Stay with the lower price as long as a sufficient gross profit and store image can be maintained.

Your pricing strategy is a key element of your marketing plan. As you've probably concluded by now, there is no easy, precise formula for pricing goods and services, but it should not be a random or impulsive process. Price-setting is a pragmatic search for what works best to achieve your overall market objectives and maximize profits. Applying these principles can help you achieve your goals.

- *Divide your price lines into three zones: prestige, popular, and competitive.* The prestige price zone is the one at the top of the line that will improve the image of your store and enhance the rest of the line, but not chase customers away. The popular zone is in the middle, where most purchases are made. The competitive zone is at the bottom, where you might buy an item simply to compete with another store located nearby. All prices in a line can fall into any of these zones.

- *Try to find merchandise that will fit into your predetermined price lines and points.* Savvy buyers are specific with their vendors. ("Do you have a silk sweater set that I can retail at $39.95 and get my regular markup?") Such a buyer knows what will attract customers under current market conditions in her market area. Price predetermination is a self-disciplinary skill you'll want to acquire. Setting specific price points before going to vendors can keep a new entrepreneur from starting out with the wrong inventory.

- *Be careful not to lock yourself into fixed lines and price points.* There are many reasons price lines must be adjusted upward and downward and price points changed. Stay abreast of economic conditions, consumer buying habits, and your competition in all channels.

Pricing Your Services

Service industries should also follow these guidelines while recognizing that the process of pricing becomes more abstract than tangible product pricing because real costs are often not directly associated with the service. Service providers often say that they enjoy what they're doing and feel guilty about getting paid for painting a picture, working in the garden, or sharing what they have learned with other people.

Competing on price until your new service business is established is a very common strategy. But if yours is a repeat business, like car maintenance, making your fees the lowest in town may not be wise because it will be difficult to raise your prices for the same service once you're established. What you charge should depend on your expenses and time, the quality of your service, your market, competitor's prices, your experience, and what your customers are willing to pay.

With some service businesses, price-charging guidelines may be available from your licensing agency or professional association. Do some research to determine the going rate. Check with your local chamber of commerce or *The Encyclopedia of Associations* in your local library. Read career, industry, and business articles in your local newspaper, trade newsletters, magazines, and online. Check with expositions, the Economic Development Department in your area, and employment agencies. Ask consumers in your market what they pay and what they expect to get in return.

Besides running his music store, Fred W. provides professional disc jockey services for weddings and formal events. The services include a professional sound system and a library of recorded music on compact discs. His library of music consists of more than 1,500 CDs and approximately 15,000 songs, representing more than 23 kinds of music. Fred consults with customers in advance to help plan how

Smart Tip

How much is your time worth? Find out what others are charging and what customers are paying. Those figures are not necessarily the same.

Beware!

Undercharging and giving away too much service and advice are among the biggest causes of financial ruin for service businesses, warns Jan Norman, author and business columnist for *The Orange County Register* newspaper.

music and his service can make their event special. They do this at the store or by phone, fax, or e-mail. A nonrefundable deposit of $50 is required to reserve his services, and the balance of payment is due before the beginning of the event. His basic rate starts at $450 for three hours, depending on the location of the event and its distance from the city where his music store is located. Lighting effects are available for an additional charge.

Once you know the minimum you should charge to avoid losses, add the following elements to determine a profitable rate for your services.

Material/supply costs (cost of goods) + your time (competitive rate for your labor) + overhead (health insurance, Social Security, taxes, loan payments, etc.) + percentage of profit you want to make (research will give you a reasonable range) = your price.

It may take some time for you to determine what price will satisfy both your needs and your customers'. With a service business, prices can fluctuate based on a particular job or extenuating circumstances. Consult with your bookkeeper or accountant for help in determining what you need to charge to build your business.

Concepts of Retail Price

The difference between the invoice cost and the original retail price is the initial markup. Maintained markup is the difference between the invoice cost and retail sale. Maintained markup differs from initial markup by the amount of any reductions.

Retail specialists suggest that you work only with the retail markup percentage. Retail markup percentages can be calculated on either a cost basis or a selling price basis. Here's how to work with the retail markup percentage: retail markup in dollars, divided by the retail selling price, multiplied by 100. Manufacturers and wholesalers generally compute their markups based on their costs: retail markup in dollars, divided by their cost in dollars, multiplied by 100. Most astute retailers rely on the retail markup approach because it is a quick and useful way to see if an item is profitable for you to carry. However, retail enterprises that

Smart Tip

All merchandise does not deserve the same markup. Markups vary depending on the price elasticity of the product, price concessions of vendors, whether the product is used as a price leader, and other variables.

sell custom-made items or have direct labor may be better off calculating their markups on the cost basis. If an item costs $9.75 wholesale, and you keystone it (double the cost of goods), you will sell it for $19.50. Your markup percentage, based on cost, is 100 percent ($9.75 divided by $9.75 times 100). Your markup percentage, based on retail selling price, is 50 percent ($9.75 divided by $19.50 times 100). Bakeries, computer consultants, appliance repair shops, embroidery businesses, and the like usually use the cost approach.

There are many practices retailers follow when it comes to markup. The approaches introduced here will provide some insight into the problems and possibilities you will encounter.

We just used the term keystone, which means "double the price." If you buy something for $5 and sell it for $10, you have taken a keystone markup. Small, less sophisticated merchants use this simple method. However, this approach does not allow for individual markup selection and often ignores what competitors are doing with identical merchandise. This method also does not account for the realities of retailing that reduce your margins, such as selling articles at markdown at lower-than-retail prices, damaged merchandise, employee discounts, and shoplifting.

Particular markup percentages are usual and customary in a number of trade areas. For example, the traditional markup for hardware is 40 percent of the retail price. If a retailer pays $6 for a hammer, he or she would sell it for $10. For jewelry, the markup range may be 400 to 800 percent. Those who follow the principle of trade acceptance want to be competitive with others in the trade and do not analyze individual items in determining markup.

> ### Fun Fact
>
> Eighty-six percent of women look at price tags when shopping, compared with 72 percent of men. As a result, men are more easily upgraded than are women. For a man, ignoring the price is almost a measure of his virility, according to Paco Underhill, founder and managing partner of behavioral market research and consulting company Envirosell in New York City.

Still other retailers believe that you should always go for the highest price for any item as long as you don't drive the customer away. Advocates of this theory usually specialize in items that are unfamiliar to customers and not handled by competitors. They are guided by the law of supply and demand, keeping prices high as long as demand is high. Many of these retailers would rather sell less at higher prices than more at lower prices. Does your business concept fit into this model, or would another markup approach be better?

The good buy theory is a popular one because it rewards good buying and can enhance the store's reputation if used well. You can increase the markup on an

Smart Tip

As far as pricing your merchandise is concerned, you want to aim at an overall markup for your business that gives you the flexibility you need to stay competitive, covers your overhead, and shows a profit at the end of the year.

unusually good buy and still offer your customers a great deal when you have scooped the competition.

Still another approach is the high start/quick drop back position. Retailers using this approach are looking for an immediate reaction from the market and are willing to drop back to a lower price to get mass distribution. They can legally advertise that an item that was offered at a higher price is now offered at a much lower price. First-of-a-kind or first-in-the-market opportunities can be leveraged to skim buyers off the top and quickly capture the secondary market by capitalizing quickly on consumer reaction.

Some retailers set pricing on the basis of achieving volume sales at different price levels. The market penetration pricing technique enables retailers who interpret and calculate correctly to gain greater volume with little loss in gross profit. Those retailers who make mistakes lose gross profit without a corresponding increase in sales. For example, a retailer aims to get 10 percent of the market on car batteries at one price—say, $69—and anticipates capturing 15 percent at $49. The lower the price, the greater the market penetration. The thinking is that many people will not buy until the price drops to a certain level below the present price.

Calculate for Competitive Advantage

How much should you mark up a product? This decision involves many factors, including the amount required to pay overhead and show a reasonable profit, and the price at which competitors are selling an identical or similar item. A third factor is the kind of purchase made. Sometimes an exceptionally good buy will allow a higher-than-normal markup that will still meet competition and satisfy the customer. If the item will be used as a leader to attract customers into your store, perhaps a smaller markup is in order.

With these and other variables to consider, there is no one absolute formula to follow. Normally, the actual markup amount is based on your best judgment. Ideally, the best markup is one that will give you the greatest gross profit and still bring the customer back to the store. The danger in determining retail prices is setting them so high that customers are lost to competitors.

The sum total of all your markups on all items during a given period of time—less markdowns—is your gross profit. Gross profit is what you pay your overhead expenses with and is one of the most important concepts in retailing. If the total income of your store for the first 12 months is $100,000, and you take a 50 percent markup on all items sold and there were no markdowns, then your gross profit would be $50,000, or half the total income. From this $50,000, you must pay all your expenses—labor, rent, advertising, etc. What's left is net profit.

The Benefits of Discounts

There are a variety of ways discounts can promote your business. The most obvious examples are post-holiday and summer clearance sales. The objective is to stimulate sales turnover during a normally quiet period and to clear remaining stock of seasonal merchandise and make room for incoming stock. Pricing can be used as a tactical tool to deal with problem products in midseason.

Loss Leaders

You can dramatically reduce the price of a single product or small group of products to bring customers to the store in hopes that they'll buy other products at full price. As a new retailer, you can use a "get acquainted" offer to drive business, placing the special merchandise at the back of the store so people will see the rest of your goods as they walk through the aisles to pick up the special offer.

Quantity Discounts

There are a few ways you can use quantity discounts. One is to stimulate volume sales and increase the size of individual transactions. For example, wine merchants might offer reductions on a case of 12 bottles. What you are essentially doing is passing back to your customers some of the savings in handling and administration costs you get from selling in bulk while increasing your net margin.

This tool can also be used to reduce the price on problem stock without putting it on sale. For instance, "buy two—get one free" on frequently purchased items such as T-shirts, underwear, file folders, and toothpaste can boost sales.

Trade and Organization Discounts

As part of your community service—or just good business—you may want to offer discounts to local clubs and associations. Sports and clothing retailers can often generate substantial incremental turnover by offering a discount to youth groups, sports clubs, and so on. Another possibility is offering discounts to electricians, firefighters, schools, or nonprofit organizations. You can establish yourself as a great source for uniforms and supplies and generate long-term loyalty and profitability.

Pre-Season Discounts

Whether you own a fashion retail outlet, holiday decoration cart, or gardening shop, you can introduce new products and build awareness of your business by offering early-season discounts. By offering sharp discounts before the start of bulb planting, the 4th of July, or a sporting season, you can identify the winning lines to invest in for the main selling months.

Voucher Discounts

Another way of quietly reducing prices and managing the timing of customers' spending is to use discount vouchers. This involves giving the customer X number of vouchers for every Y amount spent; the vouchers are redeemable against future purchases within a fixed time frame. This technique stimulates the current sales period and provides an incentive for the customer to return to the store during a specified future period to make further purchases with the vouchers. You delay having to pay for the discount, which will benefit your cash flow. Furthermore, customers usually spend more than the amount on the voucher when they come in to redeem it, and a number of customers will lose the vouchers or forget to redeem them by the expiration date, in which case your cost for the promotion goes down.

General Markdowns

Although every retailer's goal is to always sell at full retail price, everyone makes overly optimistic or bad buys. You may be forced to lower the price to attract customer attention and encourage buyers. After the holidays and between seasons, retailers must deal with markdowns and clearance items. Sometimes, especially in fashion merchandise, markdowns for the year can be more than 15 percent of original prices.

Many markdowns are due to lackluster displays, insufficient product information, improper placement, or poor customer knowledge. If you misinterpret consumer demand, buy too much merchandise, or select the wrong colors, sizes, or styles, review what went wrong with your staff and buyers. The more information you have about your market, the better you will get at having inventory that sells at full price.

Another common cause of markdowns is coming up with the wrong price to begin with. Weather, economic recessions, and

---

Dollar Stretcher

Your suppliers can be your partners in profit by working with you to promote your business. The more you sell, the more they sell to you. Ask your vendors to work with you by sharing the cost of discounts on redeemed vouchers or reducing the costs for merchandise bought for special promotions.

other unusual external events can also force you to cut prices to move merchandise.

It's easy for merchandise to become damaged or soiled while in the store. When this happens, take immediate markdowns to move the items so that returns to the manufacturer are not required. The ideal markdown is one that will move the items quickly without cutting into profits more than necessary. If an item was offered to customers at $9.95 and didn't move, try it at $6.95 before lowering the price to $5.95.

Beware!

As much as 50 percent of all markdowns occur because one or more of the six laws of marketing are broken. Pay attention to price, promotion, place, product, perceived value, and positioning.

Don't follow one mistake with another. Sometimes it is better to admit a mistake, take a deep markdown, and go on to some successful purchases with the money received and free up your buying dollars and valuable space for full-price items.

Often, entrepreneurs in the fashion business drop prices of slow-moving merchandise to 10 percent above cost. This enables them to pay their overhead and still break

Extra! Extra!

When it's time to clear out merchandise to make room for new and hotter-selling items, you want to move reduced-priced items quickly. It's difficult to close out products that are seasonal, fashion-oriented, artsy, or edible, but here are five things you can do:

1. *Use price points instead of percentages.* Customers relate to dollar signs faster and more easily than percentage points.
2. *Set up small displays in your clearance area.* The same principles used in selling your full-price merchandise apply to markdowns, too. You want it to sell, so make it attractive.
3. *Do not let your clearance items look like junk.* As much as possible, keep this merchandise looking fresh.
4. *Keep the markdown area well-lit.* Customers don't like shopping in dark corners, and the light will make items more appealing.
5. *Use tables for large quantities of clearance merchandise.* Put the tables in the traffic pattern of the customer, encouraging impulse buying.

even on the merchandise. You can use this principle when reducing prices for an annual clearance sale.

Warehouse stores use the 10/30 principle, reducing the price on slow-moving merchandise 10 percent every 30 days until it sells. Still another markdown theory is early price reduction in the season while customers are still in a buying mood. This technique can be used for newer and better styles that may be turned over many times and can generally bring in more money. When you cut prices slowly over time, you rarely stimulate any real buying, and this can damage the image of your store because you have merchandise around too long.

At the end of a season, some retailers give distressed merchandise to charity. Others prefer to recover what they can in cash quickly and sell the odds and ends to retail specialists who often bid less than 10 cents on the dollar of the retail value.

True Costs

There needs to be a healthy balance between the accountancy view of your business and the marketing view. Retailing is more than numbers—it's relationships as well as salesmanship. You have to sell the intangible (goodwill and dreams) as well as the tangible (goods and services). Successful retailers pay attention to the soft side as well as the calculated part of doing business. Are your instincts and feelings about things paying off? Will they enable you to extend your retailing experience another year or cause your store's demise? You must understand the financial consequences of your decisions and the constraints of money on your choices.

"I tried to do too much," music store owner Fred W. admits, "when I tried to become a full-time musical instrument store." The plan was to cater to professional musicians and get instruments for his personal use. "The reality was that I could travel to and from Boston or New York and still buy things for less than [what I could sell them for] being a small dealer. My market was simply too small to support my investment." It took him three years to work out payment arrangements with suppliers and to liquidate his musical instrument inventory.

The lesson? You need to stay alert to the true costs of stocking various products. Prime retail space is expensive. High interest rates punch up inventory costs. Therefore, it is vital to ensure that every foot of floor space is earning an appropriate return.

True costs include all the factors that contribute to the retailer's ability to provide a

Fun Fact

Market research shows that women always shop longer than men, which is one of the major reasons that, in a standard regional mall, women make 70 percent of all purchases.

Compete on Your Own Terms

Author and marketing consultant Benson P. Shapiro in Concord, Massachusetts, suggests that retailers focus on their own success, not on creating failure for their competitors. He offers a seven-step guide to resisting the pressure to slash prices to compete:

1. *Create customer value by providing a reason for the customer to do business with you.*
2. *Focus on the customers who want what you have.* You can't be all things to all people.
3. *Be different!*
4. *Don't compete with yourself.* Simple product lines and service offerings are the easiest to manage and the most profitable.
5. *Set your prices to reflect the value customers place on the quality or the quantity of your products or services.*
6. *Deliver on your promises.* If you don't, your customer will have a good reason to negotiate and focus on price.
7. *Be courageous.* If you set a price and say it's not negotiable, don't negotiate or you lose your credibility.

consumer with goods or services, and the way you price your inventory should cover these costs. For instance, in a menswear store, a suit will take up twice as much space as a pair of trousers but may only sell at half the rate. Therefore the "rent" cost of a suit should be four times that of trousers and the interest charge for the square footage of space it takes up should be double. Since suits require a higher level of personal selling, they should carry a higher proportion of the selling staff costs. There will be similar differences between the true costs incurred by a furniture store and those in a high-stock-turn, self-selection lamp store. From day one, you need to have a clear picture of the direct product profitability of all the merchandise ranges you stock.

Pricing menu items is difficult for the new restaurateur. Pricing can depend on volume, portion size, and seating. It may be necessary to price items according to what you feel the customer will pay. Even if you decide you have to maintain a food cost of 35 percent to make a profit, you may have to weigh various factors. For example, certain items on your menu may be priced too high to be accepted by the public, and some items will necessarily have to be priced below your targeted range in order to attract the lunch crowd to your dinner house. This policy may mean pricing one item at a 25 percent food cost and another at a 45 percent food cost. You have to determine the selling mix of these items, as well as the portions, to stay in business.

Knowing the real costs of providing goods—wholesale cost, shipping, preparation, merchandising, selling, etc.—will help you select and price the inventory that will keep your business viable.

On the Internet, just as on the boardwalk, consumers are looking for the best deal. Armed with wholesale and competitive information, consumers might try to haggle with you to lower the price you will sell a particular item for. They may also ask you for quantity, senior citizen, student, teacher, or organization discounts. These days, it's a fact of life that retailers will lose some sales to sites like eBay and Priceline.com. Because of this price pressure, one of the biggest challenges a new retailer faces is building a brand that customers will value and support with their wallets.

The Unbeatable Pricing Strategy

A new business has the ability to customize products for small market segments, to respond quickly to changes in the market, and to cultivate personal relationships with customers to satisfy their needs. Small businesses cannot compete on price with big-box retailers, but they have an equal or better chance of competing on value. As a small retailer, your best pricing strategy is to provide both tangible and intangible benefits, rational and emotional ones, to your customers.

Human
Resources

U ntil now, you've mainly been concerned about what it will take to get your store open—the location of your business, layout and image, proper pricing procedures, lining up vendors, etc. Making sure you don't burn through your money before the doors are open is no doubt at the top of your priority list. Good—you're planning to succeed.

▲

Bright Idea

Establish a mission-driven team with total customer satisfaction and company profitability as the primary goals. You and your employees are interdependent. Together, you can achieve your goals if you measure your decisions and actions against this simple two-part guideline retailers gave us: "Do what is right for the customer and what is right for the team."

Having said that, what if you get what you want? What if you are flooded with customers on opening day? How will you greet, direct, answer questions, ring up sales, and wrap and deliver the goods all by yourself? Even after the shoppers go home, your work won't be over. You'll have the store to clean, merchandise to reshelve and display, register to balance, deposits and orders to make, and other paperwork to complete before opening the next day. Still want to do everything yourself? Can't afford to hire any help? Think again.

As the quantity of work to be performed expands, you must hire employees. The positions you may need filled are a display coordinator, buyer, controller, receiving clerk, stock person, delivery person, manager, bookkeeper, operations manager, and cashier. You don't necessarily have to hire one or more people for each task. The important thing is to organize your team and hire smart.

When you start out, you will handle the lion's share, if not all, of the business functions. Small retailers usually divide the work in half: You, as the owner, manage the operations, and you're assisted by someone who manages the merchandise. At the Thomasville, Georgia, clothing boutique, Mary D. is the buyer, sales manager, and merchandiser, and Jim D. is the business manager. As your business grows, you will probably need a general manager, operations manager, merchandise manager, marketing manager, and financial manager.

Each manager has prescribed areas of responsibility with measurable goals and written procedures for each. Operations managers are in charge of building maintenance, delivery, purchasing, and personnel. Merchandise managers are responsible for the purchase, flow, and movement of merchandise to the customer. Marketing managers are in charge of all advertising, promotions, visual presentations, and public relations. And financial managers are responsible for all computer data, financial controls, and reports.

You don't want to wait too long before hiring a manager to relieve you of some responsibilities. Hiring the right professional at the right time will ensure that all the jobs are getting done, which makes the store a better place to shop and a better place to work. If you are not able to get answers back to your salespeople for customers in a timely manner, this frustrates customers and costs sales. Newport Beach, California, pet bakery owner Stephanie B. says if she had to do it over again, one thing she would do differently is, "I would have a partner because it's difficult to handle a business that is open seven days a week on your own."

Assessing Your Needs

Consumers often form their impressions of a store by evaluating its sales force. So look for initiative and problem-solving skills in employees who can ring up repeat sales for your business and keep customers satisfied.

Whether selling shoes, computer equipment, or plants, retail salespeople assist customers in finding what they are looking for and try to interest them in buying the merchandise. They describe a product's features, demonstrate its use, and show various models and colors. Therefore, you need to hire people with experience in your trade area—or at least people with a willingness to learn.

While these are the basic requirements for selling items, not all sales approaches are the same, and not all salespeople will fit your line of goods or store. For example, some sales personnel, particularly those selling expensive and complex items, need special knowledge or skills. Selling automobiles requires explaining the features of various models, the meaning of manufacturers' specifications, and the types of options and financing available to prospective buyers. Selling fine jewelry involves a certain level of expertise beyond that required for a costume jewelry clerk.

Darrell T. plans to hire a full-time person to handle his Seattle art gallery's gift registry on the Web as soon as the demand warrants it. He will use the training tools

---

Job Advertisements

Ad for a Salesperson

We want your energy and ability to contribute to our success. You must be highly motivated, enthusiastic, friendly, and energetic. You must have sales experience, a strong customer service attitude, and the ability to consult with customers on purchases. Neat appearance and the ability to work in a fast-paced environment are essential. Employee benefits and room for advancement are available to the right candidate.

Ad for a Store Manager

We're looking for candidates who are merchandise-oriented and want to be involved in all aspects of running a retail store. Candidates should have three or more years of retail store management experience, strong people and communication skills, strong sales and motivational abilities, some computer skills, visual merchandising and inventory control experience, excellent customer service skills, and a sense of style. Excellent salary, benefits, and ability for advancement for the right candidate.

> **Smart Tip** Tip...
>
> A Monday-through-Friday, 9-to-5 workweek is the exception rather than the rule in retail. Most salespeople work some evening and weekend hours— and long hours during holiday and other peak retail periods. So keep in mind that flexibility and reliability are mandatory traits for your employees.

available from his licensor to make sure new employees have all the information they need to do their jobs. Thomasville, Georgia, audio retailer Jim O. hires students from local tech schools because they have basic equipment know-how; he spends time training them for customer service and sales.

In addition to selling, all employees will need to know how to make out sales checks, receive cash, check, and charge payments, bag or package purchases, and give change and receipts. Depending on the hours they work, they may have to open and close cash registers. This may involve counting the money, separating charge slips, coupons, and exchange vouchers, and making deposits at the bank. Attention to detail and basic math skills are important.

Depending on the type of store and your policies, your workers may also handle returns and exchanges, wrap gifts, stock shelves or racks, arrange for mailing or delivery of purchases, mark price tags, take inventory, and prepare displays. Neatness and artistic talent are very useful. Salespeople must be aware of special sales and promotions. They must also recognize possible security risks and thefts, and know how to handle or prevent such situations.

How Many People Is Enough?

The quick answer is as many as it takes to ensure complete customer satisfaction. In reality, simple economics preclude this. There are as many answers to personnel needs as there are types of retail businesses. Nonetheless, here are a few points to consider in deciding how many staff members your business requires:

- *Size.* A single-floor firm will need fewer staff than a multifloor store of the same size.
- *Type of product.* The higher the price and complexity of the product, the more personal selling is required. More personal selling means more people.
- *Opening hours.* The number of work days and the hours of business may require shifts and flexible work times. Changes in holiday business will also affect staffing.
- *Patterns of trade.* The concentration of sales at certain times of the day or on certain days of the week will affect staffing needs.
- *Sales density.* The higher the sales per square foot, the more staff you'll need.
- *Business location.* A homebased business increases its chances of experiencing zoning problems with every employee it adds.

Hiring

The first phase of hiring is the more impersonal aspect of personnel administration: creating plans, formulating policies, and setting up procedures. This involves recruitment, selection, hiring, compensation, employee health and welfare, maintaining personnel records, and the like. Then comes the more human aspects of managing human resources—the personal, in-the-flesh people business.

A natural tendency of many new retailers is to hire family members and/or friends as soon as help is needed. Avoid doing this. Your relationship with these individuals may interfere seriously with your in-store supervision of them and your focus on what you need done. Of course, there are exceptions. Some partnerships are smashing successes: Jim and Mary D., the Georgia clothing retailers, are a successful husband-and-wife team. Georgia audio retailers (and brothers) Jim, Doug, and Carlos O. work well together. And Fred and Dennis W., the music store owners in Vermont, also have a good working relationship. The point is not to ever hire one of your family members and friends without seriously thinking through the possible impact on your business's bottom line.

Most retailers experience little difficulty in attracting help for entry-level positions such as salesclerk, stock manager, and delivery clerk. You can put a "Help Wanted" sign in the window, advertise in the local paper, or put signs up on community bulletin boards to attract applicants. Another option is to post your needs with your local state Department of Employment Services or nonprofit career opportunity center. Frequently, applicants will just walk into your business and ask for a job. You can also reach prospects by telephoning or visiting local high schools, nearby colleges, senior housing centers, and youth groups.

When the time arrives to hire higher-level employees such as assistant managers, buyers, and bookkeepers, you need to be more imaginative and aggressive in your pursuit of qualified personnel. You can place display advertisements in the newspaper, trade journals, or professional association newsletters or discuss your needs with suppliers and other retailers.

Labor Practices

A person who operates a business with employees outside the immediate family must comply with a host of statutes regarding fair employment practices. These statutes relate to things like terms of employment, safety on the job, provisions for retirement, and workers' compensation and unemployment insurance. The fairness principle requires that decisions related to employees aren't made arbitrarily and that policies are applied equally to all employees. The law gives employees certain rights, and as an employer, you are responsible for knowing the law and abiding by it.

Some retail employees working in large companies belong to unions that represent their common interests. The United Food and Commercial Workers International Union has 1.4 million workers at the checkout stands, in the food aisles, and behind the deli and meat counters of neighborhood supermarkets. The Hotel Employees and Restaurant Employees International Union accounts for 300,000 employees. The Retail, Wholesale, and Department Store Union has 100,000 members. Consult your lawyer and SBA counselor regarding labor laws in your state.

Hiring Procedures

There are several methods for attracting and evaluating potential employees. Educate yourself on proper hiring procedures. Information on this subject is available at local libraries, community colleges, Small Business Development Centers, employment services offices, career development centers, and seminars.

Make sure your job announcement is attractive, accurate, meets government equal opportunity criteria, and is listed in the right places. Each job posting should be well-thought-out to emphasize the positive aspects of the job, including benefits and potential for advancement (see sample ads on page 163). The medium used to advertise positions should be tailored to the job type and the type of person you hope to hire. For example, if you are looking for an experienced store manager, you may want to run an ad in the local newspaper. If you're looking for an entry-level candidate, you will probably target young people, so advertise on radio stations they listen to. Signs in the store entryway or on community bulletin boards may be helpful, too. You can also pass the word along to current employees to suggest friends or acquaintances, work with employment agencies, or list the opening with the state Department of Employment Services or on the Web.

Smart Tip

Tip...

Using friends or relatives in your store may damage your relationship with them and cause resentment by other employees. Be sure that anyone who works in your store is qualified for the job. You may find it difficult to criticize friends or relatives or to assign them tasks they don't like. Don't hire someone you can't fire.

Some firms pay a bonus to any employee who brings in a new hire. Others spend thousands of dollars on classifieds, only to report that word-of-mouth referrals still seem to bring in the best candidates. Outstanding salespeople must be recruited, developed, and then shown they're appreciated.

It is often easier to train inexperienced people to sell your line of goods than it is to retrain salespeople who have developed undesirable attitudes and habits. Productivity can be developed in candidates who have a few desirable traits: friendliness, attention to detail, persistence, patience, and creativity. For example, one La-Z-Boy franchise has had success recruiting waitresses and hairdressers, as well as people who have worked in clothing stores, to sell their furniture. These people are used to working with the public and handling difficult situations. If they're good, they have the patience and know-how to listen and work with people.

Fred W. observes prospective employees in public situations before hiring them. His manager, Kevin, has been with him 13 years. "He was a cook at a vegetarian restaurant. I used to go in and talk to him all the time about music. Then I realized this guy was an encyclopedia of information. So I asked him if he would like to get out from behind the stove and work in my store.

"For my sales counter person," continues Fred, "I'm more interested in finding someone who's pleasant and can deal with the public than someone who knows a lot about music. All kids want to work here because they like music, but then I ask them what kind of music they like because generally it's limited. They need to appreciate a wide spectrum [of musical types], particularly to be able to help customers who like something else."

Top Ten Things Employees Want

In business today, a lot of focus is placed on customer satisfaction, but without employee satisfaction, very little can be accomplished. As you hire people, establish your policies and procedures, and run your business, keep these 10 motivators in mind to develop a top-quality team that is loyal and productive:

1. *Achievement:* to be challenged by worthy goals
2. *Balance:* flexibility in scheduling to have a life while earning a living
3. *Respect:* to be considered professional and left alone to do their jobs
4. *Community:* support and validation from co-workers and customers
5. *Opportunity:* the chance to learn new things and advance their positions
6. *Stability:* leadership, fairness, organization, and job security
7. *Communication:* access to information and openness about what's going on
8. *Reward:* appreciation of their work through fair compensation and recognition of a job well done
9. *Environment:* a healthy, positive, pleasant atmosphere with comfortable working conditions
10. *Pride:* personal satisfaction in their day's work

Background Checks

There is no crystal ball to ensure that the employees you hire will be loyal, honest, and hard-working. It is wise to screen applicants more thoroughly than simply asking them to fill out a job application and calling a few of the person's friends. Since everyone from the store manager to the shipping clerk represents your business, you should either verify an applicant's background or hire someone to do it for you.

One online organization outlines information sources and procedures for you to follow at www.ahhapeopleprofiler.com. Investigation firms can also be found in your local telephone directory, and through your police department and lawyers' association. They will do background criminal checks on prospective employees for about $35 to $200, depending on the agency's fee schedule and how many jurisdictions the agency checks.

Retail jobs are an easy starting point for immigrants to get into the workplace when first coming to the United States. Employers must have proof that the employee has the right to work in the country, as required on Immigration and Naturalization Service (INS) form I-9. To find out which requirements your business must meet, call the INS information line, (800) 755-0777, or the U.S. Department of Justice. Ask new employees to provide one of the following:

- Certificate of U.S. citizenship or naturalization
- Government-issued birth certificate
- INS Form 688 or 6881
- Native American tribal document
- Proof of identity, such as current driver's license, school photo ID, or voter registration card
- Social Security card
- U.S. passport

Compensation

According to the U.S. Department of Labor, retailers hired about 4.6 million salespeople in 1998 to work in stores ranging from small specialty shops employing a few workers to giant department stores with hundreds of salespeople, and self-employed representatives of direct sales companies and mail order houses. This occupation offers many opportunities for part-time work and is especially appealing to students, retirees, and others looking to supplement their incomes. The average hourly earnings of workers in retail trade were $9.08 in 1999, compared to an average of $13.24 for all workers in the United States, according to the U.S. Department of Labor.

You can pay sales employees hourly or on commission. The commission method is generally practical only for stores providing one-on-one customer service to sell high-priced items such as expensive clothing, jewelry, electronics, furniture, and computers. The advantage of this form of pay is that it ties employees' income directly to their job performance. Some stores pay a combination of hourly salary and commission. Add to these three approaches the opportunity for employees to win special rewards or bonuses for meeting or exceeding goals for sales and service.

Most managers and full-time employees expect health coverage, paid time off for illness or vacation, and some perks like paid educational opportunities, trade show attendance, and merchandise discounts. Without offering some benefits in your compensation package, you will find it difficult to compete for quality employees. When considering what to offer your workers, compare the perks with the costs of high turnover—decreased morale, time interviewing new employees, training new people, interruption of customer service, public perception of instability, loss of person's know-how, etc.

> **Beware!**
> Employees who feel they are appreciated, compensated fairly and treated respectfully have the incentive to be more productive and positive than those who feel overworked and underpaid. If the poor performers receive the same compensation as the go-getters, it won't be long before you have a mediocre staff and lose all your best workers.

After They're Hired

Once you have invested the time and effort in recruiting and hiring skilled new employees, don't rest on your laurels. Your work's not done! There are several things you can do to make sure your diligent hiring efforts don't go to waste.

Lack of communication between management and employees is one of retailers' biggest mistakes. Don't let your business fall into this common trap. Regular store meetings are a good way to improve the situation, according to the retailers we interviewed. These gatherings are great settings for educating employees on new products or services. Let an employee explain and demonstrate benefits and features of your products. Have employees tell you what they observe customers liking or disliking and what they hear customers asking for that may not be in stock. Employees should be told when new products will be arriving and when

> **Bright Idea**
> Establish employee policies that don't attract people who are looking for an employee discount rather than a job. A lot of kids want to work in music and stereo stores, owners say, so those entrepreneurs have to screen candidates carefully to avoid low productivity and high turnover.

replacement items will be in stock. Employees want to be asked for their opinions and see some of their ideas implemented.

Provide Incentives to Employees

Employees should constantly be encouraged to perform in a quality manner. When you or a customer are pleased with an employee's performance, let everyone know about it. Personal and public recognition has a multitiered affect. It communicates what you value to your workers and customers, which can generate more achievements

Weekly Time Sheet

Date from: _____
Date to: _____
Employee name: _____
Number: _____
Department: _____

	Morning		Afternoon		For office use only	
	In	Out	In	Out	Regular hours	Overtime
Monday						
Tuesday						
Wednesday						
Thursday						
Friday						
Saturday						
Sunday						
				Total hours:		

Employee signature: _____

Approved by: _____

and satisfaction. Some rewards the retailers we interviewed use are treating a star employee to a lunch, bonus, afternoon off, or reserved parking. You will be hiring from the same labor pool as other local businesses. How can you get your employees to perform better for you? Your acknowledgment, rewards, and overall management will make all the difference.

Employee and Operations Manual

Operating a retail business can be fun and rewarding, but without effective management procedures, it can also be a lot of headaches. If you put the proper systems in place so that your store is more or less on autopilot, you'll be successful. The reason franchises generally work well is that they use proven systems; all the new retailer has to do is follow the tried-and-true policies.

The Employee Bible

Here are some of the topics you should cover in your employee manual:

- ○ Company philosophy
- ○ Company benefits, including medical care, time off, discounts, and allowances
- ○ Hours of operation and reporting hours
- ○ Procedures for reporting an illness, absences, or family emergency
- ○ Dress code, including uniforms, safety gear, or badges to be worn
- ○ Standards of behavior regarding smoking, alcohol, drugs, gum-chewing, language, personal telephone calls, and visitors
- ○ How to greet customers
- ○ Telephone etiquette
- ○ Procedures for dealing with unhappy customers
- ○ Procedures for dealing with suspected shoplifters or other illegal activities
- ○ Procedures for making suggestions for company improvement
- ○ How to use all equipment
- ○ Procedures for serving customers
- ○ Where to get product or service information
- ○ Emergency procedures

> **Bright Idea**
>
> Build strong communications with your employees through weekly store meetings, a periodic newsletter, an annual company meeting, sponsorship of academic or athletic teams, a suggestion box, and scheduled social get-togethers with families.

An employee and operations manual provides the information your people need to do their jobs and play by the rules. It gets employees off on the right foot and instills in them habits you want to see rather than those you want to break.

Many retailers are extremely dependent on their key staff members. If a management person leaves, sales suffer because of the knowledge that walks out the door with a valuable employee. Turnover is expensive, and training new staff is a tedious, time-consuming process. Written operating procedures that explain how to perform the day-to-day, week-to-week, month-to-month, and year-to-year jobs involved in running your store will help smooth employee transitions.

By having a guide for employees, you eliminate uncertainty about what your store's policies, procedures, and guidelines are. This can be of particular importance when you need to put an employee on probation or fire someone. Having clearly stated policies can protect you from the litigation that is all too common in today's world.

Your dress code should be plainly understood by everyone who works in the store. Employees should know that they will be sent home to change if they are not dressed appropriately. Clothing, makeup, and jewelry regulations should be appropriate for your clientele because poor dressing and hygiene will drive customers away.

Managing the customer's mood is not a small task. Management of the customer's experience starts when they walk in and ends when they walk out. A warm greeting from an alert, knowledgeable, and attentive (but not pushy) salesperson will make customers want to do business with you time and again. For more on store policies, read Chapter 6.

Probation

It is customary to hire new people on a probationary basis. For retail employees, this period should be relatively short—for example, 10 to 90 days. This time allows you to evaluate the new employee to measure their progress and to determine if they will fit into your organization. A probationary period also provides incentive for new employees to prove themselves and to learn their jobs quickly and well.

Training

When new employees are hired, they should be trained in a well-thought-out and thorough manner. To begin orienting them to your way of doing business, give them a complete tour of the facilities, explaining what their role is in each area, what procedures to follow, and things to watch out for. Take new employees around your store or office from the front door to the back. It is important that everyone understand how their job fits into the overall scheme of things and what each person's duties and responsibilities are so people will work well together.

Continue training on a regular basis. Training is an investment in the future—your future. With rapid changes in technology and fashion, products change frequently and the challenge to employees to keep up with them is great. Encourage employees to stay informed about the latest trends in your industry by reading trade journals, local newspapers and consumer magazines. Send employees to trade and consumer shows to pick up new ideas, interact with other businesspeople, and promote your business.

Scheduling Personnel

Scheduling employee hours is complex and can be daunting at first since you have no history to go on. In setting up the store and merchandise, employees may work longer hours during the first few weeks when the public hasn't found you yet. With time, customer patterns will emerge that make it easier to know how many staff members will be needed on certain days of the week and at what times of day.

Full-time employees work 30 to 40 hours a week and are usually paid at a somewhat higher hourly rate than part-time employees (or they are paid salary). Full-timers provide continuity for your store and develop your customer base for you. They generally have broad-based skills in the areas of sales, cashiering, special ordering, and display work. These employees make a commitment to your business and have regularly scheduled hours and days of the week. Jim and Mary D. have two employees who share a full-time position in the dress store. Jim, Doug, and Carlos O.'s audio business keeps the three brothers plus four full-time and one part-time person busy. While designer Matt M. does most of the design and marketing work himself with one full-time office assistant, he relies on subcontractors for production and delivery.

Part-time employees may work year-round or seasonally when you need additional help in sales, gift-wrapping, inventory, and service. They can be scheduled for your heavy-traffic hours and days or on an as-needed basis. These workers are frequently students,

Bright Idea

Unless an employee steals, destroys property or causes safety problems, immediate dismissal for poor performance isn't a good idea—legally or managerially. Instead, meet privately with the employee and explain the problem. To prevent misunderstandings, you might want to have your store manager follow up with the employee.

retired people, or parents of school-age children, and their schedules can be set to accommodate school and/or seasonal schedules. Establishing four-hour shifts allows you the flexibility of having people work partial days as well as adjusting staffing needs. Some of your part-time workers will stay with you for years and provide exceptional service.

Invite employees to submit schedule requests and make every effort to accommodate them. However, don't be casual on the accountability side. Let employees know you are counting on them and expect them to arrive on time and ready to work.

Staffing Calendar

Date from: _____   Date to: _____

Employee	Mon.	Tues.	Wed.	Thurs.	Fri.	Sat.	Sun.

Overstaffing, understaffing, and no-shows disrupt other workers and can jeopardize your business. By maintaining detailed sales, traffic, and staffing records, you can analyze what's working and what isn't. From year to year, you'll amass figures that will help you maximize your resources and opportunities. For a "Weekly Time Sheet" and a "Staffing Calendar," turn to pages 170 and 174.

Employee Performance Appraisals

Annual employee evaluations help you zero in on the strengths and weaknesses of your business. At the same time each year, set up appointments with your employees to review their performance. Give each employee a self-evaluation form to complete and return to you prior to your scheduled meeting. Then, review each employee's answers and prepare your points for discussion. These will include expectations for the job, personal achievements, areas where effectiveness could be improved, how you can help the employee do a better job, and the employee's new performance objectives.

From the information exchanged during the performance appraisal process, you will get a clearer view of how well your hiring, training, and management practices are working. You will also gain insight into ways to motivate employees. This is often a time when new ideas for the business surface and aspirations for promotion are revealed. Performance appraisals also provide the opportunity for clearing the air about misunderstandings or mistakes and for starting fresh.

Firing

"We're all in a tight labor market," Dadeville, Alabama, grocer Jeff P. says. "When you get somebody to do the job, you're going to have to use some discretion on occasion when they do something you don't like. You do have to put your foot down firmly and don't tolerate certain things; but you can't fire everybody and his brother because they mess up sometimes."

The laws protecting workers' rights are complex and can easily be used against you. Check with your lawyer, local Small Business Development Center, and other advisors to make sure you understand what you can and cannot do in terms of firing an employee.

If you feel you need to discipline an employee, the first thing you need to do is meet with the employee and give him or her a verbal warning. The next time the

> **Bright Idea**
>
> Learn from the experience of letting an employee go. Ask yourself what went wrong and whether improved interviewing/ screening practices might have prevented the problem in the first place. Ask yourself if there's anything you can do to improve your management to create an atmosphere where both your business and your employees benefit.

employee exhibits behavior that goes against your policies, meet with the employee and provide him or her with a written summary of things the employee must and must not do and a time period within which the employee must correct his or her performance. This is known as a written warning. Keep a copy of the warning that clearly states that if behavior is not corrected, the employee may be terminated. Ask the employee to sign the warning, acknowledging the understanding of your expectations. If, after these measures, the employee's performance has not improved in the ways you outlined in the verbal and written warnings, you may have to fire the employee.

Be humane if you have to let someone go. Meet in private with the employee and tell the person the exact reasons for termination. Create an atmosphere of fairness, if not compassion, and have the employee's final paycheck and paperwork ready to make a clean break.

You Must Remember This...

Establishing a sense of community among your employees is one of the best ways to make your store successful. Employee loyalty leads to customer satisfaction, which profits everyone. Be fair, have fun, attend to business, and you'll all be proud of what you create.

12

Marketing

Marketing is a system of business activities designed to plan, price, promote, and distribute products and services to potential customers. How well you promote what you're doing is a major factor in determining how much business you will do.

▲

Marketing is often the most creative and fun part of running a retail business. To let people know you can satisfy their wants and needs, you must be highly visible. You can publicize your business through paid or free promotions. Paid promotions include advertising, direct mail, and your Web site. Publicity and community relations are a few of the free promotional tools you have at your disposal. Since you've already identified the customer you'll serve, you know where to aim to get the returns you're seeking.

Marketing Ideas Galore

Use this list to brainstorm ways to promote your business:

- ○ Auction/raffle prizes
- ○ Bag stuffers
- ○ Balloons
- ○ Billboards
- ○ Billing inserts
- ○ Brochures
- ○ Catalogs
- ○ Celebrity guest appearance
- ○ Classes, workshops
- ○ Collectors club
- ○ Contest
- ○ Coupon
- ○ Direct mail
- ○ Event program ad (theater, sports, school)
- ○ Fliers
- ○ Frequent buyer program
- ○ Gift certificates
- ○ Gift with purchase
- ○ Group discount card
- ○ Internet e-mail, banner ad, Web site, links, search engine registry
- ○ Loyalty program
- ○ Magazine ad, article, insert, bingo card
- ○ Newsletters
- ○ Open house
- ○ Partnership with school
- ○ Patron of the arts
- ○ Photo opportunities
- ○ Pledge on sales
- ○ Postcards
- ○ Posters
- ○ Product demonstration
- ○ Radio ad, appearance, live remote
- ○ Sales
- ○ Shopping cart signage
- ○ Signs: interior, exterior, building, vehicle
- ○ Skywriting
- ○ Special events
- ○ Specialty items
- ○ Tastings
- ○ Themed events
- ○ TV ad, appearance, infomercial
- ○ Volunteer opportunities
- ○ Window displays
- ○ Yellow Pages ad, listing

When devising a plan to promote your store, these are the things you need to think about:

1. What do I want to say to potential customers?
2. How will I reach them?
3. What are my specific objectives for each promotion?
4. How will I measure the success of my efforts?
5. What is my budget?

Putting Together a Promotion Plan

Keep the big picture in mind while leveraging the benefits of the various marketing channels and vehicles to achieve your goals. A typical marketing plan may have 10 to 35 different marketing channels through which sales will come. The goal is to be as creative and playful as possible.

Next, you need to decide how you will allocate funds over the entire year. If your business does a large percentage of business in the summer or at holiday or tax time, you will probably want to budget a large share of your budget to capturing those seasons.

As in the other aspects of starting his business, Seattle-based art gallery owner Darrell T. received assistance from his licensor's marketing arm once the store was set up. "For the first 90 days, they kept in contact with us and [gave] us any help we could dream of," says Darrell. "For example, to set up our Web site, they actually sent us CDs with all the images and information on how to go about doing it. When we started advertising with local magazines and newspapers, [the licensor's marketing arm] would create the ad for us and send it directly to the publisher. It was very helpful." Since he had no previous retail experience, Darrell found the help invaluable.

Few independent retailers have this type of arrangement, though. If you're on your own, you'll have to find your own way through the world of marketing and advertising. This chapter will give you lots of ideas to get you headed in the right direction.

If you built your store, you may have had a groundbreaking ceremony to let people know you were coming to town. For most retailers, the first opportunity to blow your horn is when you're ready to open your doors for business. Some kinds of businesses need greater opening promotion efforts than do others.

Your Grand Opening

The opening of an auto repair shop might not need to be as lavish as the festivities for an interior design store. For restaurants and some other businesses, it is often wise to have a "soft" or quiet opening until all the kinks have been worked out. Still other

▲

Smart Tip *Tip...*

Retailers say your grand opening should be only the first of several special events you host throughout the year. Invitational events make customers feel special and generate enthusiasm and goodwill for your business.

---

businesses have a series of events targeting various stakeholders in their success. Suppliers, investors, family, and friends may be treated to small celebrations, with a fund-raising party for a local charity or group the night before the official opening.

How much should you spend on your grand opening promotion? Retail expert and author Carol Schroeder says a general rule of thumb is to spend 3 to 5 percent of your anticipated sales for the first year. If you expect to generate $200,000 in sales, you can probably afford to spend $6,000 to $10,000 to launch your business.

Darrell did a barrage of advertising on the radio and in newspapers for his opening, spending about $13,000 to $15,000 over a two-month period—one month before the opening and one month after. As he describes it, "When we opened the doors, we had everything decorated, served refreshments, and had a live radio broadcast from the store. It was quite a bit of fun and drew people in for at least a month. We timed it for just before Christmas, so that was really beneficial, too. Things just took off from there."

Advertising

Advertising offers a wide range of opportunities. You can pay to have your message put almost anywhere you find your customers.

Thomasville, Georgia, clothing retailers Jim and Mary D. cater primarily to teenagers and their mothers. They find that the best way to reach them is through the store's Web site, gospel radio, and print advertising. "We do a lot of radio advertising," explains Jim. "The local stations have [inexpensive] rates, so we can do a spot for $4. We do simple compositions ourselves. We have a friend who used to be in the [radio] business, and she records the 30-second spots with two people talking. We advertise periodically on the gospel station. We're not there every day; I think that wears out. We'll buy a package of 100 spots for $400 to $500 and run three a day in a two-hour period during the week. We avoid the weekends because we've found that it's not good for us. The ads draw people as far away as 120 miles."

If you open a children's store, car repair business, or fast-food business, you might want to use radio to reach commuters while they're driving. If you have a photography studio or florist shop, you may want to print an attractive brochure that can be used in many ways. Which media will give you the largest return on your investment for the least amount of money and wasted effort? Check prices against circulation figures and audience profiles.

Media Mix

What media can put consumers under your spell? Compile a list of publications and other media outlets that reach your target audience. Consider radio, TV, billboards, newspapers, transit, Internet, magazines, newsletters, fairs, and event programs. Retailers suggest you ask the sales reps of the advertising outlets you're thinking about using to give you a rate card and demographic profile of their audience. This is free market research for you and can help you decide if the price is right and the customer profile matches yours.

"[The marketing arm of our licensor] gave us suggestions about which newspapers would be good to advertise in," Darrell T. recounts. "They based their recommendations on readership and cost. We can take advantage of corporate negotiated rates with some magazine and newspaper publishers. This can mean getting 30 percent discounts because of our corporate ties."

The media mix you choose depends on the size and type of your store, the part of the market to be served, media availability, advertising budget, and other factors. A jewelry store specializing in engagement and wedding rings might concentrate on ads on radio stations broadcasting music to young adults, or on direct mailings to young adults such as graduating seniors at local colleges, and to organizations composed of this group. A small gift basket business might send direct mail to businesses and college dorms. Cable television may work well for sellers of furniture, cars, and computers.

For Darrell's art gallery, a mix of direct mail, newspaper, and radio advertising is working. Darrell plans to put up a gift registry on his Web site to leverage that vehicle as well. Direct mail pieces go to the gallery's primary audience, and the other media canvass Seattle and beyond. "We've found that a great many of our buyers have some sort of religious background, so we use the Christian music station up here to reach them," adds Darrell.

Historically, newspapers have been the primary advertising outlet for retailers. This is still true today, although other media are now playing bigger roles. Finding it hard to compete with warehouse and department stores in the major dailies, small retailers take advantage of suburban and neighborhood weekly and semiweekly newspapers at more reasonable costs and effectiveness. For more on this, read the "Print Advertising" section on page 182.

Co-Op Advertising

Get your suppliers to work with you in promoting goods. They can send consultants to talk to salespeople, provide demonstrators, and help your advertising efforts by providing camera-ready ad slicks or product illustrations for you to use.

Under certain conditions, some suppliers will pay part of your advertising bill. A cosmetic firm that supplies you with goods, for example, might wish to push a new product. As part of the purchase agreement you negotiate, the cosmetic firm might

▲

agree to pay 50 to 100 percent of the cost of a full-page newspaper ad for your store. This enables you to get good newspaper coverage at a discount (or for free); it also permits the vendor to get its product in front of the public at the lower per-column-inch for you. Look into negotiating this type of arrangement with your suppliers.

Direct Mail

You want to build a relational database that helps you identify various customer segments for direct mail and service opportunities. Segment customers by ZIP code, level of spending, buying habits, interests, family size, or other criteria that will enable you to match your offerings to their wants and needs. For example, if a customer has school-age children, you can send that person a mailer on back-to-school supplies.

"Direct mailers have been the most effective form of advertising for us," says Darrell. "We work with mailing houses, targeting our mailings to our best prospects. Because there are so many galleries around, we focus primarily on those people who live in our area. We target people 35 and over with two children and six-figure incomes who live within a 10- to 15-mile area."

Direct mail can effectively promote open houses, anniversaries, private sales, seasonal events, preview parties, factory-authorized sales, factory closeouts, or floor sample sales—and can generate significant traffic and sales.

Meticulously maintain customer lists so you can build relationships with your existing clients. When you send them a time-sensitive invitation, deliver a little something extra, like extending the terms of normal financing or offering a gift to the first 50 people who come in. You have to make a strong, sincere offer so you can get people off the Internet and out of their homes to see what you have for them.

Print Advertising

You can hire an advertising agency or graphic design firm, pay a publisher to compose an ad for you, hire a freelance professional or student, or create your own print messages. Desktop-publishing software comes with most computers, giving people the tools to produce visually attractive, legible print promotions—catalogs, fliers, newsletters, ads, posters, mailers, postcards, tent cards (seen on tables in fast-food and other types of restaurants), brochures, sales sheets, gift certificates, coupons, menus, etc. Get some instruction online or through classes at a computer store, community college, or university on how to use desktop-publishing software like Illustrator, PageMaker, PhotoShop, and QuarkXpress to produce high-quality pieces.

Take a look at what your competitors are doing. What are your prospects reading, watching, and listening to? Gather clues of style, color, language, and values from popular culture and apply them to your print materials. A lot of the research has already been done for you. Match the medium, type, content, and style of print advertising to your audience.

Be sure to tell your salespeople about the theme and placement of ads so they will be prepared when customers phone and come in. Post the print ads in the store for quick reference. Put the ad in an acrylic frame on your countertop with the headline, "As Seen On TV" (or whatever). You can also get extra mileage out of any publicity you've received by displaying it in your store, noting, "As featured in" and the name of the publication.

Stat Fact
People who have already shopped in your store are five times more likely to come in again. Look at their ZIP codes and buy a mailing list for that ZIP code so you can draw their neighbors in, too.

Web Site: a Must-Have in Retailing

The Internet is the great equalizer, making it possible for you to reach across town, the United States, or the world, if you like. There are several ways you can go about marketing your products and services on the Internet. Every retailer we interviewed for this book is marketing his or her services on the Internet or plans to do so in the near future.

Having a Web site is very important in this highly competitive industry. Having a Web site will give your customers a place to go anytime they want to learn more about your business, whether your front doors are open or closed. You can create a site by yourself with software such as Adobe's PageMill and Macromedia's Dream Weaver, or by using the instructions at sites such as www.howtointernet.com. But it might be better to hire a professional designer through a college, advertising agency, or design firm. After all, this is your company's reputation we're talking about. Your site needs to be more than just so-so. It needs to be great. The essential elements of a great Web site, according to retailers and Internet surfers, are:

- store name, location, and contact information;
- product or service descriptions with prices and fees;
- pictures of products, or pictures of services being performed;
- ordering information;
- lines carried or clients served;
- company background;
- store policies regarding payment, returns, repairs, and warranties;
- links to other interesting sites; and
- constantly updated information that entertains or informs the visitor.

So why do you need a Web site when you already have a storefront? A recent Ernst & Young survey revealed that 43 percent of consumers' online purchases were based solely on the fact that the products or services were available online. (Convenience is king.) Sixteen percent of purchases were unplanned, impulse buys. The Internet is boosting sales for mom-and-pop stores, too—not just the big guys. A survey conducted by the National Trust for Historic Preservation in Washington, DC, found that small retailers with Web sites experienced an increase of nearly 13 percent in sales via the Web during the summer of 2000. Don't you want a piece of this action?

As consumers incorporate online shopping into their daily lives, they will use the channel in more conventional ways, purchasing in more discretionary categories like apparel and food. This "normalization" of online shopping will drive total online revenues higher, according to *Chain Store Age*, but it will also reduce the amount of incremental and impulse buying. In a shopping environment with no physical barriers, online customers will continue to purchase items they could not otherwise buy—a garment not available in a local store, a hard-to-find book, etc.

"It's a very big job for the stores in our little town to keep up with the competition from bigger stores, so we are joining together to have a site for the town," says Thomasville, Georgia-based Jim D. His store was doing a healthy business in fancy

Your site needs to be more than just so-so. It needs to be great.

clothing when he and his wife/partner, Mary, decided to market their prom dresses online. The site went live in February 2000, just in time for that year's proms, and by March the company had 40,000 hits on the site. By June, the couple had received nearly 500 orders for dresses that cost $150 to $200. Requests came from Georgia, Missouri, West Virginia, Rhode Island, Hawaii, and Japan. This success is an example of the possibilities that exist for small retailers to develop a clear, narrow identity so shoppers can find what they're looking for on their Web sites.

Jim and Mary's site is primarily an online catalog. It shows pictures of the company's primary line—prom, junior prom, bridesmaids', mother of the bride, and flower girl dresses—and highlights the messages "be unique," "low prices," "great designs," and "satisfaction guaranteed." The graphics load quickly (very important in today's fast-paced world).

"Our Web designer was very good in registering our site [with search engines]. That helped a great deal. Our hits have leveled off to about a 10,000 a month," says Jim. What's one drawback to getting so much online business so fast? Fulfilling all the orders has been difficult. "Our problem was that our suppliers could not send us enough dresses, so we've lost hundreds and hundreds of sales," says Jim. "We're working with [vendors] to go interactive so we can buy designs online and they can tell us when they will be delivered. With all the buying and inventory control improvement, we expect to double or triple our e-commerce [business] this year."

Make your site a rich experience. In addition to order information, extend your brick-and-mortar line by testing market acceptance of additional items. You can give background information on the product, its materials, manufacturer, or users. Profile employees and satisfied customers. Have a treasure hunt, quiz, game, or contest. Make it entertaining.

When Internet music distributors like CDNow and MP3.com exploded onto the scene, Montpelier, Vermont, music store owner Fred W. decided to jump into the Web world rather than be left behind. His partner and brother, Dennis, put the company's site up in 1998. Since then, it has increased store sales by 10 percent by expanding their audience from 8,000 in Montpelier to millions globally.

The way people will find you on the Internet is by using search engines. Google, Yahoo, AltaVista, and Lycos are just a few of the hundreds of search engines Web surfers can use. You need to have your site listed with as many of these search engines as you can. You can do it yourself, hire someone to do it for you, or hire a service like Submit It (www.submitit.com) for about $100 to register your site on 50 to several hundred search engines.

You can link to other sites to increase traffic to and from these resources. Have major suppliers refer customers to you as the local provider of their brand, and in return, provide a link on your site to theirs. Linking is a great form of advertising for you because it's free and it refers people to you right away. Think about businesses with complementary products or services, organizations for your industry, directories, and general consumer sites. These partnerships might include either click-through or revenue-sharing agreements that give companies incentives to push your products. To make arrangements to link your site with someone else's, speak to the webmaster, company president, or marketing director. Another way to advertise on the Internet is by buying banner advertising.

For more information on starting an e-commerce Web site, read *How To Dotcom* (Entrepreneur Press).

In-Store Promotions

While advertising drives traffic to a store, the store closes the sale one-on-one with the shopper. Most successful promotions require consid-erable advance planning. A good promotion is based on good merchandise. Sometimes the merchandise is already in inventory, but many times you must make special purchases. The most common promotions include warehouse sales, parking lot sales, pre-Christmas promotions, back-to-school sales, inventory reduction sales between seasons, anniversary promotions, moonlight

Tip...

Smart Tip

Promotions have a dual purpose: to sell new merchandise in large volume and to sell regular or old merchandise, thus keeping inventory clean of irregular, outdated, or shopworn items.

> **Bright Idea**
>
> Ask manufacturers and distributors to work with you in creating sizzle for your store and their merchandise. Ceiling banners and interactive media capture consumers' attention. Many manufacturers and distributors will give or sell you videos, memorabilia and artifacts related to their brand or selling season theme to create the proper atmosphere in which to sell their merchandise.

sales, post-Thanksgiving sales, summer clearances, and end-of-the-month sales.

Merchandise displayed in high-traffic "power" aisles grabs shoppers' attention and usually yields higher sales than the same merchandise placed in a side aisle. Therefore, savvy merchants use these aisles to display special values, seasonal merchandise, and/or price-sensitive items.

Sales promotion is an important part of your marketing strategy. In order to manage the costs, you must establish an objective the same way you do for advertising, pricing, and distribution. The objectives for each promotion should be clearly stated, such as trial, repeat purchase, reducing stock levels, a shift in buying peaks, combating competition, and so on. Then select the appropriate promotional technique and dates the promotion will run, and make sure to evaluate the results once the promotion is over.

Assign dates and responsibilities for all aspects of executing the plan. In addition to briefing your staff beforehand, set target performance levels and offer incentives for exceeding goals. Don't forget to establish a procedure for collecting the required data for follow-up and evaluation. Spending must be analyzed and categorized by type of activity, such as special packaging, special point-of-sale material, special labels, extra product, loss of margin through price reductions, etc.

Special Pricing

The most obvious in-store promotion is special pricing (price reduction). Coupons, vouchers, and competitions with cash prizes are ways of attracting customers. Premium promotions (e.g., two-for-one offers), free gifts, and trade-in programs are some direct promotions of goods you can use.

Visual Merchandising

Wow your customers with exciting merchandise vistas. The exterior of your store may help attract visitors, but it is the interior décor and atmosphere, combined with the assistance and attitude of salespeople, that convert prospects into buyers. The interior of your store, like the exterior, must be compatible with your products and services and the image you are trying to portray.

Do not overcrowd displays. Crowded displays can confuse customers and may prevent them from spotting something they would buy if it were more visible. Making a choice among three similar products is easier than among six.

Group displays into obvious categories, and if your customers are generally repeat ones, do not constantly move products to different locations since that can irritate some people. This is particularly true for grocery store, office supply store, and drugstore customers.

Try to create an air of spaciousness in displays, and wherever possible avoid displays that block the view of other parts of the store or the locations of cashiers. The objective of good display is to make the items most customers want stand out. Display signs can help, but don't overdo them. Poor signs or too many signs detract from the actual merchandise, so have a professional make them neat and easy to read.

Great Displays

Arrange displays throughout the store to facilitate the shopper's journey from one area to another. Give new offerings star treatment by showcasing them either in window displays or in a prominent place near the front door. Start designing the display area by choosing a focal point for the display, such as a key piece of fishing equipment or a grouping of skin-care products. Know your merchandise so you know how to combine items into displays that make sense.

Update displays as needed to reflect items sold out or discontinued lines. Plan to change each display of large items, such as furniture or home theater suites, a minimum of four times a year with the change in season. Some markets require monthly or weekly rotations, such as music, books, food, and fashion.

You can give your store a fresh look and pump up sales just by giving items a new location. Sometimes moving a collection to a wall display or to a pedestal and spotlighting it will attract the attention it deserves. Retailers suggest accessorizing furniture and clothing to give you extra marketing mileage.

The effective use of public relations can increase the awareness, understanding, and acceptance of your business. Media contacts should be nurtured and utilized at every opportunity. Using public relations to your advantage is an important part of your marketing plan, so don't forget about it!

Stat Fact

Table tent cards work in fast-food and casual sit-down restaurants. Researchers find that tent cards are read more frequently and for more time than other in-store merchandising tools. The typical hanging ceiling sign in a fast-food restaurant is looked at by about 4 percent of all customers, whereas tent cards attract the attention of 17 percent of all customers.

▲

Public Relations

Well-prepared press releases and media kits containing photographs and background information on your company are good ways to generate media interest and articles on your new season's product line, your new employee or customer service, or a special event. When someone associated with your business is taking part in community projects or supporting a charity, let the media know. The media are often interested in human-interest stories, and the benefit to you is in keeping your company in the public eye and enhancing the relationship between your business and the community.

Getting coverage in the media is free advertising and can reach many more prospective buyers than you could hope to on your own. How do you obtain radio, television, newspaper, and magazine coverage? Write a press release with strong descriptions and relevance to the audience. Send your press packet to the media your prospective customers rely on for information.

Is It Working?

To evaluate your advertising and marketing plans, ask yourself the following 10 questions:

1. Are my objectives for advertising and sales promotion clearly stated? Do they support my marketing plan?

2. Is my media mix supportive of my marketing plan?

3. Are budgets adequate to accomplish my objectives? How are budgets established?

4. Are my creative strategies compatible with my marketing plan?

5. Do I have weekly, monthly, and seasonal plans for such activities in place?

6. Are customer service levels satisfactory? What weaknesses exist?

7. Are mail and telephone sales programs compatible with my overall marketing plan?

8. Are my after-sales delivery programs, if any, compatible with my marketing plan?

9. Are my credit programs cost-effective? Should credit options be added or deleted?

10. Is the breadth and intensity of market coverage satisfactory for growth?

13

Customer
Service

The century of the consumer has arrived. Customers have love-hate relationships with shopping, and they know they can make or break a business. If you recognize that it's your job to make shopping as pleasurable and painless as it can be, the odds of your succeeding in retail are good.

▲

"Retailers are not opening stores in the United States to serve new markets anymore," says retail anthropologist Paco Underhill, founder and managing partner of New York City-based Envirosell Inc. "They are opening stores to steal someone else's customers. As the competition gets heated, there is a need for an edge." What does this mean for you? Customer service is more important than it has ever been before, and if you can't master it, your business will probably fail.

Customer-Centric Objectives

To distinguish yourself from the competition, you will have to offer something besides reasonable prices. That something could be as simple as a quick, easy, pleasant, or exciting shopping experience. Your goal must be your customer's goal. That means you must find out what the customer wants—not just profile the demographics of the customer you want. From store concept to order delivery, you want to weave the needs and wants of customers into your store's policies and procedures so that satisfying them is part of your business's DNA.

When the first person steps up to your cash register to make the first purchase, you'll begin learning who your customers are. Until then, who your store serves is just an educated guess. You want to learn why certain people buy from you, their likes and dislikes, and their interests and lifestyles. By keeping your fingers on the pulse of consumer preferences, you can plan your inventory and sales strategies to get the most from your relationships.

Information Collection Is Key

There are several ways you can collect information to develop customer loyalty. One is by setting up shopping services and gathering personal information for creating cosmetics, travel, wardrobe, and technology profiles of your customers. You can also collect valuable information through warranty and service registration, and through continuity programs such as newsletters, order-replenishment programs, and reminder notices. Two more ways of profiling customers are by conducting an online customer survey and having visitors sign a guest book in the store with their comments.

Getting to know your store regulars is relatively easy. These are the people who come in frequently and you get to know them through

> **Smart Tip** Tip...
>
> One golf shop keeps track of each customer's store visits to document their wishes as well as purchases and sizes. When someone wants to buy a gift for the individual, they just ask the salesperson for suggestions based on information maintained in the customer's file on the computer.

casual conversation and regular contact. You can strengthen these relationships by inviting them to invitation-only events like meet-the-author nights, special VIP sales, and previews of the new season's merchandise.

Since your goal is to convert shoppers to buyers and buyers to loyal customers, you want to increase not only the frequency of purchases but also the size of each transaction. Here is where your computer system can really help. It's your best tool for developing a detailed profile of each customer's purchasing activity. You can draw conclusions about your clientele, which will be helpful in developing one-on-one services as well as in merchandising.

Customer Relationship Management

Customer relationship management (CRM) is about building old-fashioned relationships using today's technology. CRM is shifting the business from being merchandise-oriented to being customer-centric. It changes your buying process from decision-making based on historic results to looking at your best customers and understanding what they buy and why they buy it. CRM involves integrating marketing, sales, service, and other functional areas that affect your relationship with people. Instead of individual departments and salespeople keeping customer information to themselves, it is pooled in a common location.

CRM is growing in popularity because this integrated approach helps retailers discover what motivates shoppers and what items they're inclined to buy. This information can help you determine which shoppers are the most profitable, which are truly loyal, and which require additional attention.

Laying the groundwork for CRM begins by capturing data and using technology to access and massage the information. Basic information such as sales figures and customer names and addresses has value, but CRM takes your relationship with customers to a higher level. Whether the customer is a saver or a spender, how many children are at home, and where else he or she likes to shop are the nuances of the customer's character that lie at the heart of CRM. The more you know about your customers, the more personalized your service can be.

To accomplish the goal of personalized service, you need to apply the knowledge you have at various customer touch points—in-store visits, telephone calls, customer service, direct mail pieces, catalogs, your Web site, billings, off-site events, faxes—to generate repeated positive experiences.

It is much easier and less costly to set up an information-gathering and analysis system from day one than to try to do it later. Building positive experiences has to be imbedded in your company's culture. Whether you use one of the 500-some CRM software packages on the market or a simpler contact management system, ensure that your operating procedures track customer value and profitability, identify risky and unprofitable customer groups, profile lost customers, and measure customer satisfaction.

Listen to the Right Customers

You cannot be all things to all people. Your programs and processes need to be designed with the paying customer in mind. This person is not always the most vocal. Combine high technology with the personal touch, and you'll get a more accurate picture of what customers are willing to pay you for.

Listen to the customer who receives value from your goods and services, who generates demand and a market for your business. Go beyond analyzing current customers and identify noncustomers who are members of market segments you want to capture. Technology makes it possible to do this. By taking a look at the characteristics of a profitable segment and seeing if another customer segment shares characteristics with this desirable group, you can identify potentially high-profit customers within your base.

In some cases, the cost of meeting a customer group's needs is too high. Sometimes the answer to a low-profit segment is to stop attracting that group by deleting the group from your mailing list, wording your advertisements differently, or advertising your promotions in narrowly targeted publications or locations.

You may also want to vary the level of service provided to different customer groups based on their profitability. One way to do that is to provide consistent level of service to everyone, but vary the fees for that service based on the profitability of the customer. One example is home delivery. You could offer free home delivery based on order frequency or amount of goods ordered; customers who order infrequently or little merchandise could pay a nominal fee for delivery.

> **The more you know about your customers, the more personalized your service can be.**

Another approach is to provide extraordinary service only to the most desirable customers. Low-value customers get only their basic must-have needs met while high-value customers get high-value services to attract, delight, and retain them. Frequent shoppers may collect points that entitle them to special events, limited offerings, or other benefits.

Promise Only What You Can Deliver

Your customers' expectations are often based on their experiences with other retailers, both brick-and-mortar and e-tailers. You must maintain a balance between what customers value and what you can actually deliver. That's a tall order. Exceeding those expectations is how the most successful retailers manage loyalty and attract a greater share of the market.

The approach you take depends on where you are and what you need to do. If your strategy is to be the low-cost provider and you want to compete on the basis of price as a commodity vendor, you may only need to meet minimum expectations. On the other hand, if you want to distinguish yourself as a high-service, premium provider, you will want to exceed expectations. Either way, you need to find out what expectations your customers have.

"Never promise more than you can deliver," warns Newport Beach, California, pet bakery owner Stephanie B. "It sounds stupid, but the only negative experiences I have had are from saying 'X' and being unable to deliver for whatever reason."

You must align your service promises with your ability to deliver. For example, if you promise zero defects in the rooms you rent at your bed-and-breakfast, guests will expect you to deliver. That means you must set in place processes that guarantee there will be functioning televisions, clean bathrooms, and working air-conditioning before a guest checks in. Providing zero defects is the minimum expectation.

Loyalty and Retailing

In a recent Retail Advertising & Marketing Association survey, 46 percent of respondents said that discounts and savings influenced their purchasing decisions. Recognition and preferential treatment have almost twice the influence for customers when they shop stores other than grocery stores. Affluence affects participation in loyalty programs, as consumers with incomes of $75,000 or higher are more likely to participate and belong to multiple programs. It is estimated that more than 51 million people in the U.S. and Canada are enrolled in programs that give points for purchases.

Getting to Know You

Here are six quick and easy ways to find out what your customers are thinking, saying, and doing:

1. Ask front-line personnel (customer service representatives, cashiers, and salespeople) what shoppers are saying.
2. Use customer satisfaction surveys with lots of blank spaces for write-in comments.
3. Interview customers who have recently given their business to another company.
4. Interview recently lost prospects. Why did they not buy what you have to offer?
5. Use customer focus groups.
6. Read newspaper, magazine, and industry reports.

▲

You can use frequency marketing to identify, maintain, and increase the dollars spent by your best customers. If you identify those customers and methodically cultivate their loyalty, they'll give you their business repeatedly and refer others to you. Industry studies indicate that loyalty programs are growing at about 11 percent a year, with approximately 16 percent of shoppers surveyed saying benefits from the programs cause them to use one store exclusively. Ninety percent of retailers surveyed believe customers in their programs buy more.

Services Customers Value

"Service, service, service are the keys to success," says Thomasville, Georgia, clothing retailer Jim D. "That means putting the needs and desires of the customer ahead of all else." He and his wife and business partner, Mary, use the Nordstrom department store model in their small town in the south. They're counting on that approach to grow their business. "We have chosen a niche market—fancy women and children's clothing—and aim each day to make it the destination of first choice when people think of those items," says Jim. "To overcome the department stores, which are our primary competition, we price aggressively and make each customer as satisfied as possible."

Seattle art gallery owner Darrell T. says service makes one business stand out from another. "When we branch out into our second chosen location at another mall, we'll be going after the same people as the other [art] dealers, so it makes it even more important for us to be able to offer a few extras," he says.

What's In It for Me?

According to the Daily News Record, a men's fashion and retail magazine, the most popular customer services retail businesses can offer their clients to build a loyal following are:

○ All-the-time discounts	75%
○ Rewards that are easy to obtain	66%
○ Points in loyalty programs	39%
○ Private sales	39%
○ Recognition	33%
○ Special services	29%

"We are customer service-oriented. We do free home delivery. We'll actually hang the images on the wall for the customer to take a look at them. And we offer something most galleries don't—free lifetime frame-changing. Four years from now, if a customer decides to change décor and there's another frame in the gallery that works, [he or she] can exchange it as long as their frame's in good shape."

> **Smart Tip** ... Tip...
>
> Customer service is more than personal selling. It is opening on time, making sure merchandise is easily accessible, having enough baskets and carts at the entrance, clearly labeling shelves and aisles, adequate staffing, and checking shoppers out quickly and efficiently.

How to Provide Exceptional Customer Service

It's fairly easy to get people to visit your store once. In Chapter 12, you learned a number of ways to attract consumers. This chapter focuses on how to keep their business. Exceptional customer service is what it takes to get them to come back again and again. Meeting this standard begins with friendly service. It is the most effective promotion your business will ever have. For some customers, you'll need to be a knowledgeable source of information. For others, you'll be a sounding board. Whatever your role, you'll want to be caring, concerned, reliable, and trustworthy.

A Warm Welcome

Customers will frequent your business if you make them feel important. Pet bakery owner Stephanie B. in Newport Beach, California, says it's simple: Just greet visitors warmly, maintain a courteous attitude, thank them for coming in, and invite them back soon. Audio retailer Jim O. in Thomasville, Georgia, and Dadeville, Alabama, grocer Jeff P.'s employees answer the phones promptly and sound happy to hear from callers. Callers aren't put on hold at Jim and Mary D.'s Thomasville, Georgia, clothing store.

These retailers all suggest training your salespeople in the art of conversation and attentiveness. You want your employees to be able to answer questions about how to use or maintain a product, where it comes from, different things a customer can do with it, and what the warranty says. People with a positive attitude and the authority to do what is necessary to make the customer happy will help increase your sales.

Attentiveness

Look at customers when they enter your store and say hello, asking them if you can help them find something in particular. This will tell you what mission they are on. If they're "just browsing," smile and let them know you are there to answer any questions and continue your work. Since a lot of people like self-service, don't hover and interfere with the customer's shopping. Give him or her space and some time, and then approach them again to begin a conversation by making a comment on the merchandise they're handling or pointing out something interesting about the store.

Creature Comforts

Comfort is a service you can easily offer. Retail analysts have discovered that, with attention to a few important details, the dressing room area can be an effective closing tool. To encourage sales, make sure that the place where customers try on clothes has adjustable, flattering lighting and ample room to turn around in and to park a stroller. Remember that most consumers shop in pairs, so don't forget the companion. Have a chair or place for the adult or child to sit. When people have a chance to try something on and do not feel rushed, they are more inclined to buy, whether you're selling jewelry, makeup, shoes, or clothing.

> ## Smart Tip
> Tip...
>
> Think of customers as your guests. You want to make their time in your store as relaxing and enjoyable as possible. Studies show that the longer customers are in your store, the more they buy—provided that they have a basket or cart and a helpful salesperson ready to ring up purchases.

While children may not be your target audience, your prime customers with children appreciate the courtesies you provide for them. With the growth of single-parent and dual-earner, two-parent families, adults taking their children shopping is a frequent occurrence, so you'll want to address these people's needs. Have a kids' corner with some children's books and safe toys, maybe a VCR playing children's videos, or a storyteller at scheduled times. Many restaurants give crayons and coloring pages to little guests and then hang up the completed artwork by the cash register.

Waiting for a meal or in line is annoying for adults, but it's worse for children. When children go "ballistic" while shopping, they often take everyone on the launch pad with them, including other customers in line. Clever retailers have displays, balloons, puzzles, word games, coloring tools, activities, or toys available to distract, entertain, and calm the wee ones so the adults can finish their shopping in relative peace.

Warm, Fuzzy Policies

In a customer-friendly store, shoppers can pay by cash, check, credit card, or debit card. The store's Web site provides information and ordering opportunities to extend store hours to accommodate a shopper's schedule. The store is open at least one night a week, and hours are extended during busy holiday seasons. The dressing rooms and bathroom are clean, the store is well-lit, and the signage is readable and helpful. Free gift-wrapping service is offered for items that cost more than $5. Shoppers can take their clothing purchases home on hangers. Gift certificates are presented in a box with a bow, and boxes are available for presents customers want to wrap themselves. Customers are kept informed about the status of their special orders, and rain checks are honored within 30 days. Items are held 24 hours for customers making up their minds about a purchase, and a layaway plan is available. All these policies and services will make customers want to buy from you.

High Value-to-Price Ratio

Employees at a durable-goods store need to provide a higher level of customer service than those at a convenience store. Computers, furniture, carpeting, cars, snowmobiles, and other infrequent purchases are carefully considered and researched by shoppers before they buy. The decision to buy from you will be heavily influenced by delivery and installation capabilities, warranty periods and conditions, credit options, training, and after-sales service. As a rule of thumb, the higher the price to be paid by customers, the more they will want to confirm that they are getting the best value for their investment.

> Employees at a durable-goods store need to provide a higher level of customer service than those at a convenience store.

Personalized Shopping

Mary D. adds value by personalizing the shopping experience for her clothing customers. She asks a lot of questions about the occasion and what the shopper wants. She listens to their hopes and concerns and then suggests the colors, style, and materials she thinks will make the customer feel beautiful and confident. She takes the time to find out how the customer wants to feel rather than trying to sell her a dress.

Saks Fifth Avenue, Nordstrom, and Neiman Marcus have formalized the approach to personalized service into personal shoppers. Independent stores can develop their own models. Invite your customers to sign up for this free service. Place ads, put signs in your store, and/or send a mailing to let people know that you can help them select personal or corporate gifts, furnish a new apartment, or pull together wardrobes for special occasions (a cruise or a honeymoon, for example). Invite an image consultant or savvy traveler to kick off the program with a demonstration of accessorizing a desk or wardrobe, or showing people how to pack. Have special business cards for employees skilled in personal shopping who will develop this special clientele.

Delivery

Florists, dry cleaners, large appliance dealers, pizza outlets, and furniture retailers are usually expected to offer delivery services. However, in these time-scarce times, customers now expect home delivery of groceries, pharmaceuticals, videos—the list goes on. You can provide this customer service in many ways.

If you intend to buy a delivery vehicle, be sure that your truck or van is attractive and clean and advertises your business name, address, telephone number, and Web address. Delivery personnel should be neatly dressed (perhaps even wear uniforms), have good driving records, and be trained in customer service. Employees need to know what to do if they are late making a delivery, the customer isn't home, or the customer refuses to accept the order. There is more to "service" than dropping off something on your way home. If you're going to offer delivery, do it right.

> **There is more to "service" than dropping off something on your way home. If you're going to offer delivery, do it right.**

If your budget won't allow for buying commercial vehicles, you might use a local courier or taxi service. Or consider cooperating with a noncompeting store to share the cost of deliveries. Many retailers use United Parcel Service or an overnight carrier. Montpelier, Vermont, music store owner Fred W. says his customers are really happy with his ability to deliver a special order within 48 hours, thanks to FedEx.

Gift Registry

Gift registries are increasingly popular customer service programs, and they are no longer just for brides. With today's gift registries, presents for any occasion can be bought off a gift registry in stores or online. Grandparents in particular appreciate guidance in selecting toys for children and gifts for hard-to-please teenagers.

Some retailers still use the traditional approach of walking people through their

---

Bright Idea

For gift items, prepare two receipts—one regular receipt for the customer and a second gift receipt with the date of purchase and coded price. Retailers also suggest putting a coded sticker on the inside of the gift box to make returns easy for everyone.

store and writing down the brand, make, model, size, color, or other description of the desired items. Other merchants have printed lists to work from. Some do telephone consultations and have toll-free phone and fax numbers, while others use a printed or faxed catalog. The Internet marries high technology and old-fashioned TLC with global online access and 24-hour ordering and shipping opportunities. Some other gift registry ideas include putting together a network of stores that offer a range of gift items, including travel packages, charitable donations, and escrow account deposits.

Gift Certificates

Another popular customer service is gift certificates. The retailers we interviewed for this book all agreed that no store should be without them. They are an effective way to solve your customers' gift-giving dilemmas, and they bring new customers into your store or to your Web site. Many certificates are never redeemed, or recipients buy additional merchandise above the gift amount, making the certificates very profitable for retailers. Certificates help customers find "the perfect gift" so people can get exactly what they want.

Retailers advise you to number each gift certificate for tracking purposes. A sample gift certificate can be found below. To make your gift certificate extra special, have an artist create a unique design for your store, print it on card stock, and present it in a box or an elegant envelope.

Gift Certificate

Susie's Fashions
1234 Style Parkway
Peoria, IL 12345
(012) 345-6789
www.susiesfashions.com

To:_____

From:_____

Gift certificate value: $_____

Message:_____

_____

_____

Authorization No.:_____

▲

How to Handle Unhappy Customers

What happens if you don't concentrate on customer service? Research shows that people who have received poor customer service tell an average of 10 others about their bad experience, and 10 percent of those told tell 20 other people. Unfortunately, good news does not travel as fast as bad news. Fewer people pass on the good news when they have been treated exceptionally well.

The poor handling of complaints can damage your reputation very quickly. Take everyone seriously, but look at them objectively. What can you learn about your market and your operation? Separate complaints into those about products and their performance and those about customer service. Complaints about products can alert you to vendor problems, advertising glitches, faulty delivery, or quality control problems. Do you have signs up that say, "One-hour photo processing," but rarely deliver in less than three? Are you getting frequent complaints about customers receiving incorrect change? Complaints about customer service should stimulate better training, hiring, and review practices.

Nearly every business encounters difficult customers. How these people are handled can make a big difference in the success or failure of a business. Remember that it takes months to gain a new customer but only seconds to lose one.

Listen and empathize, ask questions, and resolve the problem. Keep in mind that there is always room for improving your relationship with your customers. Always acknowledge the customer's concerns and clearly state how they will be addressed.

Sometimes you'll make mistakes, and at other times you'll encounter someone you can't please despite your best efforts. To resolve a problem, the most effective method is merely to ask the customer what you can do to make things "right." Surprisingly often, many don't want anything other than an apology or a sincere promise to do better next time.

Handling Returns

When a customer wants to return a purchase, you have the opportunity to demonstrate your commitment to customer satisfaction. Listen to the reason for the return, have a clearly defined policy, and then calmly and pleasantly tell your customer what you can (and in some circumstances, cannot) do for him or her. All three components of dealing with a potentially difficult situation must be present to build trust: Listen, stay calm, and be pleasant. You want your customer to feel confident that you treated him or her fairly and professionally.

Apologize to your customer and take back any defective merchandise sold in your store. Offer store credit when confronted with a questionable return. You'll find the majority of your customers will be honest. Tagging merchandise and the box with a store ID can help reduce incidents of people trying to return something to you that they didn't buy in your store.

For some clearance sales and second-quality merchandise, you may want to have a no-returns policy. For items you do accept returns of, it is customary to give the customer who purchased with a credit card either a credit card credit, a store credit slip (see below), or a merchandise exchange. For purchases of more than $100, pay refunds by check. Some stores have a no-exceptions policy requiring a receipt for large purchases.

You will encounter your share of people who will show up with an unfounded complaint or request for a refund or exchange when it is obvious the item has been used or worn. The retailers we interviewed expressed different ways of handling these inevitable situations.

If you get strong support from your suppliers and are confident that you can send the merchandise back to the source for full credit, you might feel comfortable having a "no questions asked" policy on refunds and exchanges. Small retailers usually aren't able to get that kind of cooperation from suppliers, particularly when they're new and haven't established their value to distributors and manufacturers. Your return policy should reflect the support available to you from your suppliers. Their warranties, service, and return policies are a significant part of how you serve your customers.

Store Credit Slip

Customer name: _____

Address: _____

City: _____ State: _____ ZIP: _____

Home phone: _____ Work phone: _____

Date of return: _____

Merchandise description: _____

Amount: _____

Received by: _____

Total credit: _____

Please note that store credits are valid for 12 months.

You should have a clearly stated policy posted by your checkout stand(s) and printed on the back of your receipts. This will help avoid customer dissatisfaction with the way you do business. Ten to 30-day returns with receipts are standard policies. If you sell or repair any kind of equipment, you may want to set up a loaner program while the customer's computer or fax machine is being repaired in your shop.

Over time, you're bound to encounter some customers who intend to bully you into accepting an obviously mistreated, old, or worn item. Don't give the stage to dissatisfied customers intent on making a scene. Take them aside and listen politely to their complaint. Then address the facts, offer to do what you feel is fair (or whatever you are authorized to do), and be done with it. You can't please all the people all the time.

In all return situations, retailers say it's important to treat everyone with respect. Some customers you'll like, others you'll tolerate, and in rare circumstances, you will refuse to do business with someone.

The Internet
Raises Consumer Expectations

The Internet gives consumers the power of information immediacy, so they now have greater control over what they buy, what they pay, and from whom they purchase. Customers can shop in many ways—through catalogs, stores, or Web sites, or all three in the same day. For a retailer to become and remain customer-centered requires constant vigilance. You must continually monitor changing customer and market perceptions.

The pressure for your company to stay in touch with potential customers will only increase as more and more consumers get used to doing business on the Internet. In light of these realities, you have no choice but to hone your ability to understand customer needs. If you apply the lessons you learn to your daily business, you can be the leader who sets the standard others will have to meet.

The Customer Is Always Right

Fierce competition means that many of the products you offer will be of comparable quality, price, and value as the products of other local and online retailers. Therefore, the attention you give to the planning and delivery of consistently good levels of customer service will determine your level of success and profitability.

Customers are the final arbiters of your fate. Retailers who are successful over the long run are those that meet the true wants and needs of their customers. You have to deliver this message to every one of your new employees.

Unfortunately, many small retailers refuse to accept the premise that the customer is always right. We all know that the customer is not always right. However, if you want them patronize your business, you need to treat them as if they are. This begins with you instilling in your employees a real concern for the customer. Get employees to consider how they can go the extra mile for their customers. These are the most effective ways of developing loyal customers. Consumers quickly recognize businesses that have well-trained employees who work together as a team, and they reward those businesses by spending money in those stores and referring others to them.

Fun Fact

Stu Leonard, the hugely successful dairy/grocery in Connecticut, has two basic laws of customer treatment set in stone in the front of its stores. Rule one is, "The customer is always right." Rule two is, "When you think the customer is wrong, refer back to rule one."

Risk
Management

Your business operates every day with the possibility of damage, injury, or loss. Small businesses are generally less able than big businesses to absorb the expenses incurred from risk, so it's important that you understand the kinds of challenges you might encounter in your new business. Initially, there is the threat of disputes with partners, investors, landlords, and employees, and accumulation of debt. Add to that heightened competition, merchandise shortages, theft, fines, bad debt, collection problems, and being underinsured.

Today's retailers must learn to anticipate legal and or consumer action. Government agencies are ready to take action if you don't conform to the laws, and customers can turn to consumer groups or the media—or seek legal remedies—if they believe they have been mistreated. Therefore, you must be alert and sensitive to the perceptions and implications of your operation. All those concerned with retailing activities must be aware of federal, state, and local regulations concerning business activities. As with all legal matters, consulting a licensed attorney is advisable.

The Law

You may already be aware of a few basic rules governing retail trade. For example, you are not allowed to ship merchandise that has not been ordered to the consumer, and consumers are likewise not required to pay for items they do not order. Advertising out-of-stock items is forbidden. Retailers must have enough of the advertised item to meet a normal level of demand. Retailers selling items by mail must disclose how long it will take to deliver the items to the consumer. If you cannot deliver the merchandise by the stated time, the buyer can cancel the order. There are a few more regulations you should be familiar with in operating your business.

The Sherman Antitrust Act (1890), the Clayton Act (1914), and the Robinson-Patman Act (1936) were all designed to prevent businesses from engaging in activities that could injure the public or competition. Courts have ruled that retailers cannot pressure manufacturers to refuse to sell to competitors, acquire other firms if the intent is to lessen competition, or conspire to fix prices. Under the Robinson-Patman Act, retailers and manufacturers may face discrimination lawsuits if they charge different prices to different people on unequal terms.

The Federal Trade Commission (FTC) is an independent administrative agency that determines what business methods, acts, and practices are deceptive or unfair. Most cases brought against businesses by the FTC deal with deceptive advertising and mislabeling of retail products. The agency requires door-to-door sellers to identify themselves as salespeople before entering a person's home, and to allow three days for the customer to decide if they want to cancel an order.

Retailers are sensitive and vulnerable to charges of discrimination of many kinds. Bias because of race, color, creed, sex, national origin, and sometimes age is expressly forbidden by the Civil Rights Act of 1964.

When your business reaches a yearly gross business volume of $500,000, you are subject to the National Labor Relations Act of 1935. Under this law, employees have the right to organize and bargain collectively through a representative of their own choosing without interference from the retailer. The act also states that no employee and no one seeking employment shall be required as a condition of employment to join any company union or to refrain from joining, organizing, or assisting a labor organization of his or her own choosing.

There are several laws that affect your consumer credit policies and practices: the Consumer Credit Protection Act (Truth in Lending), Fair Credit Reporting Act, Fair Credit Billing Act, Equal Credit Opportunity Act, Consumer Leasing Act, and Fair Debt Collection Practices Act.

Insurance

Retailers have diverse needs that go beyond the average small business. Use the "Insurance Coverage Checklist" on page 208 to make sure you have sufficient insurance. Since you can never afford to insure your business 100 percent against all hazards, it's a good idea to think in terms of the two major categories of risk you face: those over which you have little or not control, and those you can control to some degree. Extended coverage covers the property against any direct loss or damage due to such things as explosions, riots, windstorms, hail, aircraft, vehicles, and smoke. Glass insurance protects against replacement of plate-glass windows accidentally or maliciously broken. Vandalism and malicious mischief insurance protects against losses caused by either of these possibilities. Sprinkler insurance covers against leakage, freezing, or breakage of sprinkler installations. Both building and contents should be insured. With the recent floods, hurricanes, and earthquakes many areas of the country have been experiencing, the added expense may be worth it. There is even coverage for rock throwing at windows or exterior signs.

Your business is liable for injuries to customers, employees, and others with whom you do business, either on or off your premises. A comprehensive general liability policy can include liability coverage for defects in merchandise that your business has sold, food poisoning from your restaurant, or bodily injury and property damage caused by an accident in the garage or on the parking lot of your business.

There are many types of crime insurance policies. Fidelity bonds insure against losses due to theft or other misappropriations of cash, inventory, or other business property by employees. Money and securities insurance covers losses that occur away from your firm's premises—for example, a robbery of daily receipts being transported to the bank.

> **Tip...**
>
> ## Smart Tip
>
> Don't skimp on disability insurance. According to the National Association of Insurance and Financial Advisors in Falls Church, Virginia, if you're between the ages of 35 and 65, your chances of becoming disabled are greater than your chances of dying.

▲

Robbery insurance covers loss of goods stolen where there is an assault or threat of an assault, as in a holdup. As you might expect, burglary insurance covers the loss of inventory, money, or equipment due to a break-in at your store. Losses of inventory, money, or equipment due to theft or shoplifting by employees, customers and others can be covered. Surety bonds protect you from losses caused by the failure of others to produce on schedule. If your contractor does not complete your ski outlet on time for the snow season, you may recover your losses from the insurance company.

While insurance against burglary and robbery is available, there are so many restrictions and the cost is so great that most retailers do without it. This usually means that the result of merchandise losses due to such thefts must be passed on to the consumer in the form of higher prices. Higher prices put you at a competitive disadvantage, so see what you can do about safeguarding your store against pilferage. Many retailers buy sophisticated alarm systems, many of which are connected directly to police stations. Solid building construction, metal grids over windows, good outside lighting and strong locks are also helpful in preventing burglary.

A standard fire insurance policy pays you only for losses directly due to fire. Business interruption insurance can reimburse you for loss of earnings that occur until normal business resumes. Things such as payroll costs for key employees, interest

---

Insurance Coverage Checklist

Discuss your options for insurance coverage with an insurance agent who is familiar with your type of retail business. Check the boxes for the coverage you must have now to start up, "X" those you can get later when you have more money, and "O" the type(s) you don't need or that don't apply to your operation.

❏ Automobile	❏ Health
❏ Boiler and machinery	❏ Inventory
❏ Business interruption	❏ Key-person
❏ Business life	❏ Liability
❏ Crime	❏ Power plant
❏ Disability	❏ Property
❏ Earthquake	❏ Sprinkler
❏ Fidelity bonds	❏ Tradesmen's liability
❏ Fire	❏ Unemployment
❏ Flood	❏ Vandalism
❏ General liability	❏ Water damage
❏ Glass	❏ Workers' compensation

expense on a mortgage or rent, and other ongoing expenses can be covered for a specific period of time.

Consult with your insurance agent and get competitive bids for the insurance package that best suits your financial and business situation.

Product-Related Issues

Let's take a look at the goods you're selling. There are the risks associated with the conditions under which they're made, and there are those associated with how they're sold, shipped, handled, used, and presented.

Pricing

Make sure you price your goods honestly and fairly and avoid being guilty of deceptive pricing. There is nothing illegal about trading a customer up to a better quality item when they shop with you, but it is illegal to advertise an item that is not available in the store and to try to sell the customer a higher-priced item instead of the cheaper one promised: For example, if you advertise an AM radio for $19.95 (perhaps as a loss leader) in the hope that customers can be persuaded to purchase an AM/FM boom box at a much higher price. You will be subject to prosecution if you don't have the AM radio to sell to the customer who wants it.

Price comparisons must be honest and legal. If you feature an item in a promotional display at $8.99 claiming that it regularly sold at $14.99, you must have sold the identical merchandise at the $14.99 price in the past. Likewise, you cannot mix scarves bought at a special purchase price of $3.95 with $9.95 scarves that regularly sold at $19.95 and are on sale for $12.95. Avoid false comparisons.

Many merchants have "half price," "buy one item and get another for one cent," and "two for one" sales. Most are honest representations. Be aware that inflating the price a few weeks before the sale in anticipation of the specials to be offered later is illegal.

Another practice that could get you unwanted attention is nonuniform pricing. Consumer groups are pushing for unit pricing—computing and showing the price per ounce or other standard unit—in addition to the total price to permit easier price comparisons. Pricing that varies from packages in different sizes and brand to brand irritates consumers.

Product Safety Information

Retailers should provide customers with adequate product safety information. If you fail to give adequate warning of possible injury that may result from the use of the product, you can be charged with negligence. The Consumer Product Safety Commission (CPSC) has the authority to take legal action against both the retailer and manufacturer who are found to be in violation of the Consumer Product Safety Act (CPSA) of 1972. The CPSC keeps close watch over products that have high frequencies of injury, such as bicycles, football helmets, power lawn mowers, space heaters, personal watercraft, spas, baby cribs, and swimming pools. Product liability insurance can protect you against injury suits. Stores that sell potentially hazardous goods such as recreational equipment and items for children are usually willing to pay the high premiums for this type of insurance.

The Consumer Product Safety Act requires retailers to report a product that they believe fails to comply with a voluntary standard or creates an unreasonable risk of serious injury or death. Call the Consumer Product Safety Commission at (202) 442-9139 or contact the consumer protection agency in your state, which can be located in the government listings of your telephone book or online at www.cpsc.gov.

False Claims

A salesperson's verbal promise that a product will perform in a certain way is an express warranty and will often hold up in court if your customer files a lawsuit. Typical selling statements like, "These tires should last as long as you own the car," and, "Your daughter will probably outgrow these shoes before they wear out," are considered sales talk. However, if a retailer claims that a suit "will not wear out for two years," the customer may have legal grounds for compensation if the suit wears out sooner.

The best way to reduce product-related risk to your business is to inspect or test the merchandise you sell. Make sure that the claims made and promotional materials you give out are truthful. The retailers we interviewed for this book were quick to say that they only sell goods that come with adequate instruction booklets and labels. Read the fine-print terms in purchase orders and sales contracts for boilerplate disclaimers or indemnities, cautions a California store owner.

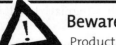

Beware!

Product tampering, whether by employees or others, is damaging to brand images, consumer confidence and profits. Keep your eyes open for containers that look different from the same kind, wrapping or safety tabs that have been repositioned, nonuniform contents in a container, signs of tampering at the top or bottom of a tube, or unusual sediment or liquid around a product.

Packaging and Labeling

The Food and Drug Administration has established rules concerning labeling requirements and health claims for foods and nonprescription drugs. Small businesses can be dragged into product liability lawsuits when the goods they sell, service, manufacture, or lease cause injury to someone. Failure to provide adequate warning labels and instructions as well as design or manufacture flaws can have harsh financial consequences.

Warranties

The Federal Trade Commission's Rule on Pre-Sale Availability of Written Warranty Terms requires that manufacturers provide retailers of their products with the warranty materials they will need to meet FTC requirements. They can do this by providing you with copies of the warranty to be placed in a binder; providing warranty stickers, tags, signs, or posters; or printing the warranty on the product's packaging. As long as manufacturers provide you with the warranty materials needed to comply with the rule, manufacturers cannot be held legally responsible if the retailer fails to make warranties available.

You are required to make available the written warranties to consumers before they buy consumer products costing more than $15. You must do this with all written warranties of the products you sell—warranties from manufacturers as well as any written warranties you extend. You can do this by displaying warranties in close proximity to the warranted products or by furnishing them prior to sale and posting prominent signs to let customers know that warranties can be examined upon request. One appliance retailer, for example,

> **Tip...**
>
> **Smart Tip**
> A guide to the legal and business requirements of buyers is available through the National Retail Federation (www.nrf.com; (800) NRF-HOW2), or you can order The Management of Retail Buying by Cash, Friedlander, and Wingate at www.amazon.com.

suggests posting a refrigerator warranty on the front of the appliance. A retailer of small products, such as watches or tape recorders, might keep warranties indexed in a binder behind the counter or in the department.

Mail order companies who accept orders for warranted consumer products through the mail or by telephone must include either the warranty or a statement on how consumers can get a copy of the warranty in their catalogs or other advertising. This information should be near the product description or clearly noted on a separate page.

Door-to-door retailers must offer the customer copies of written warranties before the sale is completed. For more detailed information, go to www.ftc.gov and read the requirements for making warranties available prior to sale.

Sales Contracts

Have your attorney review all sales contracts before you have them printed. You must specify all the terms of agreement—price, quantity, method of delivery, time of arrival, time of payment, buyer inspection, and seller protection. There are many controlling laws and regulations regarding agents of a company and that company's liability for any laws violated by your buyer's actions.

▲

Transfer of Title

It's important for you to know at what point the title of goods shipped to you is transferred because the owner of the merchandise is responsible for loss or damage before and during transport. F.O.B. (free on board) is the most common shipping term to describe transfer of title. When merchandise is shipped to you "F.O.B. destination," the seller pays the freight and other charges—including damages—until the goods reach the F.O.B. point (your store). You're responsible for getting the merchandise to your place of business.

Customer-Related Issues

There are two sides to every customer: profitability and liability. You can't live without them, but sometimes you can't work with them. Accidents and mistakes happen, and regrettably so do problem customers. The majority of complaints can be solved amicably. For others, the customer is not worth keeping. To keep the peace and your piece of the action, be forewarned that there are risks involved in dealing with John Q. Public.

Physical Safety

When you invite customers into your place of business, you are to some extent responsible for their safety on your premises. You can be found negligent if you don't maintain your business or you fail to correct a situation that could lead to injury. An icy walkway, loose step, or wet floor could cause a customer to slip and fall. As this injury could have been prevented by removing the ice, fixing the step, or mopping up the floor, the store could be found negligent if a suit is filed. Performing an audit of potential risks can help you minimize the number of incidents as well as the amount of money you'll have to pay out to remedy problems. Here are four things you can do to identify potential risks:

1. Evaluate your liability risks from your customers' point of view by walking through your business, from curb to alley, noting various sources of possible danger:
   - Are the front of the store and sidewalk well-maintained?
   - Is the parking lot uneven or poorly marked?
   - Do the entry and exit doors open easily?
   - Do the aisles, restrooms, and access meet Americans with Disabilities Act (ADA) standards?
   - Are the aisles wide enough for easy passage?
   - Do lights shine in customers' eyes?
   - Are the edges of counters and displays safe?

2. If you provide a service at a customer's home, evaluate your liability risks.

3. Walk through the store and look at things from an employee or delivery person's point of view:

  • Where are the cleaning materials stored?

  • What kinds of protective gear or procedures do you have for cleaning, repairing or packing the store and inventory?

  • Are all the tools and equipment in good working order?

  • Are the loading dock, storage units and utilities safe?

4. Go over your list of risks with your insurance agent to decide the best and most economical method of handling the risk of loss and protecting your business.

Customer Property Loss

To ensure the protection of a customer's personal property, advise them not to leave their briefcases, purses, cellular phones, and jackets unattended while shopping. Some stores have cubicles or coat racks near the checkout stands for customer convenience. Check with your insurance agent to see if an insurance rider is necessary and what security you are required to provide. Train your employees to keep a close eye on what customers arrive and leave with, and to report any irregularities or claims for lost items to you immediately.

Handling Bad Checks

Handling bad checks is a necessary evil for retailers. There are two ways you can combat this expensive aggravation: Have a rigorous policy on accepting checks that requires at least two pieces of identification, and use a check verification service such as TeleCheck (www. telecheck.com) or XpressCheX (www.xpress chex.com). These services electronically read the account data encoded on the check and reject any check reported lost or stolen, or from an account that has had overdraft problems. In most states, retailers can recover merchandise from customers who have paid with a bad check, but not always. Remember that not all bounced checks are criminal acts; some are honest mistakes, so use discretion and diplomacy to tell the difference.

Smart Tip

If you used a business lawyer to help you set up your business, he or she can advise you about risk management. However, if you need someone to represent you in claims brought against you or lawsuits you initiate, check with your local chamber of commerce or the state bar association to provide you with information about the reputation, expertise, and fees of attorneys in your area.

▲

Counterfeit Money and Merchandise

With the high quality of graphics programs and printers these days, counterfeit money is not always easy to spot. Add to this the uncertainty and confusion many people feel about the new U.S. currency, and you will be relieved to know that your bank can give you an instruction sheet on how to identify a counterfeit bill. You can also buy pens to test the authenticity of cash received. These are available at most office supply stores.

Counterfeiting merchandise is a $250 billion industry. Work only with established suppliers and ask your manufacturer's representative for ways to authenticate merchandise. The fraud unit of your local law enforcement agency can give you a briefing on counterfeit money and merchandise.

Extending Credit

It is not uncommon for retailers to extend credit to customers on expensive purchases such as furniture and major appliances. Often this financing is given simply on the credit worthiness of the buyer, but in other instances the seller or lender demands that the purchaser's promise to pay be backed with some security.

Before you offer financing to your customers, there are a few basic things you should know. Usually, the retailer asks for a conditional sales contract on the merchandise purchased, or a legal hold on the merchandise until full payment is made. If a customer fails to pay on an unsecured debt, you can collect the money owed only by suing. If he fails to pay on a secured debt, the retailer may repossess the security and sell it, or keep it, in full satisfaction of the debt.

The Truth in Lending law (Consumer Protection Act of 1969) requires you to inform customers of the terms and conditions of your credit policies when finance or other charges are assessed. When you let a customer buy a dining room set on an installment plan, you need to advise the buyer of the cash price for the merchandise, the down payment required, the amount of the contract to be financed, the annual percentage rate charged, and the amounts and due dates of payments. You should also know that customers have the right to change their minds (right of rescission) within three days of purchasing a "big ticket" item on an installment plan, and you must void the contract.

Shoplifting

Retail stores report losing $26 billion a year to shoplifting. Approximately 5,400 people are detained for shoplifting every day, according to security management consultant Charles A. Sennewald, founder of the International Association of Professional Security Consultants. You basically have three ways to combat this problem:

1. You can vigilantly watch everyone who comes into your store to make sure they don't steal anything. You can do that by assigning employees zones to protect, hiring security guards, or using video surveillance systems.

2. You can use cable, security bars, and locking racks.

3. You can use electronic article surveillance (EAS) systems that attach special tags onto everything so that an alarm goes off if someone tries to walk out with merchandise without paying. EAS tagging is extremely labor-intensive.

EAS systems are almost an unbeatable anti-shoplifting tool. The systems are useful anywhere there is an opportunity for theft of items of any size. Using EAS devices enables retailers to display popular items on the floor, where the merchandise can be seen, rather than putting items in locked cases or behind the counter. The use of these systems does not completely eliminate shoplifting; however, experts say theft can be reduced by 60 percent or more when a reliable EAS system is used.

There can be large differences in cost of an EAS system, depending on the system, the size of your store, and the amount of merchandise to be protected. Considering that store personnel will have more time to assist shoppers if they're not preoccupied with watching for potential thieves, experts estimate that a reliable EAS system can pay for itself within two years. Today, there is a push for a common industry standard and manufacturer-added EAS source tagging. With source tagging, an inexpensive label is integrated into the product or its packaging by the manufacturer.

Everyone in your business should be involved in controlling shoplifting. This takes training. Your local police or sheriff's department, mall security, or merchants association can help. Stay in touch with them and other retailers to be alert to illegal activities that may be going on in your area and to learn what you can do to avoid becoming a victim.

Here are a few preventative measures you should always take: Employees need to be aware of a customer's presence as soon as they enter your business. Making eye contact with every customer within 25 feet of you lets visitors know you are there. Even when talking to a customer, employees need to remain aware of other customer activity. Know where the vulnerable merchandise is in your store. Frequently raise your eyes from your work and look around. Train your employees to be alert for suspicious customers. Customers carrying open bags or wearing loose-fitting clothing in which merchandise can be easily concealed should be watched. People who

Stat Fact

Merchandise valued between $1 and $50 accounts for more than 66 percent of all merchandise stolen, and merchandise worth more than $100 accounts for more than 16 percent of all thefts, according to the *1997-1998 Retail Theft Trends Report* published by Loss Prevention Specialists Inc. and Sensormatic Electronics Corp.

Beware!

According to National Loss Prevention Associates Inc., a licensed private investigative firm, one out of 10 customers will shoplift from you if given the opportunity. About 15 percent of shoplifters are professionals who steal for profit or lifestyle. If shoplifters get away with it once, they will return for another try.

appear nervous or apprehensive and are spending a long time browsing may be suspect.

Tact must be exercised at all times to avoid improper accusations or embarrassment. If a customer appears to be about to walk off with an item without paying for it, you might say "I can ring that up for you here if you like." When it is obvious that shoplifting is taking place, call security, dial 911, or activate a silent alarm. Do not attempt to apprehend a suspect by yourself.

To control losses from price tag switching, securely fasten all price tags or use tags that shred when tampered with. Double-mark major items with the price on one tag and a price code attached elsewhere. If the two do not match, you will know that the item's price tag has been switched.

The retailers we spoke with feel fortunate not to have had many problems with theft. They say a combination of employee vigilance, store layout, and tagged packaging assists their efforts to minimize loss. Having a buzzer or bell by the door and using mirrors are a couple of the strategies our retailers use.

When designing the layout of your store, try to eliminate blind spots that enable shoplifting. An open layout makes it easier for employees to see what's happening in

Watch Out!

Here are six things you must do before detaining a person for shoplifting:

1. See the person approach the merchandise.
2. See the suspect take possession of the merchandise.
3. See where the person conceals it.
4. Maintain uninterrupted surveillance to ensure that the person doesn't dispose of the merchandise.
5. See the person fail to pay for the merchandise before leaving the store.
6. Approach the person outside the store.

various departments and aisles. Two-way and convex mirrors, closed-circuit TV, video cameras, and other surveillance devices may also deter would-be criminals.

Some stores employ uniformed guards as deterrents to shoplifting and robbery. Others have plainclothes security guards circulating throughout the store. At least one employee should be working in every department at all times, or have a manager circulate throughout the store.

To combat a common shoplifting technique of wearing one garment under another, many clothing stores require customers to use locked dressing rooms and/or check each garment with a designated employee. Employees should clear out the dressing room, look for torn-off tags, and count hangers after each customer leaves.

Bathrooms are another vulnerable area in your store since there are usually no monitoring devices there. Post signs on doors directing customers to leave carts and unpaid-for merchandise outside the bathrooms, and have an employee check the stalls periodically.

Especially valuable or easily concealed merchandise can be displayed in locked cabinets. Some retailers attach leather coats to racks with chains that allow for the garment to be tried on but not removed from the rack. Hand calculators are kept in locked cases; videos, CDs, and DVDs are displayed in visual cases with hand holes so they can be examined but not removed without the assistance of an employee. Oversized, stiff packaging makes items difficult to hide.

Posting signs from law enforcement that your premises are under surveillance and that you will prosecute under the full extent of the law will deter some amateur thieves.

Employee-Related Issues

When you think about staffing your business, give some thought to the legal consequences of how you fill those personnel needs. Areas where you might be vulnerable to lawsuits involve on-the-job injuries, family and medical leave conflicts, pay and privacy disputes, and discrimination charges.

Occupational Safety and Health Administration

If you have employees, you are probably covered by regulations set forth by the Occupation Safety and Health Administration (OSHA). If you are a sole proprietor with no employees, you generally aren't covered, but if you use independent contractors, the law still may cover you. Check with your local OSHA office—(800) 321-OSHA—for a checklist of policies and procedures your business must follow.

▲

If you have fewer than 10 employees, you are exempt from most of the injury- and illness-recording requirements. However, you must report any accident that results in one or more deaths or the hospitalization of three or more employees.

Retailers with any employees, regardless of the size of your business, must display posters that inform employees of their job safety rights. Spanish and English copies of these posters are available by contacting the OSHA office in your area.

Americans with Disabilities Act

The Americans with Disabilities Act (ADA) says that stores, day-care centers, hotels, theaters, pharmacies, and restaurants must have reasonable policies, practices and procedures to avoid discrimination on the basis of disabilities. Be sure you provide an accessible path of travel throughout your business, including bathrooms, dressing rooms, telephones, drinking fountains, activity centers, and checkout stations. Auxiliary aids and services must be provided to individuals with vision or hearing impairments and other individuals with disabilities, unless this would be particularly burdensome to you.

ADA accessibility requirements also apply to Web pages. If you have a Web site, the information on your site must be presented in text format that is compatible with screen-reading devices. (People with visual impairments use these.) You can also provide accessible formats such as Braille, large-print or audiotaped information, or an electronic file on computer disk or an electronic bulletin board.

Employee Theft

It is sad but true: Research indicates that more than 80 percent of all employees steal from their employers. The five main categories of employee theft are:

1. Merchandise
2. Supplies
3. Cash from the register
4. Conspiracy with shoplifters
5. Conspiracy with delivery persons

The incidence of employee theft is higher in retailing than in nonretail operations because employees have greater access to a wide range of consumer goods. The financial impact of employee theft on your business goes beyond the items stolen to the indirect costs of lost productivity, turnover, hiring, and other expenses.

Stat Fact
According to the *1997-1998 Retail Theft Trends Report* published by Loss Prevention Specialists Inc. and Sensormatic Electronics Corp., inventory shrinkage nationwide accounted for almost 2 percent of total retail sales. Employee theft accounted for a record 43 percent of merchandise losses.

Most retailers bond employees who handle large amounts of money. Through fidelity bonds, the retailer is reimbursed for losses up to the amount specified in the policy if an employee takes off with any of the retailer's funds.

One important way to avoid employee theft is to carefully screen all job applicants. When making key hiring decisions, there are eight basic areas to look into before entrusting someone with the keys to your store. These are: an applicant's driving history, criminal record, previous residences, prior employment, educational achievement, character references, credit check, and professional licenses and certificates. Omissions and inconsistencies on job applications should be questioned. References and past employers should be contacted by telephone.

Retailers are also very vulnerable to theft by delivery personnel. Some of these problems are short counts and merchandise removal. Some security procedures you can use to reduce supplier pilferage are:

- Establish a receiving area for all incoming merchandise and restrict access to the area to authorized store personnel only.
- Employ security officers to monitor the store and inspect packages.
- Employ outside security agencies to "shop" your store to detect dishonest employees who may be conspiring with suppliers to remove merchandise under the guise of legitimate transactions.
- Require employees to store their handbags and backpacks in lockers before beginning work, or use clear plastic bags.
- Use video cameras.
- Install mirrors.

Combatting Shrinkage

Shrinkage is the loss of merchandise for unaccountable reasons. Some results from: vendor fraud, employee theft, external theft, clerical mistakes, or bookkeeping errors. Losses can be caused by unrecorded markdowns, unrecorded allowances, unrecorded breakage, and mistakes in pricing or charging the wrong price. To minimize such shortages, take the following measures:

- Catalog merchandise upon arrival at the store.
- Properly mark, price, and identify merchandise before transfer to the selling floor.
- Record all price changes.
- Record each transaction at the computer terminal or cash register.
- Change records before transferring merchandise from one branch store to another.

▲

Shrinkage from all causes has become more and more of a problem. Today, a 2 percent loss in sales volume is considered acceptable in the industry, although many stores experience heavier losses. Shrinkage losses cut deeply into net profit. For example, 2 percent shrinkage for a store doing $5 million in annual sales means an actual loss of $100,000 per year.

Tighten Store Security

Here are six simple things you can do to tighten security in your store:

1. Equip your store or warehouse with a security alarm system hooked up to a central service company.
2. Use locked trash dumpsters to decrease the risk of merchandise being thrown into the dumpster to be retrieved later.
3. Do not permit personnel to park near docks or exit doors. A long walk to stash or transport items can be a deterrent to theft.
4. Strictly enforce inventory-control and tracking procedures.
5. Follow up on all references when hiring any new employee, including relatives and friends of friends.
6. Implement an anonymous tip program that motivates employees to report theft, drug abuse, and other business abuses by co-workers and outsiders.

Emergency Preparedness

Take advantage of the free or low-cost services offered by the Red Cross and your local police and fire departments to train you to cope with natural disasters and accidents. They will show you what to do in case of fire, hurricanes, tornadoes, earthquakes, floods, and lightning. Learn what actions to take and who to call in case someone gets sick in your store or falls on your sidewalk, or a car runs into your store. What will you do if there's a gas leak, power failure, or hazardous waste situation? Find out ahead of time—the things we're talking about here are not for on-the-job-training. You don't want people to panic and cause more problems.

A number of the risks discussed in this chapter can be reduced or controlled by taking precautions and using common sense. Being aware of what could happen—and learning what to do if the unthinkable occurs—can minimize damage to the reputation and operation of your business.

Planning
for the Future

In the next few years, what can you expect to see in retailing that you can capitalize on to grow your business? Let's drag out the crystal ball and see what lies ahead.

▲

The demand for a quality experience, price value, and time savings will continue. You always need to look for ways to improve your retail environment. The retailers we interviewed for this book gave us these seven "must dos":

1. Make sure your store is easy to navigate.
2. Make the merchandise accessible.
3. Have product information readily available.
4. Ensure that sales associates are focused on providing personal assistance.
5. Find and keep good employees.
6. Help customers help themselves in your store.
7. Offer 24/7 shopping convenience online.

Also, don't forget to educate your customers every way possible—through signage, personal selling, videos, Web links, newsletters, and so forth. Give them information about products, fashions, trends, solutions to problems, safety, and usage tips.

Change Is an Everyday Challenge

The life spans of retail stores and retail concepts keep getting shorter and shorter. One of the things being heavily looked at in the 21st century is the extent to which the Internet liberates retail. Industry watchers predict that most consumers will go back and forth between the Web and local stores. The lines will blur between who does what in terms of service, purchasing, delivery, returns, and information.

No formula lasts forever. Customer needs and preferences change constantly. The good news is that in the United States, there are an average of 76 people per square mile, with disposable income to spend on goods and services. The bad news is that there are more outlets selling more products to the same 76 people per square mile. Be ready to reinvent yourself and your company to survive and thrive.

Top Ten Causes of Retail Failure

Ever wonder why retail businesses go under? Take a look at the top 10 reasons, listed below:

1. Economic factors
2. Management incompetence/lack of experience
3. Poor sales
4. Heavy expenses
5. Neglect
6. Disaster
7. Capital problems
8. Fraud
9. Customer problems
10. Overexpansion

Here are five guidelines to follow:

1. Clearly define what success looks like, and make sure that everyone on your team understands and focuses on that definition.

2. Do not be complacent no matter how well things seem to be going. A false sense of superiority makes it easy to ignore encroaching competitors. To stay relevant, stay alert.

3. If you are a new brand, you need to advertise that fact heavily and provide clear evidence that you offer something unique. Innovate.

4. Leverage technology to collect information about consumers; then act on that information. Analyze and apply demographic and psychographic data to improve customer service.

5. Cultivate loyal relationships with employees, suppliers, and customers through regular interactions, innovative programs, and fair practices.

Every attempt to reinvent the company must begin with a total approach to doing everything better. The Japanese call it *kaizen*. Initiate vitality in everything from store planning and design to assortment, service, and marketing. Approach every day with fresh eyes: What does your signage say about you? Your customers? Community involvement? Pricing strategy? Your promotions? Your salespeople? Your displays, colors, hours—everything talks to your bottom line. What messages are you sending, and who do you need to reach to remain in business?

Rethink the Rules

Retailers are becoming quite creative when it comes to integrating the various channels they do business in. Starbucks and Blockbuster Video recently put a deal together where the Starbucks stores are being used as a repository for Blockbuster videos. Use your imagination to come up with new ways to deliver goods to the consumer quickly and economically. Capture the magic of retailing by thinking of new ways to leverage the physical properties of your business—the look, feel, smell and ambiance of your environment and tactile sensations of experiencing the merchandise.

Encore?

What do the retailers we interviewed see in their futures? Would they do it all over again? What advice do they have for you?

Music store owner Fred W. in Montpelier, Vermont, advises new retailers to "concentrate on doing a few things really well, and don't try to be everything to everybody and end up doing that poorly."

Fred doesn't know how the consolidation of banks is going to play out and what impact that will have on him and his business. "Already, the bank I've been doing business with has been sold, and someone else is ready to buy it from the new owners. We're still on a month-to-month lease, but because of our history with the bank, the owners are willing to let us set the time frame for the new lease terms for one, five, or 10 years. They have a formula they'll be instituting for rent increases, so my overhead will be going up."

Fred's business is successful even in the face of fierce online competition (Napster, MP3, etc.)—and traditional competition. Why? Because of the niche he's dug out for himself and his business in a small community. "Montpelier is one of the few places where a small retailer like me can make it. People are supportive. We're a part of the community, and we've been here for so long that people know about us and tell their friends."

In Newport Beach, California, pet bakery owner Stephanie B. is enjoying the support of a beach community. She also advises entrepreneurs, "I would follow my heart more than my mind because that's where my successes have been. I would always listen when people give you advice because some of my best ideas have come from conversations with customers." Stephanie wants to warn would-be retailers that "It [running a store] is a lot of work! You have to take time off. Otherwise, you'll get burned out."

> "Some of my best ideas have come from conversations with customers."

"I love this business," says Dadeville, Alabama, grocer Jeff P. "If we can get the debt down in this store a little bit, there are probably two different places in Alabama I'd like to look at to build a store like this one." Jeff has three children, and the two stores he owns currently provide a good living for his family, so he doubts that he'll get the grocery business out of his blood.

"The trend in the apparel business is toward casual clothes and away from fancy," says Thomasville, Georgia, clothing retailer Jim D., "but that doesn't bother us. Our target customers will always need special-occasion clothing. Also, e-commerce is where we will find real expansion. Technology will make buying clothes on the Internet more and more desirable and easier. We will be there." If they can institute the buying and inventory-control improvements they've planned, Jim and wife/business partner Mary expect to double or triple their e-commerce in a year. "If we do that, we would go to the next level of business," says Jim. "Both sides [of our business] are growing now, so the percentage of our Web trade to our store business is a moving target. We are developing a second Web site for brides because of the success of our prom site. We also have plans to expand, acquiring the spot next door and remodeling the store to double our space."

Jim doesn't want the store to get any bigger than about 4,000 square feet. "That will be just about the right size for what we want to do. Any bigger than that and you become tied to larger inventories and all kinds of problems. What we really want to do is to continue what we're doing and just do it a little bit better. We want to make ourselves more of a target destination."

New York City-based luxury handbag designer Matt M.'s five-year goals are "perpetual and innovative handbag and accessory collections; excellent international distribution and customer loyalty through escalating quality; a successful introduction of a furniture and furnishings collection; development of men's and women's clothing; and a shop to house everything in."

"My only concern so far is saturation," says art gallery owner Darrell T., noting that his original plan was to open five stores in the Seattle area in five years. "One of the key indicators of how we're doing is how many images we're selling and how many clients are coming back requesting us to sell an image they've purchased. When the number of resale requests goes up, this will be the first indication that the market is being saturated with too much product."

The home theater business is growing, and the live recording side is steadily expanding as well, comments audio retailer Jim O. in Thomasville, Georgia, who's in business with his brothers, Doug and Carlos. All three brothers really like the audio business, the people they work with, and the opportunities to invent specialty products that are "better than anything else out there." With 20 years of experience in audio engineering and a global network of customers, they expect to stay up to date with the new sound technologies and can't imagine doing anything else.

The Future of Retailing

The basic premise of successful retailing is to know your merchandise, give your business a recognizable personality, maximize product presentation, and make the purchase easy for the shopper. While few people believe that virtual retailing will make shops obsolete, retailers will need to justify and adapt their physical presence to remain profitable. Some retail experts believe that retail's street presence will become more about building an emotional bond with the consumer than

Tip...

Smart Tip

The future of the retail industry depends on your ability to enhance the quality of the human experience. You need to create an enjoyable shopping environment so people will leave their houses to buy goods and services.

about buying. Whether online or offline, the dividing line between retailers that survive and those that don't will be brand strength—offering visitors more than the simple purchase of a product and creating a memorable brand experience.

Down the road, you may be incorporating video touch screens, virtual reality experiences, and multimedia sensory stimulation into your store's interior. In the future, stores will be less utilitarian and more of an emotional experience. Destination purchases are price-sensitive, but impulse purchases are not. To win over customers in a market saturated by sameness of merchandise, retailers will offer customers gathering places that are hard to duplicate. Stores are experimenting with various forms of entertainment, such as jazzy piano bars, esoteric coffee clubs, and kiddie play lands. They are also reaching out to an aging population with seating areas, easy-to-read tags and signs, and easy access to merchandise. Some say that in the future retail experiences will provide an oasis in the middle of an overburdened world. Retail will be the conduit of fantasy in a 3-D, physical space choreographed to stimulate shoppers' senses.

Know Your Customers

Baby boomers represent a large pool of older, richer, well-educated consumers spending their earned and inherited incomes. Seventy-six million strong, their median age is now 40 years old. The youngest households today belong to the "Echo Boom" generation. These are 72 million people now 22 years old and younger. This generation is currently forming first households. Householders under the age of 25 claim less than 4 percent of all household spending in the United States, but their influence is growing in several markets. They account for more than 5 percent of the market for men's apparel, women's apparel, and footwear, and they claim more than 10 percent of spending on infant clothing. Also very noteworthy: This generation of highly educated shoppers is embracing e-commerce.

Thanks to the many retailers who took time out of their busy schedules to speak with us and offer their advice, you are starting on sound footing with the wisdom of experienced entrepreneurs. Plan well, work hard, and reap the rewards of retailing. This is an exciting business. The one thing we can guarantee is that no two days will ever be the same. Enjoy!

Appendix
Retail Store Resources

They say you can never be too rich or too thin. While these can be argued, we believe you can never have too many resources. Therefore, we present for your consideration a wealth of sources for you to check into, check out, and harness for your own personal information blitz.

These sources will get you started on your research. They are by no means the only sources out there. We have done our research, but businesses tend to move, change, fold, and expand. As we have repeatedly stressed, do your homework. Get out and start investigating.

As an additional tidbit to get you going, we strongly suggest the following: If you haven't yet joined the Internet Age, do it! Surfing the Net is like waltzing through a vast library with a breathtaking array of resources literally at your fingertips.

Association

Adventure Travel Society, 228 N. F St., Salido, CO 80121, (719) 530-0171, www.adventuretravel.com

Alliance of Professional Tattooists, 428 Fourth St., #33, Annapolis, MD 21403, (410) 216-9630, www.safetattoos.com

American Amusement Machine Association, 450 E. Higgins Rd., #201, Elk Grove Village, IL 60007, (847) 290-9088, www.coin-op.com

American Association of Franchisees & Dealers, P.O. Box 81887, San Diego, CA 92138-1887, (800) 733-9858, www.aafd.org

American Booksellers Association, 828 S. Broadway, Tarrytown, NY 10591, (800) 637-0037, (914) 591-2665, www.bookweb.org/aba

American Disc Jockey Association, 10882 Demarr Rd., White Plains, MD 20695, (301) 705-5150, www.adja.org

American Franchisee Association, 53 W. Jackson Blvd., #205, Chicago, IL 60604 (312) 431-0545, www.franchisee.org

Association of Wedding Professionals, P.O. Box 6080, Silver Spring, MD 20916, (301) 350-3068, www.weddingpros.org

Cosmetic, Toiletry and Fragrance Association, 1101 17th St. NW, #300, Washington, DC 20036, (202) 331-1770, www.ctfa.org

Food Marketing Institute, 655 15th St. NW, #700, Washington, DC 20005, (202) 452-8444, www.fmi.org

International Association of Professional Security Consultants, Charles A. Sennewald & Associates, 28004 Lake Meadow Dr., Escondido, CA 92026, (760) 749-7527, www.shoplifting.com

International Franchise Association, 1350 New York Ave. NW, #900, Washington, DC 20005, (202) 628-8000, www.franchise.org

National Association of Chain Drug Stores, 413 N. Lee St., Alexandria, VA 22314, (703) 549-3001, www.nacds.org

National Association of College Stores, 500 E. Lorain St., Oberlin, OH 44074, (440) 775-7777, www.nacs.org

National Association of Convenience Stores, 1605 King St., Alexandria, VA 22314, (703) 684-3600, www.cstorecentral.com

National Association of Recording Merchandisers, 9 Eves Dr., #120, Marlton, NJ 08053, (609) 596-2221, www.narm.com

National Community Pharmacists Association, 205 Daingerfield Rd., Alexandria, VA 22314, (800) 544-7447, www.ncpanet.org

National Grocers Association, 1825 Samuel Morse Dr., Reston, VA 20190, (703) 437-5300, www.nationalgrocers.org

National Home Furnishings Association, 305 W. High St., #400, High Point, NC 27260, (910) 883-1650, www.nhfa.org

National Retail Federation, 325 Seventh St. NW, #1100, Washington, DC 20004, (202) 783-7971, www.nrf.com

National Retail Hardware Association, 5822 W. 74th St., Indianapolis, IN 46278, (317) 290-0338, www.nrha.org

National Shoe Retailers Association, 7150 Columbia Gateway Dr., Columbia, MD 21046, (410) 381-8282, www.nsra.org

National Trust for Historic Preservation, 1785 Massachusetts Ave. NW, Washington, DC 20036, (800) 944-6847, www.nthp.org

Retail Advertising & Marketing Association, 333 N. Michigan Ave., #3000, Chicago, IL 60601, (312) 251-7262, www.rama-nrf.org

Books

The 11 Immutable Laws of Internet Branding, Al Ries and Laura Ries, HarperBusiness

201 Great Ideas for Your Small Business, Jane Applegate, Bloomberg Press

Advertising Handbook for Retail Merchants, Judy Y. Ocko, National Retail Federation Publication, Washington, DC

The Age of E-Tail, Alex Birch, Philipp Gerbert, Dirk Schneider and Geoff Mott, Capstone Ltd.

Bond's Franchise Guide, 2000 Edition, Source Book Publications, 1814 Franklin St., #820, Oakland, CA 94612, (510) 839-5471, www.sourcebookpublications.com

Chase's Calendar of Events, NTC/Contemporary Publishing Group, 4255 W. Touhy Ave., Lincolnwood, IL 60712, (800) 621-1918, www.ntccpg.com

Clicking Through: A Survival Guide for Bringing Your Company Online, Jonathan Ezor, Bloomberg Press

Dictionary of Retailing and Merchandising, Jerry Rosenberg, John Wiley & Sons

Employee Theft—The Profit Killer, John Case, John Case & Associates, 2310 Coast Blvd., Del Mar, CA 92014, www.employeetheft.com

Encyclopedia of Associations, The Gale Group, 27500 Drake Rd., Farmington Hills, MI 48331, (248) 699-4253, www.galegroup.com

E-Service: 24 Ways to Keep Your Customers When the Competition Is Just a Click Away, Ron Zemke and Thomas Connellan, AMACOM

Shoplifters vs. Retailers, Charles A. Sennewald, Charles A. Sennewald & Associates, www.shoplifting.com

The Soul of the New Consumer: The Attitudes, Behavior, and Preferences of E-Customers, Laurie Windham and Ken Orton, Allworth Press, 10 E. 23rd St., #210, New York, NY 10010, www.allworth.com

Web Rules: How the Internet is Changing the Way Consumers Make Choices, Tom Murphy, Dearborn Trade, 155 N. Wacker Dr., Chicago, IL 60606, (312) 836-4400, www.dearborn.com

▲

Consulting Services

Fitch Inc., 10350 Olen Tangy River Rd., Worthington, OH 43085, (614) 885-3453, www.fitch.com

National Decision Systems, (973) 285-3337, www.natdecsys.com

Retail Planning Associates, 580 N. Fourth St., Columbus, OH 43215, (614) 564-1000, www.rpaworldwide.com

Retail Management Consultants, 1635 S. Rancho Santa Fe Rd., #206, San Marcos, CA 92069, (800) 766-1908, www.whalinonretail.com

Retailer News, 120 Walton St., #201, Syracuse, NY 13202, (315) 423-0548, www.retailernews.com

Threat Analysis Group, 1503 Meadowsweet Dr., Sugarland, TX 77479, (281) 494-1515, www.threatanalysis.com

Consumer Research

BrainReserve, Faith Popcorn, 59 E. 64th St., New York, NY 10021, www.brainreserve.com

Envirosell Inc., Paco Underhill, 907 Broadway, 2nd Fl., New York, NY 10010, (212) 673-9100, www.envirosell.com

Trends Research Institute Inc., P.O. Box 660, Rhinebeck, NY 12572, (888) 668-7363, (845) 876-6700, www.trendsresearch.com

Jupiter Communications, 627 Broadway, New York, NY 10012, (212) 780-6060, www.jupiter.com

Specialty Retail Report, (800) 936-6297, www.specialtyretail.com

Equipment

Advanced Communication Design Inc., Marco Scibora, 7901 12th Ave. S., Bloomington, MN 55425, (952) 854-4000, www.acdstar.com

Checkpoint Systems Inc., www.checkpointsystems.com

MUSE Services & Products, P.O. Box 495, Gulfport, MS, (228) 865-9558, www.museusa.com

National Cash Register (NCR), www.ncrdirect.com

Specialty Retail Report, (800) 936-6297, www.specialtyretail.com

Symbol Technologies Inc., One Symbol Plaza, MSA-12, Holtsville, NY 11742, (800) 722-6234, www.symbol.com

Wordstock P.O.S. and Inventory Control, 69 Grove St., Watertown, MA 02472, (800) 753-9673, www.wordstock.com

Franchise and Business Opportunities

Franchise Opportunities.com, 1085 Powers Pl., Alpharetta, GA 30004, (888) 363-3390, www.franchiseopportunities.com

Grow Biz International Inc., 4200 Dahlberg Dr., Minneapolis, MN 55422 (800) 567-6600, www.growbiz.com

Media Arts Group Inc., 521 Charcot Ave., San Jose, CA 95131, (408) 324-2020, www.mediaarts.com

Merchandise and Visual Display

Institute of Store Planners, 725 Wilshire Blvd., #210, Los Angeles, CA 90010, (213) 388-5510, www.ispo.org

Risk Management Resources

National Loss Prevention Associates, 1307 W. Sixth St., #119-A, Corona, CA 92882, (909) 280-0619, www.nationallossprevention.com, www.shopliftingexpert.com

John Case & Associates, 2310 Coast Blvd., Del Mar, CA 92014, (858) 755-2931, www.employeetheft.com

Threat Analysis Group, 1503 Meadowsweet Dr., Sugarland, TX 77479, (281) 494-1515, www.threatanalysis.com

Social Responsibility

Fair Trade Federation Inc., P.O. Box 698, Kirksville, MO 63501, (660) 665-8962, www.fairtradefederation.com

Software

MYOB US Inc., 300 Roundhill Dr., Rockaway, NJ 07866, (973) 586-2200, www.myob.com

Peachtree Software, 1505 Pavilion Pl., Norcross, GA 30093, (770) 724-4000, www.peachtree.com

QuickBooks, (800) 264-5643, www.quickbooks.com

Successful Retail Business Owner

The Barkery, Stephanie Bailiff, 322 Marine Ave., Newport Beach, CA 92662, (949) 675-0364, www.b-barkery.com

▲

Buch Spieler, Fred Wilber, 27 Langdon St., Montpelier, VT 05602, (802) 229-0449, www.bsmusic.com

Chez Panisse, Alice Waters, 1517 Shattuck Ave., Berkeley, CA 94709, (510) 548-5525, www.chezpanisse.com

Matt Murphy Design, Matt Murphy, (800) 434-6900, www.mattmurphy.com

Oade Brothers Audio, Jim Oade, 316 S. Broad St., Thomasville, GA 31792, (229) 228-0093, www.oade.com

Parker Food Land, Jeff Parker, 483 N. Broadnax St., Dadeville, AL 36853, (256) 825-4461

Thomas Kinkade Westlake Gallery, Darrell Taylor, 400 Pine St., #304, Seattle, WA 98101, (206) 625-9945

Unique Boutique, Jim and Mary DeFore, 111 N. Madison St., Thomasville, GA 31792, (229) 226-4301, www.timeforprom.com

Trade Publications

Apparel News, 110 E. Ninth St., Los Angeles, CA 90079, (213) 627-3737, www.apparelnews.net

Chain Store Age Magazine, 425 Park Ave., New York, NY 10022, (800) 216-7117, www.chainstoreage.com

C-store Central, 1605 King St., Alexandria, VA 22314, (703) 684-3600, www.cstorecentral.com

C-store e-magazine, 6039 Beverly Hills Rd., Coopersburg, PA 18036, (610) 282-9978, www.c-store.com

Discount Store News Retailing Today, 425 Park Ave., New York, NY 10022, www.discountstorenews.com

eRetail.net, 6312 Seven Corners Center, #263, Falls Church, VA 22044, www.eretail.net

Franchise Times Magazine, 2500 Cleveland Ave. N., St. Paul, MN 55113, (651) 631-4995, www.franchisetimes.com

Journal of Retailing, 655 Avenue of the Americas, New York, NY 10010, (212) 633-3730, www.haas.berkeley.edu/jr

P.O.P Times, 7400 Skokie Blvd., Skokie, IL 60077, (847) 675-7400, www.hoytpub.com/poptimes

Progressive Grocer, 770 Broadway, New York, NY 10003, (646) 654-4500, www.grocerynetwork.com

Retail Newsbeat, www.retailnewsbeat.com

Retail Strategies, 1326 Fifth Ave., #620, Seattle, WA 98101, (206) 623-3974, www.outcaltjohnson.com

Shopping Centers Today, 1221 Avenue of the Americas, New York, NY 10020, (646) 728-3800, www.icsc.com

Web Sites

www.4anything.com (a network of Web guides with access to numerous topics of interest)

www.bizbuyer.com (customized purchasing services)

www.dealtime.com (a site for comparing products, prices, and stores)

www.ebay.com (an online marketplace)

www.lowe.org (the Edward Lowe Foundation's Entrepreneurial Edge Web site; provides resources for entrepreneurs)

www.i2iretail.com (a site for buying and selling overstocked merchandise, or fixtures and equipment)

www.killerbiz.com (streamlines small business purchasing)

www.m4r.com (also www.kennethmorrisgroup.com; retail technology and solutions)

www.mynetsales.com (sales process management and automation)

www.mysimon.com (a pricing and comparison service)

www.priceline.com (an e-commerce site where you name your own price)

www.retail.com (retail solutions and services)

www.retailexchange.com (excess inventory solutions)

www.tradeweave.com (retail network portal)

www.uccnet.com (electronic trading; enables forming trading partnerships)

Glossary

Above-market pricing: pricing above the normal market value for trendy or scarce products or services.

Advisory board: a cross section of community citizens appointed by a retailer to offer advice and counsel to management on a variety of issues.

Aggregation: an approach to target market selection whereby retailers assume that most consumers are alike in their needs and wants.

Anchor tenants: the major tenants in a shopping center that serve as the primary attraction.

Assignment: the transfer of title, right, and interest in certain real property; the document used to convey a leasehold is called an "assignment of lease" rather than a deed.

At-the-market pricing: when retailers set prices that are about the same as competitors'.

Balanced tenancy: the types of stores in a planned shopping center chosen to meet all of the consumers' shopping needs in the trading area.

Base rent: minimum monthly rent payments, as set forth in a retail lease, excluding pass-throughs, percentage rents, and other additional charges.

▲

Base year: the year in a lease term used as a standard in a rent escalation clause; operating costs in the next year are compared with costs in the base year, and tenant's rent is adjusted either up or down.

Basic stock: the amount and assortment of merchandise sufficient to accommodate normal sales levels.

Below-the-competition pricing: setting prices lower than competitors' prices.

Boutique department: small specialty shops within a larger store that feature a narrow range of exclusive, fashionable merchandise in an attractive atmosphere; a boutique layout approach is adopted by many department stores as a variation on conventional departmental layouts.

Breadth: the width of a merchandise assortment; the number of different styles, colors, sizes, and other variants a retailer carries.

Brick-and-mortar merchants: traditional retailing in physical businesses as opposed to virtual retailing, which is conducted online without a physical headquarters customers can visit.

Bulk marking: a merchandise marking practice (used for items that sell at very low prices and are subject to rapid price changes) whereby items are not marked until placed on the selling floor.

Buying groups: organizations that coordinate or pool the buying needs of many small businesses into larger orders with major manufacturers or suppliers.

Cashwrap: cash register or checkout stand.

Category management: emerging practice that brings suppliers and sellers together to determine the right product mix within a specific food category; the goal is an efficient assortment of profitable products.

Chain: a retail organization consisting of two or more centrally owned units that handle similar lines of merchandise.

Channel: the medium through which a message-sender communicates with an audience.

Checking: a phase of the physical handling process that involves matching the store buyer's purchase order with the supplier's invoice (bill), opening the packages, removing the items, sorting them, and comparing the quality and quantity of the shipment with what was ordered.

Circular: a store promotion printed on one page and distributed by third-class mail or by hand; also called a *flier*.

Classification dominance: displaying and arranging merchandise in such a way that psychologically the consumer is convinced the firm has a larger assortment of merchandise in the category than competitors.

Clayton Act: declares certain practices illegal even if they do not actually restrain trade or do not constitute a monopoly or an attempt to monopolize.

Click-and-mortar strategy: a strategy of physical businesses to incorporate the Internet in buying and selling.

Cluster anchors: a group of small stores that sell similar or complementary merchandise and operate in the place of the traditional anchor tenant in certain specialty centers.

Come-on item: an item that a retailer sells at a loss (below cost) to draw customers into the store; also known as a *loss leader*.

Community shopping center: a shopping center in which the leading tenant is a variety store or junior department store.

Comparison goods: merchandise that consumers will usually shop for at several stores before buying.

Consignment: a situation in which suppliers guarantee the sale of items and will take merchandise back if it does not sell; the store does not pay for the inventory, but rather keeps a percentage of the receipts from each sale.

Consumer Credit Protection Act: requires retailers to explain in easily understood language the finance charge and annual percentage rate on the merchandise they finance.

Consumer Leasing Act: requires a leasing company to make an accurate and detailed disclosure of all terms and costs in leasing contracts.

Convenience center: a small shopping center anchored by a quick-stop food store and occupied by other service-oriented tenants.

Convenience goods/products: frequently purchased items for which consumers do not engage in comparison shopping before making a purchase decision.

Cooperative advertising: promotional programs in which wholesalers or manufacturers pay a portion of the retailer's advertising cost under specified conditions.

Core service: the primary benefit customers seek from a service firm.

Debt service: regular payment made on a loan.

Depth: the number of pieces stocked of the different styles, colors, sizes, and other variants in each line a retailer carries.

Developer: the individual or entity that invests in building a retail property and is responsible for construction, marketing, and leasing; this person may also be the owner of the land.

Dual distribution: a situation in which wholesalers also operate retail outlets.

e-Commerce: buying and selling over the Internet.

Effective space: the amount of retail space in a given trade area that is capable of drawing consumers.

▲

Electronic cash register (ECR): a point-of-sale register that uses electronic light beams to enter information at a very high rate of speed.

Electronic data interchange (EDI): a computer network that links manufacturers, distributors, and retailers for streamlined ordering.

Electronic funds transfer system (EFTS): a system for the automatic transfer of cash from a customer's account to a retailer's account.

Endcap: a display set up at the end of a store aisle; always well-stocked and changed frequently.

Equal Credit Opportunity Act: prohibits discrimination on the basis of race, color, religion, national origin, age, sex, marital status, and receipt of income in any aspect of a credit transaction.

Experience qualities: attributes, such as taste, that can only be discerned after purchase or during consumption.

Express warranties: written warranties for products or services.

Fair Credit Billing Act: legislation establishing a billing dispute settlement procedure for "open-end" credit; also imposes certain other requirements on retailers to assure fair and accurate handling of credit accounts.

Fair Credit Reporting Act: protects the consumer's right to an accurate, up-to-date, and confidential credit report.

Fair Debt Collection Practices Act: designed to eliminate abusive debt collection practices and to protect the consumer from harassment and unfair collection procedures.

Federal Trade Commission: a government agency responsible for enforcing the Clayton Act and other antitrust laws.

Federal Trade Commission Act: legislation passed in 1914 to create the Federal Trade Commission.

Fixed-payment lease: a rental agreement in which rent is based on a fixed payment per month.

Food court: an area in a shopping center, usually in an enclosed mall, where different kinds of food are available from individual vendors selling from separate stalls.

Franchise: an exclusive right to sell a product or perform a service; in retailing, an individual will purchase this right from a chain store or other type of a parent corporation and operate at the store according to the rules and regulations of the franchisor.

Free-standing retail space: a store that is not an integral part of a shopping center, enclosed mall, or mixed-use development; also called *pad space*; many downtown department stores are free-standing.

Frontage: the section of a store that faces the street or the pedestrian walkway in a mall; also refers to window display area and entrance.

Generic merchandise: merchandise that is unbranded and which is typically somewhat lower in quality than brand-name merchandise.

Implied warranty: a provision of the Uniform Commercial Code that requires that all merchandise sold be fit for the purpose for which it is intended.

Impulse items: items purchased on impulse when they are seen by a shopper without prior intent to buy.

Independent retailer: a local, nonchain store owned by a single individual or family.

Industrial shopping center: a type of specialty center based around stores and services having to do with plumbing fixtures, hardware items, or the care of automobiles.

Initial markup: in pricing merchandise, the first markup of a new item after purchasing it wholesale.

Keystone: a standard apparel markup that sets a selling price for merchandise at double its cost (a 100 percent markup).

Kiosk: a booth or stall set up in a shopping center, sometimes on a temporary basis, to sell goods such as tobacco, newspapers, magazines, seasonal merchandise, candy, keys, and other small impulse-purchasing items; also, a multimedia electronic selling or information tool set up inside stores or malls.

Layaway: customer service in which the shopper makes a down payment on an article, pays the balance due in installments, and the retailer retains ownership until the customer has paid in full.

Lifestyle presentation: arranging merchandise in such a way that it is compatible with the consumer's activities, interests, and outlook on life.

Loss leader: a product intentionally sold at a loss to attract customers; also known as a *come-on item*.

Manufacturer's brand: a brand, often referred to as a national brand, owned by a manufacturer who may sell to anyone who wants to buy the brand.

Maintained markup: the average markup of an item sustained over a period of time, allowing for future markdowns and other reductions in selling price.

Margin: refers to the amount of profit a retailer makes from a certain item; it is always expressed as a percentage of the sales price.

Markdown: a reduction in the original selling price of an item.

Market development: a strategy that focuses either on attracting new consumer segments or completely changing the customer base.

Marketing fund: an account controlled by the landlord that is specifically for funding shopping center promotions and advertising, and to which all merchants in the center must contribute based on a predetermined amount stated in their leases.

Market price: the amount actually paid for a property.

▲

Market rent: the rent a retail site could command under prevailing market conditions.

Market share: that portion of consumer dollars spent on a particular merchandise category that a given retailer can capture.

Merchandise distribution: an aspect of merchandise management in multiunit organizations related to getting merchandise from consolidation points/distribution centers to the individual stores.

Merchandising: having the right merchandise, at the right price, at the right place, at the right time, and in the right quantities.

Merchant wholesalers: wholesalers who take title to the goods they sell.

Merchants' association: an organization formed in shopping centers and controlled by the tenants to plan promotions and advertisements for the good of the center as a whole; usually all tenants are required to participate, and both tenants and landlord pay dues.

Minimum rent: the rent which will always be due each month in a tenant's lease term, regardless of sales volume and exclusive of any additional charges; often used in conjunction with a percentage rent arrangement and sometimes called fixed minimum rent.

Mom-and-pops: small stores, generally operated by members of a family with limited capital; typically locally owned and operated; can be three or four-store chain if the owners are involved on a daily basis at each store.

Nonmarking: the practice of not price-marking individual merchandise items; usually the display fixture will indicate prices.

Off-price retailers: outlets offering well-known brands of merchandise at substantial discounts compared to conventional stores handling the same products.

Order point: the level of stock below which merchandise is automatically reordered.

Original retail price: the first price at which an item is offered for sale.

Outlet center: a type of specialty center comprised of at least 50 percent factory outlet stores offering name brand goods at discounted wholesale prices; the manufacturer will usually operate the store, eliminating the retail markup.

Power retailers: merchants with sufficient financial strength, marketing skill, and price/value relationship to enter a market, however saturated, and make a profit.

Price discrimination: varying the prices charged to different retailers for identical merchandise without an economic justification for doing so.

Price line: a limited number of prices that reflect varying levels of merchandise quality; price lining may occur either in the context of rigid price points or price zones.

Price point: a small number of different prices; for example, a merchant might price all "good suits" at $175, all "better suits" at $225, and all "best suits" at $350.

Price-sensitive: the tendency of the demand for an item or service to vary based on the demand, availability, and competitor pricing.

Price zones: a pricing strategy in which a merchant establishes a range of prices for merchandise of different quality; for example, prices for general kitchen items might be $10 to $200 lower than prices for gourmet kitchen versions.

Private brands/labels: brands owned by a retail or a wholesale firm rather than by a manufacturer.

Promotion: any form of paid communication from the retailer to the consumer.

Quantity discount: a reduction in unit cost based on the size of an order.

Reach: the number of persons exposed at least once to a message during an ad campaign.

Receiving: a phase of the physical handling process that involves taking possession of the goods and then moving them to the next phase of the process.

Regional dominance: a location strategy whereby a retailer decides to compete within one geographic region.

Remarking: the practice of changing the prices marked on merchandise to reflect price changes.

Retail decision support system: the structure of people, equipment, and procedures which gathers, analyzes, and distributes the data that management requires for decision-making.

Retail marketing mix: those variables—product, price, presentation, promotion, personal selling, and customer services—that can be used as part of a positioning strategy for competing in chosen markets.

Retail saturation: the extent to which a trading area is filled with competing stores.

Robinson-Patman Act: says that manufacturers must sell the same quantities of the same goods at the same price; they cannot discriminate regardless of the buyer.

Sales promotion: marketing activities other than direct selling, advertising, and publicity that stimulate consumer purchasing; examples include displays, sales, exhibits, and demonstrations.

Sales retail price: the final selling price or the amount the customer pays for the merchandise.

Same-store retail sales: anniversary (annual) comparison of sales from the same store at the same period from year-to-year to measure business health and growth.

Scanner: a permanently fixed device which emits a laser beam for scanning the bar codes on merchandise and which can provide automatic price readouts, automatic updates of inventory, and similar features.

Seasonal discount: a special discount given to retailers who place orders for seasonal merchandise in advance of the normal buying period.

Seasonal merchandise: merchandise in demand only at certain times of the year.

Shelf space: amount of point-of-purchase space occupied by food products in a grocery store, as measured by square feet, linear feet, or number of facings.

Sherman Antitrust Act: federal legislation declaring that price-fixing is illegal.

Shopping goods/products: merchandise for which consumers engage in a price- and quality-comparison process before making a purchase decision.

Showing: a term that describes the way in which outdoor advertising space is bought or sold; a 100 showing in a market means that advertising space was purchased on enough posters to reach 100 percent of the audience in an area at least once each month.

Shrinkage: stock shortage determined by discrepancies between book and actual inventory values.

Single-price policy: all merchandise in a store is sold at the same price.

Site plan: a drawing of the retail site as it will look when it is completed, including individual tenant spaces, common areas, elevators, escalators, food courts, service areas, parking, and access routes.

Slotting fee: fee that food manufacturers pay retailers for shelf space and/or to have products promoted in the highest-profile slots.

Source marking: the practice of the vendor, rather than the retailer, marking the goods.

Specialty goods/products: products that consumers know they want and that they are willing to make a special effort to acquire.

Stock turnover: the rate at which inventory is sold in a retail store, normally expressed in turns per year; also called *stock turn*.

Stock-keeping unit (SKU): specific measure of an item of merchandise for inventory purposes; SKUs can refer to anything from the size of a bottle of aspirin to the type of photo film.

Strip center: a type of shopping center designed in a single, unenclosed strip facing the street.

Super regional center: a shopping center anchored by at least three full-line department stores.

Target market: the specific group of consumers whom the retailer wishes to attract.

Tenant mix: the combination of retailers and service vendors leasing space in a shopping center.

Trade area: the geographic area from which a shopping center will obtain most of its customers; size depends on the type of center, location of competition, and other factors.

Trade area zones: a way of subdividing the trade area on the basis of distance, travel time, and other factors; usually classified as primary, secondary, and tertiary.

Trade discount: a reduction off the seller's list price that is granted to a retailer who performs functions normally the responsibility of the vendor.

Universal product code (UPC): a standardized form of product marking for electronic reading of price and other information that is used for food and health-and-beauty aids.

Upscale retailer: a retailer specializing in goods at the high end of the scale in price, quality, and consumer served.

Wand: an electronic device that can be passed over merchandise for reading machine-coded information.

Index

▲